CIVITAS DEI

MACMILLAN AND CO., Limited
LONDON · BOMBAY · CALCUTTA · MADRAS
MELBOURNE

THE MACMILLAN COMPANY
NEW YORK · BOSTON · CHICAGO
DALLAS · ATLANTA · SAN FRANCISCO

THE MACMILLAN COMPANY
OF CANADA, LIMITED
TORONTO

CIVITAS DEI

BY

LIONEL CURTIS

MACMILLAN AND CO., LIMITED
ST. MARTIN'S STREET, LONDON
1934

COPYRIGHT

THIS book is dedicated to friends, too many to name, for the most part members of the Round Table, Chatham House and All Souls College, in grateful acknowledgment of the help they have rendered by criticising the Studies upon which this attempt to discover a guiding principle in politics is based.

CONTENTS

CHAPTER I

Development of caste in India, leading to absorption of Aryans into Hinduism, 13. Association of crafts with castes. Temporal existence conceived by Hinduism as unreal and evil. Hence belief in asceticism, 14. Chinese in contrast with Indians a vigorous and cheerful race. How the Indian philosophy influenced their outlook, 15. Effect of Indian philosophy in arresting development of civilisation in China as well as in India, 16.

CHAPTER IV

Dawn of Semitic civilisation, 17. The desert as nursery of prophets. Nomad antipathy to town civilisation. Conquests by nomads leading to creation of states, based on divine right. Effect of monotheism in promoting conquest, 18. Expulsion of Shepherd Kings from Egypt may explain stories of Exodus. The God of Israel as conceived by Moses. Hebrew tribes as separated from other tribes and united together by this conception, 19. Monotheism, a philosophic idea as contrasted with polytheism, considered by Hebrews as divinely revealed to Moses. Worship of Yahwe as personified goodness incompatible with idolatry. Conquest of heathen nations in his name a pious duty. 'The day of Yahwe' a term for 'victory', 20. Origin of the word Jehovah explained. Egyptian garrisons in Canaan attacked by Habiru (i.e. Hebrews), 21. Adoption by Hebrews of Canaanite superstitions. Development of a priesthood hostile to prophets. Israel reclaimed from idolatry and human sacrifice by prophets, but not from animal sacrifice, 22. Canaanite ritual ascribed to Moses by priestly scribes. Condemnation of animal sacrifice by prophets. Hebrews united by Philistine pressure in one monarchy, with Jerusalem as capital. Solomon's temple. Hebrews weakened by schism and oppressed by Egyptian and Mesopotamian Empires. The prophets produced by this tribulation, 23. Syrian invasions due to Phoenician enterprise. Teaching of Elijah. Assyrian conquest of Israel. Her leaders exiled, 24. Babylonian conquest of Judah. Deportation of leading Jews to Mesopotamia. The Jewish diaspora. Synagogues as centres of prophetic teaching, 25. Conquest of Babylon by Persia, 539 B.C. Jews authorised by Cyrus to rebuild the temple at Jerusalem, 444 B.C. Rival worship of Israelites at Gerizim, 26.

CHAPTER V

The law of Judaism as codified by priests. Effect of writing in establishing its sanctity. Prophetic teaching when recorded also regarded as divinely inspired, 27. How the canon was closed. Hostility of aristocratic priests to peasant

CHAPTER VIII

CHAPTER IX

CHAPTER XV

CHAPTER XVI

CHAPTER XVII

CHAPTER XVIII

CHAPTER XIX

CHAPTER XX

CHAPTER XXI

CHAPTER XXII

CHAPTER XXIII

miracle. Belief in the resurrection forced men back on the
principle of authority, 194. It obscured individual conscience
as the final criterion of conduct, and also the doctrine of
Jesus that the divine element in men must also be realised
in the structure of society, 195. The real meaning of Jesus is
clearer to us who have lived under commonwealths than to his
disciples who knew only the Roman Empire but who yet
faithfully preserved sayings which show what he really
meant, 196. Belief in his resurrection led them to identify
Jesus with the Messiah of prophecy, 197. Their belief in his
second coming and the judgement day of Jewish folk-lore to
inaugurate the Kingdom of God, to inherit which Gentiles
must be circumcised as well as baptized, 198.

CHAPTER XXIV

The Church in Jerusalem headed by James. Saul of Tarsus
sent by Sanhedrin to purge synagogue at Damascus, 199.
His account of his own conversion. His mission to the Gentiles, 200. He persuades the Churches to reject circumcision.
Spread of monotheism as conceived by the prophets limited
by Jewish nationalism, 201. Christianity saved from this
limiting factor becomes religion of the Roman Empire. His
belief in the second coming to be hastened by spreading the
Gospel. The Kingdom of God thus restored to the supernatural plane, 202. How the Gospels came to be written in the
next generation, 203, when the truth had become encrusted
with legends, 204.

CHAPTER XXV

Persecution of Christians who cease to be identified with Jews,
205. Their refusal to recognise emperors as divine. Their conception of themselves as a separate people, the Kingdom of
God, 206. The Empire regarded as the kingdom of Satan.
Belief in divine revelation, 207. The Holy Spirit conceived as
a person. Effect of these ideas in producing a hierarchy. The
hierarchy strengthened by conflict with Gnostics, 208. Origin
and meaning of the word 'Church'. Varieties of church organisation. Origin of bishops as the vehicle of apostolic authority,
209. Influence on church organisation of Roman Empire and
army, 210. Regarded by emperors as a dangerous rival. The
Church purified and strengthened by persecution, 211. Final
attempt of Diocletian to extinguish the Church. This attempt
fails, 212.

CHAPTER XXVI

The Church legalised by Constantine and established by Theodosius as the recognised religion of the Empire. The capital transferred to Byzantium by Constantine. Division of the Empire into east and west, 214. Rome sacked by Alaric the Goth. St. Augustine writes *De Civitate Dei.* Its argument as summarised by himself, 215. His postulate that truth can be known to men only by divine revelation, 216. The heavenly and earthly cities, the earthly city, identified with the Roman Empire, 217, is the city of Satan doomed to destruction, 218. The Church is the city of God founded by Christ but imperfect until he returns to purge and perfect it. The Church as so conceived is Judaism freed from its nationalist limitations assimilated to the Roman Empire and based on authority and is thus the antithesis of the commonwealth of God as conceived by Jesus, 219. The spiritual autocracy established by Pope Leo was the logical outcome. Leo persuades Attila to spare Rome and saves its people from massacre by Gaiseric, 220. Odoacer abolishes the western Empire. The Empire reunited under Justinian. The Papacy acquires vast estates in Italy. Exercise of political power by Gregory the Great, 221. His authority recognised throughout the Empire. Conversion of England by Augustine and of Germany by Boniface, 222.

CHAPTER XXVII

Christendom threatened from the south by a rival religion. The hungry tribes of Arabia disabled from plundering the Roman Empire by their own disunity, 223. Mobility of desert nomads enabling them to pillage and trade with each other and the Roman Empire. Paganism of the Arabs with its focus at Mecca. Mahomet goes as a trader from Mecca to Syria, 224, where by contact with Jews and Christians he must have learned the meaning and implication of monotheism. His belief in a moral code and in bodily resurrection, 225. His reforms compared with those of modern Hinduism and Buddhism. His conception of himself as the medium of a final revelation brings him into conflict with Judaism and Christianity, 226. Effect of his creed in uniting tribal society of Arabia in a state not limited by nationalism which rivals Christendom as a project of world government. His initial methods in Mecca. Their non-political character. Opposition to his teaching in Mecca which threatens his life, 227. Like Jesus he turns to the pilgrims who invite him to Medina. His conflict with Jews in Medina. He begins to organise the Arabs about Medina as a theocratic state, 228. In attacking Mecca he acquires credit for miraculous powers. He captures Mecca, A.D. 630, and conciliates its people by conces-

CHAPTER XXVIII

CHAPTER XXXIII

CHAPTER I

THE art of writing, which made it possible for men to record events and their feelings about them, was only invented in the last few thousand years. A progressive improvement in these records has enabled historians to frame an ever fuller account of human activities. For this latest period of human existence the outline of its story can be gathered from witnesses, though circumstantial evidence is used to check their testimony and to fill in the details. We have thus been led to think of society as a whole, to see the problems by which we are faced and to study their solution. But when we ask how such problems were first set the historians fail us, because they arose in an age when men were unable to record what they saw or heard. Our knowledge of this age is derived from circumstantial evidence only. From ever-increasing material the anthropologists and archaeologists are slowly compiling the preface to history, and this, at least, we know with certainty, that the preface covers a period greater than the human mind had ever conceived until recent years.

The exact length of the prehistoric age is, of course, a matter of weighing and valuing inadequate evidence. According to a recent computation our ancestors were assuming a human character somewhere short of a million years ago.[1] One branch of the primitive half-human stock described as Pithecanthropus, though now extinct, was still living in Java about 200,000 years ago. Other species, definitely human, developed later. One, the Neanderthal stock, whose remains were first discovered in Germany, is thought to have branched off some 300,000 years ago. Two other species, whose bones have been found at Piltdown in Sussex and in Rhodesia, separated later.

These three species seem to have perished, but a fourth survived to become the progenitor of all the races that now inhabit the earth. From this surviving stock offshoots found their way to the habitable parts of the globe and so for long ages lost sight of each other. In the course of those ages their bodies and minds were responding to the physical conditions of the country and climate in which they lived. In tropical climates, for instance, the colour of the skin darkened to blackness and the absence of cold gave little incentive to continuous exertion. In temperate zones complexions whitened. Continuous exertion was the price of existence in the colder and damper climates of the north. In order to live through the winter, food, clothing, fuel and shelter had to be provided in the warmer months. The necessity for continuous work tended to method in working. In the temperate zones was developed a more vigorous physique, a higher sense of the value of time and a greater capacity for sustained and methodical action.

The great families of mankind have thus grown for many generations in separate worlds to be what they now are. The varieties of country and climate in which they developed have reacted on their physical structure and still more on their habits of life and thought. Yet all these races can still mix their blood with each other; for, as in the countries they inhabit, there remains beneath all these diversities a nature common to them all. In the course of a few brief centuries they were brought into contact, made to depend on each other and merged in the framework of a single society.

Till a few generations ago it was commonly supposed that the life of man on the earth began about

4000 B.C., as the dates printed in editions of the Bible which are not very old continue to remind us. The Christian world was long taught to believe that its end would come in a sudden cataclysm, which might be expected at any moment. The idea of society as something recent and essentially transient has profoundly influenced political thought for eighteen centuries. As noticed in the opening paragraph of this chapter, we now have to think of men as living their lives on this earth aeons before the few thousand years of which we have record.[2] Yet this change in our estimate of the past is of minor importance when compared with the change that the recent growth of our knowledge has wrought in our estimate of the future. We now have reason to believe, as firmly as we are able to believe anything for practical purposes, that the aeons in front of us are immeasurably greater than those behind us. Astronomers and physicists encourage us to assume that our earth will continue to support human life for millions of years. Yet political thinking is still slow to absorb the idea that human society is yet in its infancy, with vast spaces of time in which to fulfil the destiny that awaits it.

While astronomers and physicists regard this as probable, they are also able to predict with certainty that an age, however distant, must come when this planet will cease to support any form of life. The cold face of the moon is there, like the mummied corpse at Egyptian feasts, to remind us of a time when human history, however prolonged and however glorious, will be as a tale that is told, with no one to tell it and no one to hear it.

NOTES

[1] Keith, *The Antiquity of Man*, p. 714 (1925 edition).
[2] *Ibid.* p. 560.

CHAPTER II

THE GENESIS OF THE STATE

FROM bones and teeth discovered in the floors of caves it is clear that the people who lived in these natural shelters obtained their food by hunting and fishing. That they gathered the berries, leaves and roots of wild plants which they found to be wholesome may be also assumed. In these conditions human life, like that of the lower animals, was confined to the places where natural conditions provided the necessary food and shelter. The dawn of civilisation opened as men discovered how to cultivate edible plants, to tame and breed animals and birds and construct for themselves shelters other than caves. As these arts were acquired the regions where human beings could live were extended, and their numbers must have increased. They spread to the countries in which both soil and climate were suited to agriculture. Where land was brought under cultivation families clustered together for mutual help and protection. They were thus able to provide their food with a greater economy of time than was possible for families living in caves by hunting and fishing. They had leisure to develop such crafts as the making of pottery, spinning and weaving; crafts which led on to the decorative arts and finally to writing. Their power of providing for the future by storing preservable foods was increased.

The land within reach of one centre would only support a certain number of villagers. When their numbers had exceeded this limit new villages would naturally be formed in the neighbourhood. A certain number of such villages could be held together by a sense of kinship. The head of the senior family would be recognised as chief. In a tribal society the basis of authority is in theory parental.

In the village community subsisting on agriculture a variety of questions affecting the relations of the various families in the settlement and their rights to the land would begin to arise, creating the need for some kind of government. The village assembly was the natural outcome, for the heads of families could easily gather and try to discuss a settlement of questions at issue. In his famous book Sir Henry Maine has described these village communities as infant republics. That the principle of the commonwealth has its roots in village meetings and tribal assemblies is certainly true, but the process by which they developed into genuine organs of government was exceedingly slow. When a number of people meet to discuss some question at issue between them, they naturally assume that a settlement must be based on agreement of all concerned. This assumption governed Homeric assemblies and those of the Celtic, German and Slavonic tribes. It still prevails in the families of China, in the gatherings of North American Indians and in the Pitsos and Indabas of the Bantu races. It survived in the Polish Diet till the eighteenth century, to the ruin of Poland, and still survives in the English jury, as litigants sometimes find to their cost.

It is needless to dwell on the difficulty of basing a system of government on assemblies which decide nothing till all are agreed. Unanimous decisions are possible only where the issues in question are simple, where peace or war is to be declared, or the heir of a dead ruler to be recognised as chief. Even so, such decisions must usually be reached by coercing the minority or shouting them down. The supposed unanimity is often unreal.

Experience is the food by which commonwealths

are nourished; and until decisions can be freely made the growth of experience is fatally clogged. The assumption that a number of persons can decide nothing except in so far as they all agree is mainly responsible for arresting the natural development of popular government in primitive societies. With us the habit of dividing a meeting and allowing the majority to decide is now so confirmed that we scarcely realise how difficult it was for our ancestors even to conceive the idea.

The village community based on agriculture was the nucleus of political society. In Europe it was destined to act as the seed-bed for commonwealths. At an earlier period in Asia and Egypt it served as the brick from which monarchies were built on foundations of agricultural revenue.

By learning to cultivate grain and to breed domesticated cattle and birds, men ceased to live from hand to mouth. But this new power of making provision for the future was fraught with trouble. The accumulated wealth of a village or group of villages was a natural temptation to the predatory instincts of more powerful neighbours. As tribes began to raid each other, capacity for leadership in chiefs became a factor of importance. The prizes would fall to the chief with the greatest talent for organising his clansmen. Amongst such conquerors the more intelligent would realise the folly of massacring the people of a conquered village or of leaving them to starve—of killing the goose that laid the eggs. The expedient of blackmail appeared. The conquered villages were suffered to live and retain their lands in return for a share in the produce to be paid each year to the conqueror. The shrewder conquerors realised their own interest in maintaining some kind of authority and justice. Life and property in the village community thus tended to become safer than under a merely tribal regime.

By the crude process of conquest, the state in its primitive form of a kingdom began to replace a form of society which was merely tribal.

This process was not confined to the conquest of its neighbours by a stronger agricultural tribe. There were large areas of the earth's surface where climatic conditions were not suited to the methods of primitive agriculture, but would none the less support herds of camels, donkeys, horses, cattle and sheep. The steppes of Siberia and the deserts of Arabia are regions of this nature, where a pastoral society developed which was utterly different from that which grew up in the belts suited for agriculture. The sparse vegetation was sufficient to support animals so long as they moved over vast areas. So their owners travelled in tribes on camels, donkeys or horses, driving their herds to wherever pasture could be found. As they lived for the most part on the milk and flesh of their herds, their commissariat moved about with them on its own hooves. Intensely mobile and warlike, these nomadic tribes were constantly fighting each other to retain or acquire the best pastures. Their manner of life inured them to extremes of hunger and thirst, heat and cold. Nomadic society was naturally fertile in military leaders.

From time to time these wandering tribes outgrew the capacity of the steppes or deserts to support them. Their cattle were also liable to wholesale destruction by storms or droughts. On the steppes a blizzard would wipe out a great part of their herds in a few hours. In periods of scarcity due to these causes they naturally turned their hungry eyes on the stores of food garnered and herded in the villages of the agricultural regions. Apart from periods of unusual scarcity, the comparative wealth of the cultivated regions was a standing temptation to the formidable nomads of the desert and the steppe. Kingdoms created by one agricultural tribe conquering a number of others were thus liable to conquest in turn by pastoral hordes. A group of kingdoms would be thus conquered and made subject to tribute by some nomad chief whose genius for leadership had enabled him to organise a number of pastoral tribes. By this process were created autocracies in the form of great empires, which in one case, that of Genghis Khan, covered nearly the whole of Asia and eastern Europe.

That tribal societies were merged into states by the process of conquest is undoubtedly true. But while brute force can change or destroy, it creates nothing of permanence without the aid of a moral idea. As Bismarck said in his famous aphorism, "You can do almost anything with bayonets, but sit on them". In tribal society the authority of the chief is in theory parental. The authority of one conquering chief over a number of subject tribes cannot be based on a fiction of parentage. Kings by virtue of conquest, or at any rate their heirs, were driven in course of time to find some moral authority for the power they exercised. The maintenance of such power depended, of course, in the long run on the ruler's ability to afford his subjects the security which enabled them to produce and so also to pay him the taxes he levied. But the theory that political power was based on deliberate contract between the king and his subjects is now generally recognised as a figment. "Men cannot live by bread alone", and the bonds which unite human beings in a state, however primitive its form, can never be explained merely in terms of material interests.

Archaeologists, helped by the spades of industrial excavators, have now shown that belief in a world other than that which men touch and see is older than some geological formations. The manner of burials made aeons ago proves no less. The spirits of the dead were held to survive and to punish or reward their descendants. In the fury of a storm or convulsions of an earthquake, so suggestive of human passion, the primitive mind saw the rage of invisible persons, not the blind energy of mechanical forces. So also with floods, droughts and plagues. The natural calamities that visit mankind were attributed to conscious and malignant powers. The first reaction of men to things they perceive without understanding is fear. As primitive man came to think of his life as controlled by forces other than those of nature, he ascribed his misfortunes to malignant spirits and ceremonies were devised to appease their wrath. It is only at a later stage in human development that gods are thought of as capable of goodness; and even so through long ages they were still regarded as beings whose will to do good to men must be excited by offerings of food. Fear of power not understood is the ruling motive in primitive society. Power, even when exercised by men, was readily assumed to be vested with supernatural sanctions.

A conqueror able to enforce obedience from his subjects was thus regarded by them as the agent of spiritual powers. That the ruler himself should accept the idea, and believe in it, was natural enough. It provided a moral basis for the absolute power he desired to wield. As the agent of supernatural authority there were no limits to his right to exact obedience. And the ultimate faculty of knowing what was right or wrong in matters of government was naturally confined to himself. For, if Heaven entrusted him with absolute power, it was logical to suppose that Heaven would also inform him with knowledge how it should be used. The organisation of society in states began before men had learned to study the working of their own minds. They thought of knowledge no less than of power as derived from supernatural sources. The priest or seer, like the king, was a man in touch with invisible powers, who was told by them what ordinary mortals could not know. It was, in a word, the age of authority, in which it was impious even to examine the basis on which authority rested. A state of society in which a large number of human beings obeyed the authority of a single ruler was the natural outcome of this attitude of mind. A power divinely bestowed and inspired is from its nature unlimited. In the primitive and absolute kingship such a right to obedience was deemed to exist. The state in fact comes to exist in so far as its members accept an authority which is, in principle, without limits. The idea of sovereignty was from the first implicit in the state.

The effects of conquest in creating a state could acquire no permanence without some belief to justify the claim of a ruler to his subjects' obedience. The connection of power with supernatural sanctions in the mind of the primitive world provided the conqueror with a moral claim to collect taxes and enforce the order without which the surplus wealth required for taxation cannot be raised. An administrative system, however simple, is highly precarious so long as it depends on orders given by word of mouth. The state in its crudest form could not be established over wide areas or with any degree of stability before the invention of writing.

We now know that ages before the invention of agriculture primitive men had been able to depict with masterly skill things which they saw, especially animals. In the better security afforded by agriculture villagers were contriving to use pictures to record their thoughts, their judgement of things which had happened, and also measures of quantity. To put the matter in another way, they learned to convey meaning, not merely by sounds which vanished the moment they were uttered, but by signs and marks visible to the eye which were also capable of remaining visible for long periods.

The art of writing was developed in Asia and Egypt, and was only conveyed at a much later date by Asiatics to tropical Africa. This fact of itself is sufficient to explain why political society developed in Asia and Egypt so long before tropical Africa began to emerge from tribal conditions.

The instinct of a conqueror must often have been to take from the conquered villages whatever he could get. But conquerors found that they could not hope to obtain a share of the village produce year after year unless they agreed to leave the villagers enough to support themselves and their families. So long as such agreements existed only in the memories of the ruler, of his officers and of his subjects, they were utterly precarious. There was nothing to prevent a rapacious officer from plundering a village till the cultivators starved, nor yet to secure that the ruler received his legitimate share of the produce. No real system of public finance was possible until the art of recording accounts was invented. And the same principle applies to the whole field of administration. Government was possible only within restricted areas and on very rudimentary lines until rulers were able to convey their orders and receive the reports of their officers in writing. We can therefore assume that states in the real sense of the word could scarcely be organised before the art of writing was known. Scribes were the necessary condition of states. They could also record for our knowledge what happened to those states. For this reason the history of states is coincident with the period of recorded history. The art which made a political organisation possible also enables its beginnings to be seen by evidence which is other than circumstantial.

CHAPTER III

WHEN the period of recorded history opened the greater part of humanity was living in south-eastern Asia. Then, as now, India and China were enormous reservoirs of population.

In India the tropical sun and torrential rains produced by the trade winds combine to multiply human beings and then sweep them away by millions. Fear of invisible powers which besets the primitive mind is here at its highest. The mass of the people have always lived dangerously near to the margin of subsistence: yet their aggregate wealth has constantly attracted invaders from the north.

The country was peopled by Dravidians, a submissive, industrious and intelligent race with exceedingly dark complexions. In the neighbourhood of the Baltic were a vigorous people with the lightest of all complexions, who, for want of a better name, have been known as the Aryans. Some thousands of years before the Christian era they were set in motion by some social or economic disturbance. From their home in north-western Europe migrations began to move to the south and the east. In course of time some of them reached as far as India. They seem to have overrun the peninsula, conquering, dominating and perhaps enslaving the Dravidian people wherever they came. It is probable that most of their women perished by the way. The light-skinned invaders found themselves mates from the dark-skinned peoples they conquered.

This was much what happened when, in the seventeenth century, Europeans first came to South

Africa and began to make their homes in the country. The males, who were largely in excess of the
females, began to mate with African women. Their
children, who were darker than their fathers, were
none the less disposed to look down on pure-bred
members of the subject race with skins blacker than
their own. While the white man does not like to
associate with the Cape-boy or Griqua, as these
mixed races are called, the half-breed in turn holds
himself aloof from the Kaffir and Hottentot.

The first result of contact between a northern
and tropical race is thus to produce three castes, the
white, the black and the half-breed between them.
But the process of stratification continues, for the
reason that some half-breeds are lighter than others.
In families born from the same parents one child
will be almost white and another nearly as black.
The half-breed girl is usually anxious to mate with
a husband as light as herself. Half-breeds with skins
of the same shade thus incline to marry each other.
In course of time they are thus stratified into castes
which try to avoid intermarriage. This process is
also at work in the coloured communities of North
America.

In India the process of stratification has continued
for thousands of years, and Hindu society is now
divided into more than two thousand castes. At the
top of the scale are the Brahmins, whose skins are
sometimes no darker than those of the French. The
Aryans who invaded India brought with them a
joyous creed. Their hymns, recorded in a later age,
reflect the gladness of life in a temperate climate.
But their outlook was presently coloured by the
gloom of the Indian jungle and the withering heat
of the tropical sun. The demon-worship of their subjects and wives began to affect them, much as the
Hebrew tribes were affected when in Canaan they
came into contact with beliefs less pure than their

own. So also the Christian Church absorbed the
beliefs of the older paganism. In India the result
was Hinduism, a system which finds room for almost
every grade of religious practice and thought, from
the profession of a lofty philosophy to the cults of
primitive animism. But Hinduism is more than a
religion. It is a whole system of life in which the
purest remnant of white invaders are held by the
darker strains to be the repository of knowledge and
power. The twice-born Brahmin is a man who knows
how the ill-will of the powers behind nature may be
avoided or appeased. This belief has given the
Brahmin caste an influence in Hindu society greater
than any hereditary class has ever acquired elsewhere.

Below this powerful hierarchy were the castes
identified with professions, the warriors, the scribes,
the bankers and so on. The practice of crafts was
abandoned to castes which could claim some slight
intermixture with the conquering race. To the pure
Dravidian was left the removal of filth and other
unsavoury tasks. They were treated as people necessary to Hindu society, but beyond its pale.

The religious belief of the Hindu grew out of this
social structure. The caste into which one is born is
determined by conduct in a previous existence. The
virtuous man when he dies will be born to a higher
caste, the impious man to a lower. Through an infinite series of successive rebirths the balance of
merit and reward is established. The final goal is
conceived as deliverance from birth by absorption
into the infinite. For behind the whole system lies
the conception that the visible world and the life men
lead in it are evil rather than good. Hence the idea
of asceticism which permeates Hindu thought. In
the Hindu mind pain, and especially self-inflicted
pain, is the road to merit and spiritual power.

To the north-east of the Indian peninsula is a belt of

almost impenetrable mountains, forests and deserts. Beyond this barrier is China, a country designed by nature to seclude an important section of the human race from the rest of mankind. This country was thickly inhabited by people of Mongolian origin, whose peculiar physique and outlook on life was formed, so anthropologists think, in the stress of combat with nature on the steppes before they invaded China and took to agriculture. Though subject to intense heat in the summer, China for its latitude is the coldest of all countries in winter, a fact which may have helped to preserve the vigorous nature of a race bred in the steppes. Whatever the reason may be, this fact at any rate is sure, that the natural outlook on life of the Chinese is as different as anything can be from that of the Indians. They are certainly not disposed to regard the good things of this life as illusory or unreal. They show more than the average capacity of men for cheerfulness and vigour in the presence of disaster. At one period they outdistanced the rest of the world in the standard of civilisation they reached. They produced for themselves a notable philosophy, but no great religion. They are, by general acceptance, the least religiously minded of people, and, for that reason perhaps, were susceptible to religious influence from without. Ideas are more portable than goods and, through barriers difficult for commerce to penetrate, religious conceptions bred in the climate of India spread to China and beyond it to Japan. The conception of life, not as something worthy of improvement but rather as something to escape from, travelled to the east and coloured the outlook of communities larger and more vigorous than those of India.

This explains why the vast mass of the human race congregated in south-eastern Asia reached the level of civilisation which is capable of philosophic reflection, and also of religion in the real sense of the word, and then failed for a long period to advance beyond that level. It is obvious enough that no great community will go on to improve its manner of life so long as it accepts the belief that the world about it is without value and without reality. The idea that the universe and the life men lead in it are real and valuable was destined to come from fragments of the human race which found their home to the west of India.

CHAPTER IV

WE have seen in the last chapter how an offshoot of the stock which was destined to people Europe found its way to the Indian peninsula. In an earlier age, say 25,000 years ago,[1] another group from the same primitive stock had found its way to the regions washed by the Mediterranean, the Persian Gulf and the Red Sea. Where the soil was fertilised by rain, wells or the waters of rivers like the Tigris and Euphrates, they developed the life of an agricultural people; and as in India, these settlements furnished material for the structure of monarchies at a later date. The fertile countries were a narrow fringe sur-rounding great areas of desert, where tribes lived a migratory life, subsisting partly on flocks and partly by carrying goods produced in the settled communi-ties. They thus developed an aptitude for commerce, which in course of time sought for an outlet beyond the seas. Trading villages grew on the coast to be-come vast emporia like the Tyre and Sidon of historical times. In these maritime settlements their zest for trade led the Semites to acquire the habits of a seafaring people. The Greeks described these sailors as Phoenicians or red-skins, an adjective latin-ised in the form 'Punic', names under which they figure in classical history. Their traffic spread through the Mediterranean and beyond as far as the British and Canary Isles. Towards the close of the ninth century B.C., a colony was founded in the Gulf of Tunis called Kirjath Hadeshath (the Semitic equiva-lent of Naples or Newtown). It was known to the Greeks as Carchedon and to the Romans as Carthage.

In the deserts which extend from Syria and Mesopotamia to the Red Sea wandering tribes continued to lead a life different from that led in the settled areas, and in violent contrast to the busy, varied and luxurious life of the town. From these wastes, where nature defies human control and society can exist only in a simple and primitive form, have emerged prophets with a deeper insight into ultimate truths than is given to men in less awful surroundings. From the age of the Patriarchs to the present day the religious revivals of the Semite world are largely connected with desert life. The message of Moses was delivered in the desert. It runs through the stories of Elijah and John the Baptist. Even Jesus, who came 'eating and drinking', withdrew to the wilderness to prepare for his mission. St. Paul retired for some years to Arabia after his conversion. The reforms of Mahomet were conceived in those regions.

There was thus developed from the desert a puritan outlook which condemned the ritual practised in the agricultural regions and in cities. We can see this attitude in the story of Sodom and Gomorrah. It runs through the book of Joshua and partly explains the evil repute of Tyre and Sidon at a later age. We can see it to-day in the attitude of Wahabi fanatics towards Medina and Mecca.

The tribes of Arabia have thus been moved by religious and moral feelings, as well as by economic motives, to conquer the settled areas beyond their desert home, whenever a leader emerged whose genius enabled them to combine in numbers sufficient for the purpose. In the Semite world, as elsewhere, monarchies were founded by pastoral chiefs, and their titles were based on a claim to divine right in its clearest and most definite shape. So long as each tribe or nation was held to have gods of its own there were limits to the pious duty of conquest. But as one nation came to believe in its own god as the universal deity, the duty of conquest was deprived of all theoretical limits. Universal dominion was the necessary dream of a people who held such beliefs as Israel held at the Christian era, and as Islam adopted centuries later. We must therefore study in some detail the gradual growth of this potent idea.

Some seventeen hundred years before Christ, Egypt seems to have been conquered by Semitic hordes from the deserts of Arabia. The rulers they placed on the throne are known as the Hyksos or Shepherd Kings. From two to three centuries later the Egyptians rose under native leaders and enslaved or expelled the invaders. It is natural to suppose that the return of some of these nomads to the desert occasioned the stories we read in the book of Exodus.

At Kadesh, which lies some eighty miles north of the Gulf of Akabah, a number of these tribes were collected by Moses. From him they acquired religious ideas which gave them a sense of unity so close that after-generations explained it on the theory of common descent from a single ancestor. They learned to regard themselves as a people standing alone and apart, not merely from alien breeds like those of Egypt, but even from the kindred tribes of the Semite world. Their God Yahwe, so Moses taught them, was their only God, a spiritual being to be worshipped in the form of no visible image. He was to be served, not in shrines by priests offering sacrifices, human or animal, but by the faithful observance of moral laws, which Moses enunciated in a brief code.[2] Their relation to this national God was conceived as a covenant, by which he was bound to save them in war from their enemies so long as they kept his law.

The first commandment delivered by Moses to the children of Israel was "I am the Lord thy God.

Thou shalt have no other gods before me." Somewhere back in the twilight of history this idea that they had one God and one only served to unite the tribes of Israel wandering in the desert of Sinai. It raised their minds from superstitions which divide the world to spiritual truths which bind it together.

Polytheism arises by the personification of natural forces. Sunlight, thunder or pestilence are conceived as the work of invisible beings. Monotheism arises from an effort, whether conscious or otherwise, to explain by hypothesis a psychological fact—the sense men have of a difference between right and wrong. In a world saturated by polytheism the idea could only occur to a mind of exceptional power. The children of Israel, when they had grasped it, assumed that Yahwe must have revealed the secret of his nature to Moses in the wilderness.

As compared with the heathen gods and goddesses Yahwe was a spiritual and ethical conception. He was never to be worshipped in the form of an idol or with rites tainted with any kind of obscenity. The God of purity, he was also the God of justice. Righteousness was conceived as the will of God. As Yahwe was the God of Israel, so Israel was the people of Yahwe. Other nations had their gods and goddesses of whom Yahwe was jealous, and against whom they fought under his leadership, as a war God. For Israelites to yield to a primitive craving and to worship the idols of surrounding tribes was not merely a crime against Yahwe but treachery to the national idea. As the jurisdiction of Yahwe was coincident with the territory of Israel, so to conquer and exterminate heathen nations was to extend that jurisdiction, an act in which piety and patriotism were combined. They spoke of victory in battle as 'the day of Yahwe'.

When in after-ages the Hebrew legends and law were recorded in scriptures, the name of Yahwe was

deemed too sacred for ordinary lips to pronounce.
In order to remind those reading aloud to substitute
the word Adonai (Lord), the vowels in Yahwe were
omitted. At a later date the vowels of Adonai were
inserted beneath the consonants, and, in ignorance
of this, the Christian scholars who learned Hebrew
read the name as Jehovah.[3] This erroneous form
became familiar in English translations, and now
suggests to our minds the tremendous attributes
which the Hebrews learned to associate with a word
that they dared not pronounce. To them in course
of time Yahwe came to imply the one universal God,
and that is the idea which Jehovah conveys to our
minds. To us the name Yahwe suggests a Semitic
God who stands some way removed from the level
of Baal or Chemosh. The value of a word should be
judged, first and foremost, by its power of conveying
ideas. Attempts to force our lips to pronounce what
can never be more than a bad imitation of the sounds
made by those who first uttered them will, if they
succeed, impoverish a living tongue. The scholars
who shortened the first syllable of Satan did more
to diminish his terrors than the sceptics who questioned his very existence. In these pages we shall
follow the tradition of the Bible and Milton, and
refer to the God of Israel as Jehovah.

The native Pharaohs, after ousting the Shepherd
Kings, had conquered Canaan. By the fourteenth
century they were losing their hold on the country.
In letters found at Tell-el-Amarna, the captains of
hard-pressed garrisons report an inroad from the
desert of tribes called Habiru. The date of these
letters is about 1350 B.C., and according to philo-
logists "the equation of Habiru with 'Ibhrim or
Hebrews is perfect".[4]

Canaan was the causeway, easily traversed because fertile, which connected Asia with Egypt and
Africa. As in China and India, a people who live by

tilling the soil are apt to develop elaborate cults. As the Hebrew nomads conquered the country and took to agriculture they began to temper the severity of the creed which Moses had taught, and copied practices followed by their Canaanite neighbours and serfs. They adopted their elaborate rites and learned to propitiate Jehovah by the sacrifice of animals and even of men, women and children. At times they worshipped their god in the form of a calf, a relic, as with the Brahmins, of an age when herds had furnished their means of subsistence. The superstitions of Canaan were thus grafted onto the teaching of Moses. Judah and Benjamin in the barren south were less exposed to such influence than the tribes which had conquered the fertile country to the north.

The adoption of ritual presently led to the development of an organised priesthood. In course of time the priests became a professional caste with a vested interest in ceremonial. There were seldom wanting, however, successors of Moses, who raised their voices against these practices. The priests, who figured as the guardians of established custom, were in frequent opposition to the prophets, whose sanctuary was often the desert.

But for the prophets, the teaching of Moses might have been buried as deeply in paganism as the teaching of Gautama is now buried in some sects of Buddhism, or the teaching of Jesus in some of the Christian Churches. In course of time they brought their people to abandon the worship of Jehovah in the form of an idol. The story of how God first commanded and then once for all forbade Abraham to sacrifice Isaac, his son, records their success in weaning Israel from a horrible rite. But animal sacrifice and a vast fabric of Canaanite ritual remained as an integral factor in Hebrew religion until the Romans destroyed the temple.

In an age when priests had begun to prepare

manuals of worship, these rites were ascribed to Moses himself. The idea that God could be pleased with the smell of an animal's blood and of its roasting flesh became a part of the national faith. To the last there were prophets who openly condemned such beliefs.

In course of time Hebrew ascendency in Canaan was threatened by a Cretan people who had settled on the coast opposite their island home. The pressure of Philistine armies forced the tribes of Israel to unite under one military leader. Saul of the tribe of Benjamin for a time rolled back the invaders. Later on he was beaten and perished in battle; but the fortunes of Israel were presently retrieved by David, a shepherd of the tribe of Judah. In the course of his reign he stormed the citadel still held by a Canaanite tribe in the country of Judah and made it his capital.

To unite the tribes by building a great shrine at Jerusalem was an obvious expedient; but David seems to have shrunk from a step which suggested that Jehovah could inhabit a house made with hands like a pagan deity. His powerful son Solomon had no such scruples. With the aid of Phoenician craftsmen he raised a temple to Jehovah, which also included shrines for the gods of his foreign seraglio.

Had the kingdom as founded by David and enlarged by Solomon endured, its history would scarcely have differed from that of other Semitic autocracies. Original thought would have languished under its rule and the Hebrew prophets might never have emerged to change the course of human destiny. But the centralised policy of Solomon had overstrained the national loyalty of the northern tribes. They grudged the revenues drawn from their richer country to embellish the capital in the sterile south. So after his death they seceded and established for themselves a separate monarchy with its seat at Samaria. The house of David continued to rule over Judah and Benjamin. The two Hebrew kingdoms were often at war with each other. When the monarchies of Mesopotamia and Egypt, strong in the wealth of their great riverine systems, came into conflict the Hebrew tribes were like grain between millstones. But foreign oppression may strengthen and purify native religion. In the debris of national ruin the fire which Moses had lit burst into flame from the hearts of the prophets.

The revolt of Israel from Judah seems to have occurred in the tenth century before Christ. The Phoenicians were now actively pushing their trade through the Mediterranean, and Carthage was founded in the ninth century. Damascus needed an outlet to the sea south of Phoenicia. Syrian armies invaded Israel, and in this struggle emerged Elijah, the central link in the chain which connects Moses with the prophets. In the cleft of Horeb where Moses was said to have talked with God, Elijah learned to divine his purpose for Israel in the quiet promptings of conscience, and not in the loud forces of nature.

And behold, the Lord passed by, and a great and strong wind rent the mountains, and brake in pieces the rocks before the Lord; but the Lord was not in the wind: and after the wind an earthquake; but the Lord was not in the earthquake: and after the earthquake a fire; but the Lord was not in the fire: and after the fire a still small voice. And it was so, when Elijah heard it, that he wrapped his face in his mantle, and went out, and stood in the entering in of the cave.[5]

With the rise of empires, which was now beginning, the Syrian kingdom was swept aside. First Nineveh and then Babylon aspired to dominate the Nile and Mesopotamia. In the eighth century Israel became an Assyrian province, and military colonies were planted to hold down the Hebrew peasants. The leaders were removed to another part of the empire; hence the legend that the ten tribes were exiled and lost.

Judah was overrun and her shrines destroyed, all save the temple which Solomon had built. The walls of Jerusalem alone resisted the onset of Assyrian armies; but her kings had to render tribute to Nineveh. Towards the close of the seventh century, as Nineveh began to weaken, the patriots of Judah raised their heads. Under the rule of the young Josiah they sought to make Jerusalem the centre of national worship, not only for Judah, but also for Israel. In 612 B.C. Nineveh was destroyed by a combination of Babylon with the Medes and Scythians. Pharaoh, hastening to the help of his suzerain, seized and executed Josiah at Megiddo, but was presently crushed by Nebuchadrezzar. So Judah became a province of Babylon. In 588 B.C. Pharaoh Hophra drew Judah into rebellion. They were both crushed. The armies of Babylon sacked Jerusalem and burned the temple. Zedekiah, the last king of the house of David, was deported to Babylon with some of his subjects. Those chosen for deportation were of course leading spirits, and included the party who had sought to make the worship of Jehovah in the temple on Mount Moriah the axis of Jewish life. Exile strengthened the instinct to crystallise their creed into codes and hold themselves aloof from people not of their blood. But even so, they acquired certain ideas from the Babylonian myths. The belief in angels is probably due to this source.

Among the exiles, however, was a school more influenced by prophetic than by priestly thought, who did not regard the temple in Jerusalem with its organised ritual as essential to the faith. Jews of this way of thinking were freer to follow their instinct for trade. In the ports of the Mediterranean Jewish communities began to collect. No doubt they attracted some of their kindred from Palestine. For their public worship they established meeting-houses, which, as they adopted the Greek language, were called synagogues. They were not shrines or places for sacrifice, but centres of teaching as little adapted for dramatised worship as a Methodist chapel.

To the east of Mesopotamia was Persia, which was partly inhabited by vigorous nomads. While the Jews were in exile an Aryan leader, Cyrus the Great, emerged from these regions, and conquered the kingdoms west of Persia as far as the Black Sea and the Mediterranean. About 539 B.C. Babylon was subdued and incorporated in his empire, which his son Cambyses afterwards completed by conquering Egypt.

The Persians were followers of Zoroaster, who conceived the principle of goodness as one, though opposed in secular conflict to the principle of evil. This explains the sympathy which Cyrus clearly felt for the monotheist exiles from Palestine, and why he allowed those who regarded Jerusalem as the necessary centre of worship to return and rebuild their city and temple. By 444 B.C. the work was complete. The Jews had abandoned idolatry, but a shrine arose once more where the unseen God was supposed to dwell. An altar smoked to Jehovah and an organised corps of priests enacted a highly dramatised ritual.

The restoration of the temple and its worship revived the old antagonism of Israel and Judah, and the northern Israelites established another centre of worship on Mount Gerizim. This estrangement was still acute in the time of Christ. To this very day Samaritan worship with blood sacrifice is practised on Mount Gerizim.

NOTES

[1] Keith, *The Antiquity of Man*, p. 40.
[2] *The People and the Book*, p. 236.
[3] Moore, *Old Testament and Semitic Studies* (1908), i. p. 145.
[4] *The People and the Book*, p. 123.
[5] 1 Kings xix. 11-13.

CHAPTER V

THE LAW AND THE PROPHETS

BEFORE the exile the priests of the temple had reduced to writing the traditional ceremonies together
with a number of social ordinances. These writings
came to be known as 'the law'. It is needless to argue
that civilisation could never have passed certain
points without the invention first of writing and also
of printing. But none the less real progress has often
been hampered or embarrassed by both. Time and
again the fluid ideas and customs of a primitive age
have been cast by scribes into rigid moulds and
forged into chains for after-generations. Writing,
moreover, like printing, has a curious psychological
influence. Even educated people will sometimes support a statement they have made by adding that
they have seen it in print. The influence of letters on
a primitive community was infinitely greater. The
ideas and usages of the Mosaic age, when written
out, acquired a sanctity which tended to increase
rather than diminish with time. Moses was believed
to have taken them down at the dictation of Jehovah
himself. The books of the law prescribed in minute
detail the manner in which the God of Israel was
to be served. And as they were inspired, so every
sentence was equally important—the directions for
sacrifice and ceremonial cleansing not less than the
ten commandments. In time they came to be regarded as containing not merely truth but the whole
of the truth. An attempt to add anything which was
not implicit in those writings was blasphemous presumption. The priestly caste which recorded the law
had an obvious interest in fostering such notions.

That Israel was none the less able to produce a long line of successors to Moses, who, like him, were profound and original thinkers, was due to its struggle for existence in the conflicts between Egypt and the northern and eastern despotisms. The ideas through which genuine religion has been gradually freed from primitive superstitions rooted in fear came from these prophets. Though prophets were sometimes found working in alliance with the priesthood, the two callings were profoundly opposed. The teachings of the prophets when written down came to be regarded, like the law, themselves as sacred and inspired. After a time the priests contrived to terminate the nuisance. They encouraged the idea that the age of the true prophets was finally ended, so that Israel had merely to obey the law and the prophets as they stood. By this process the 'canon was closed' and the Scriptures confined to the library known to the Christian world as the Old Testament.

The inveterate hostility of priests to prophets is recorded in a passage inserted by a priestly hand somewhere about 160 B.C. into the book of Zechariah (xiii. 2-5):

I will cause the prophets and the unclean spirit to pass out of the land. And it shall come to pass that, when any shall yet prophesy, then his father and his mother that begat him shall say unto him, Thou shalt not live; for thou speakest lies in the name of the Lord: and his father and his mother that begat him shall thrust him through when he prophesieth. And it shall come to pass in that day, that the prophets shall be ashamed every one of his vision, when he prophesieth; neither shall they wear a hairy mantle to deceive: but he shall say, I am no prophet, I am a tiller of the ground; for I have been made a bondman from my youth.

The hereditary priesthood in Jerusalem regarded the prophets, who often sprang from the peasant class, with the jealousy of a cultured and privileged nobility. Jerusalem was a place dangerous to prophets.

Up to and during the period of the exile the prophets were patriots who believed intensely in the moral nature of the God of Israel. They thought out the consequences of that premise up to certain limits and arrived at results from which those who followed them reached far wider conclusions. They passed from the Mosaic stage of regarding Jehovah as the one God of Israel to the conception of Jehovah as the only God of the universe. "Thou shalt have none other gods before me" of the Mosaic law becomes in the prophets "There are no other gods than I".

On the other hand, their view of the life which awaited men after death had not emerged from that stage of paganism which is closely connected with ancestor-worship.[1] The souls of the dead were conceived as continuing some kind of ghostly existence in a place called Sheol under the earth. It was very like Hades as depicted by Homer, when he tells how Odysseus went down to it to visit the soul of Achilles. "Sooner would I be the slave of a landless man on earth than king in the realm of shadows" is the best that Achilles can say of the lot beyond death which awaits even the hero. So Sheol was a place of ghosts where good and evil alike met a fate faintly removed from annihilation. They had there no relations with God. "For Sheol cannot praise thee, Death cannot celebrate thee; they that go down into the pit cannot hope for thy truth."[2] These early prophets were not looking beyond the grave. The life in communion with God, the only life worth considering, was the life of the nation and not the life of the individual. It was to be lived not merely by punctilious observance of the minutiae of the law, as the priests taught, but by purity of life, righteous dealing, mercy to the weak, humbleness of heart.[3]

The people of Israel had been chosen by God to fulfil his will upon earth, and if they were faithless and disobedient God would destroy them.[4] This was the message of Amos (*circa* 760 B.C.), a shepherd who came from the edge of the desert to the south of Jerusalem. 'The day of Jehovah', he warned Israel, would mean destruction not to their enemies, but to themselves.[5] So also the first Isaiah in the closing years of the eighth century.[6] In this last prophet there is one concession to the popular hope that in the end Jehovah will pardon and restore his people.[7]

The second half of the seventh century was the era of the great reforms carried out by Josiah in the kingdom of Judah after it had survived the destruction of the northern kingdom. In consequence we find a different note in Nahum, Habakkuk and Zephaniah, the prophets of this period. The people of Judah are now regarded by these prophets as a righteous people in contrast with the wickedness of the heathen, who are doomed to destruction. Henceforward the habit develops of distinguishing Judah as the righteous and the Gentiles as the wicked. The destruction of the Gentiles in 'the day of the Lord' appears as a feature in Jewish conceptions of the future. In Nahum and Habakkuk the enemies of Judah are to be destroyed. In Zephaniah the idea of Jehovah as the one universal God of the earth has advanced a stage further. His judgement will apply to all the nations alike. At the close of it will be saved a righteous remnant of Israel.[8]

So far the prophets had thought of the 'day of Jehovah', the day of judgement, as applying to the nation as a whole. The idea that a remnant will be saved marks a change. Separation of the righteous from the wicked as the consequence of judgement implies that the prophet is beginning to consider the fate of the individual as distinguished from the fate of the nation. This idea comes strongly to the front in Jeremiah, who lived to see the fall of Jerusalem in 586 B.C., and also in Ezekiel, who went into exile in Babylon. The destruction of the Hebrew state forced the prophets to consider the fate of the individual Hebrew. But as their thoughts scarcely extended to a future life, the hopes of the individual are encouraged by a promise that the Hebrew state will witness a glorious revival. A new and regenerate Israel is to result from rewards and punishments assigned to individual Hebrews.

In one passage Jeremiah foretells that a scion of the royal house will govern the restored kingdom:

Behold, the days come, saith the Lord, that I will raise unto David a righteous Branch, and he shall reign as king and deal wisely, and shall execute judgement and justice in the land. In his days Judah shall be saved, and Israel shall dwell safely.[9]

So, in the minds of this primitive and tortured Semitic community, ground between the millstones of Nineveh, Babylon and Egypt, was born the dream of a righteous kingdom established by God himself, a dream destined to influence the course of history and to mould human society for over two thousand years.

In the view of Jeremiah the Gentiles will be admitted to the Kingdom of God if they repent.[10] In the view of Ezekiel salvation is only for the righteous in Israel. For the Gentiles there is no room for repentance. They must either perish or, at best, survive as helots in the Kingdom of God.[11] Both Jeremiah and Ezekiel had arrived at absolute monotheism. But Jeremiah had divined that if there be one righteous God of the whole universe there must be room for repentance for all peoples of the earth, for the Gentiles as well as for the Jews. Ezekiel asserts that spirit of exclusion, which led the Jews to hold themselves aloof from other civilised nations, as they came in touch with them. In his view the Kingdom of God is for Hebrews alone. In Jeremiah the Kingdom of God is open to all, to Gentiles no less than to Jews. His idea led on to Christianity. The soul of Ezekiel issued in Judaism.

In the mind of that age there was no distinction between natural and supernatural events. In rain or droughts, in famine or plenty, in victory or defeat, they saw the direct and conscious working of Jehovah. God was the final reality, the absolute master of forces natural and human. For the prophets the only question was how far Israel could realise this truth and act upon it. Their future prosperity depended on obedience to the unseen spirit of righteousness who governed the laws of the universe. But as yet that conception was not fully thought out to all its conclusions. After death the righteous and the wicked alike passed to Sheol, a place beyond the divine jurisdiction.

The Kingdom of God for which they were looking was in fact an earthly kingdom established in Canaan with its centre in Jerusalem, such as had once been realised in the golden age of David. Its ruler would be Jehovah, issuing his edicts from his seat in the temple, though, perhaps, through a visible ruler descended from David. This kingdom would be everlasting. Its citizens would enjoy it, but only for their natural lives.

But what of the righteous in Israel who had died before the day of Jehovah and the final establishment of his kingdom? In answer to this question the prophets began to conceive the idea that the righteous would be raised to life from their graves to experience in the flesh the benefits of the Kingdom of God. His justice seemed to require no less, and the miracle involved was no difficulty to their minds. Thus came into being that strange idea that, in the day of Jehovah, the day of judgement, the bodies of

the dead would rise from their graves and live once
more.

> Thus saith the Lord God: Behold, I will open your graves,
> and cause you to come up out of your graves, O my people;
> and I will bring you into the land of Israel.[12]

The vision of Ezekiel in the valley of dry bones
was in process of time to pass into dogma.

> And at that time thy people shall be delivered, every one
> that shall be found written in the book. And many of them
> that sleep in the dust of the earth shall awake, some to
> everlasting life, and some to shame and everlasting con-
> tempt.[13]

The reference to the book was no metaphor, for
it seems that priests actually kept in a roll the names
of those entitled to rank as members of Israel.[14] The
tremendous privileges claimed for the people of God
in contrast with the Gentiles required no less. This
roll was known as the book of life. In the day of
judgement it would be opened, and the names of
those entitled to inherit the kingdom of God would
be found in its pages.

By slow degrees the Hebrew seers were destined
to realise that the facts of life could not be reconciled with the righteousness of God, so long as the
relations of God to man were limited to physical life
on this earth. The wicked not seldom prosper, while
the righteous are found begging their bread. There
is in this life no adequate adjustment of merit to
reward. Jeremiah admits but cannot explain this.
Ezekiel, with his narrower outlook, ignores the
evident facts by assuming that in this life the righteous
will be blessed and the wicked be punished, as they
deserve.

Some centuries later the problem was faced with
superlative courage. A nameless poet took for his
hero a powerful sheik on the border of Edom and
Arabia. The attention of Satan is drawn by God

to the perfect virtue of the prosperous Job. To this Satan replies with a sneer that Job does not 'fear God for nought'. He is good because he is prosperous. The challenge is accepted and God authorises Satan to test the virtue of Job by taking away all his prosperity, sparing only his life. So Job is reduced to beggary, his children perish, and he himself is afflicted with leprosy. In the depths of his misery he is visited by friends who, true to the doctrine of Ezekiel, exhort Job to admit that he must have sinned to deserve such pain. Job, conscious of integrity, calls on God to justify his treatment of one whom he knows to be innocent. He is answered by God out of the whirlwind. The Creator of all things asks Job to consider whether he can explain the earth and heaven; the alternation of night and day, the order of the seasons, or the animal kingdom. If the human mind can grasp so little of the ways of God in the natural world, why then expect that the ways of God in the spiritual world can be fathomed? In a few closing words Job humbly admits the force of this argument, and falls back upon sheer faith in the justice of God, though it seems contrary to the facts of life.

The book of Job is a milestone in the progress of thought. It shows the Semitic mind approaching the truth reached by Socrates that if virtue and happiness, sin and pain are accurately balanced, in this life, as Ezekiel assumes, then virtue and sin lose their essential qualities. The Satanic sneer would remain unanswered.

The conception of reality as a spirit creative, righteous and existing beyond time and space, could not in the end be sustained without a further hypothesis. The souls of the righteous must also be assumed to be capable of inheriting the qualities of the spirit from which their being is derived. They also must know an existence beyond the limits of time

and space, an existence in which such temporal conditions as pleasure and pain would have no rele-
vance, where righteousness would need no extrinsic
reward. For a moment this conception seems to have
flashed through the mind of the poet, but only for a
moment.

But I know that my avenger liveth, And that at the last
he will appear above my grave: And after my skin hath
been thus destroyed, Without my body shall I see God:
Whom I shall see for myself, And mine eyes shall behold,
and not another.[15]

This idea which had thus begun to dawn on the
Hebrew mind was utterly different from the notion
mentioned above, that the bodies of righteous men
would rise from their graves and live on the earth
once more. This last idea was a product of folk-lore.
The idea of the soul as immortal was a genuine
product of thought. A confusion between them in
creeds and liturgies continues to darken the popular
mind.

In the Hebrew prophets we can thus discern great
philosophic ideas emerging in a tangle of notions
generated by the history of the Hebrew polity mixed
with folk-lore. The idea of a righteous God, of
society ordered in accordance with his laws, and of
that society as subsisting beyond time, hypotheses
which have vitalised civilisations, grew out of ideas
of a Hebrew kingdom ruled from Jerusalem by a
son of David, of a day of judgement at which it is
initiated and a book of life in which the names of his
subjects are enrolled. So from fields choked by the
superstitions of astrologers, alchemists and magicians
came the truths of astronomy, chemistry and physics.
The wheat and the tares must grow together to be
separated at the harvest.

This process is nowhere more evident than in the
opening chapter of Genesis, beyond all question the

work of a Hebrew exile in Babylon. The writer
accounts for the universe by adapting for the purpose
one from a number of Babylonian legends. In Mesopotamia he had obviously met and disputed with
people whose minds were tinged with the pessimism
of the further east.

Nowhere as in India has the idea of the impermanence
of the transient and the unreality of the phenomenal entered
so deeply into the national soul, and become, even for the
uneducated, an unconscious presupposition of a practical
philosophy for everyday life.[16]

At this period, as Streeter shows, Hindu paganism
was undergoing a reform analogous to that which
Christianity afterwards produced in the Jewish religion. Its essential idea was cleared by Gautama of
polytheism and also of rites by which the favour of
deities could be won. This reforming process served
to emphasise the idea native to India that "all things
material, all the ordinary activities of daily life . . .
are essentially maya or illusion", and therefore worthless. "The real is the unchanging." The best hope for
the human soul is escape from the world where things
happen, to merge like a dew-drop and lose its iden-
tity in the infinite ocean where nothing can happen.
To the north of India the Persian Zoroaster had
founded another religion, based on a dualism which
identified goodness with spirit and matter with evil.
In the Indian view the world of sense was without
value, in the Persian positively bad.
To anyone who holds this in mind it is clear that
the Hebrew exile who wrote the first chapter of
Genesis had in the great emporium of Babylon met
and disputed with people whose minds were possessed by conceptions of the universe which came
from India or Persia. At each of the stages of creation he meets those views with aggressive contra-
diction. Six times he asserts, "God saw that it was

good", and when all is complete, he declares "And God saw everything that he had made, and, behold, it was very good". The origin of evil he relates in a legend but cannot explain any more than we in these days can explain it. Faced by a mystery, he reverts like Job to an attitude of faith in the goodness of God and therefore of his works. If reality, as the prophets had taught him, was a spirit creatively righteous, then the life he created was essentially good. We in this age may go a step further and say it is something in which the work of creation is worth continuing. Did the spirit of God really rest after his labours; or did he not rather call the beings he made in his likeness to join in his work? Is the age in which we are living not really the greatest of all the days of creation?

Gautama, who reformed and purified the Hindu religion, was perhaps contemporary with the Hebrew exile who wrote the opening chapters of Genesis. In the course of centuries Gautama's teaching pene-trated the great barriers to the north-east of India and China adopted a religion which this cheerful people would certainly never have produced for themselves. In the view of Dr. Hu Shih, the greatest of living Chinese philosophers, the genius of China was diverted by Buddhism from its natural course.[17] This vast section of human society was taught by India to regard the world of sense as illusory, at best worthless, and something from which to escape. The conception of life which could vitalise man's creative energy and make it continuous was a product of Hebrew thought, proclaimed on the first page of the book which Europe learned to accept as the manual of truth.

The riverine systems of Egypt and Mesopotamia were the natural homes of powerful monarchies based on agricultural revenue. In the country between them, where these monarchies met and fought, lay the Hebrew kingdoms. Here was nothing to develop political society except in its primitive form of monarchy. In the books of the prophets we can see how the institutions under which they lived reacted on their minds. They thought of Jehovah as the King of Kings and of righteousness as a law enacted by him. They conceived the ideas which they gave to the world as oracles of God revealed through their lips, and not as the products of human thought. They accepted without question the view that truths which govern human existence are revealed to man by God through supernatural means, and not otherwise.

The first people who dared to question the principle of authority were the Greeks. Truth, as they came to perceive, is discovered by human intelligence applied to the facts of life. In the word intelligence is included the faculty of imagination. Our perceptions enable us to observe a certain number of facts, which we then try to explain. We imagine a possible explanation, and conceive what the Greeks called an hypothesis; and then in the course of time we proceed to observe how the facts fit the hypothesis. If they do not fit it, we try to think of some new theory to explain the facts. So in course of time certain ideas, the fruits of a vivid imagination, are established as truths. In the physical world many theories are finally accepted as truths. For example, all educated people who are normal accept the Copernican view of the earth as a ball revolving in space round the sun.

In the metaphysical field we can never expect this degree of certainty. If we say that ultimate reality is made of the same stuff as our minds, rather than of the same stuff as our bodies, we cannot expect all reasonable people to agree, as when we assert that the earth is a sphere. The facts of the spiritual world cannot be measured and weighed like the facts of the natural world. The idea of the earth as a sphere is merely a high probability. A physicist would advise us to act on it with unquestioning faith. But our practical conduct depends even more on the view we take of metaphysical truths. A people who think that right and wrong are valid distinctions will develop one kind of society and those who deny the distinction will develop another. "In the long run", wrote Bishop Gore at the close of his life, "what any society is to become will depend upon what it believes, or disbelieves, about the eternal things."[18] Whether we like it or not, we must form an hypothesis as to the nature of things beyond those that we touch and see. But here like Job we are driven to adopt beliefs which do not satisfy everyone, which do not satisfy even ourselves. We choose what seems, in spite of difficulties, the wisest basis for human existence. As we recognise the limits of our own minds, we are led to rely on faith to a greater extent than we have to rely on it in the natural world. As Mark Rutherford says:

God vouchsafes to Job no revelation in order to solve the mystery with which he was oppressed. There is no promise of immortality, nothing but an injunction to open the eyes and look abroad over the universe. Whatever help is to be obtained is to be had, not through an oracle, but by the exercise of Job's own thought.[19]

The author of Job was in fact approaching the point which the Greeks in his time had begun to reach. As to whether ideas were already passing from the Greek to the Semite world we can only conjecture.

In its long struggle with kindred races Israel had won its way to monotheism cumbered and obscured by a mass of pagan traditions and beliefs. The impact of these ideas on Graeco-Roman civilisation was to shape the life of the modern world; and though Greece and Rome conquered Judea, the race was not always to the swift, nor the battle to the strong.

NOTES

[1] Charles, *Eschatology: Hebrew, Jewish and Christian*, chapter i.
[2] Isaiah xxxviii. 18.
[3] Hosea vi. 4-11.
[4] Amos iii. 1, 2.
[5] Amos v. 18-20.
[6] Isaiah xxix. 6.
[7] Isaiah i. 24-27.
[8] Zephaniah iii. 12, 13.
[9] Jeremiah xxiii. 5, 6.
[10] Jeremiah xvi. 19-21 and xii. 16, 17.
[11] Ezekiel xxxviii., xxxix.
[12] Ezekiel xxxvii. 12.
[13] Daniel xii. 1, 2.
[14] Charles, *Eschatology*, p. 165.
[15] *Ibid.* p. 71; Job xix. 25-27.
[16] Streeter, *The Buddha and the Christ*, p. 43.
[17] Hu Shih, *Religion and Philosophy in Chinese History*.
[18] Gore, *Jesus of Nazareth*, p. 250.
[19] Mark Rutherford, "Notes on the Book of Job", p. 197, in *The Deliverance* as reprinted by Jonathan Cape, 1927.

CHAPTER VI

When the Aryan invaders descended on India some other hordes of this restless race seem to have moved on south-eastern Europe. The village communities on the coasts and islands of the eastern part of the Mediterranean had already achieved a definite civilisation of their own. They also were mastered by those forceful invaders; but the racial difference between them was not wide enough to establish any permanent system of caste. Conquerors and conquered blended as thoroughly as, in a later age, Saxons with Celts or Normans with English.

The mixture of bloods was in varying proportions. The southern race was a maritime people, who were best able to hold their own where they rested on the sea. In coastal regions they absorbed their conquerors as thoroughly as the native Irish afterwards absorbed Norman invaders. On the shores and islands of the Aegean the Mediterranean stock prevailed, and hence a more versatile genius marked the Ionian branch of the Greeks. The Dorian branch was produced in the inland communities where the mixture of northern blood was richer. This process of fusion in various proportions was already complete in the Greek world as revealed in the *Iliad* and *Odyssey* of Homer. In its village communities there are headmen whose office is hereditary. They have priestly functions and are called kings. But the village meeting is a definite factor which rulers know that they cannot ignore.

In Hebrew literature we are always conscious of pressure from without. On one side is Egypt, on the

other Damascus, Nineveh or Babylon. In the poems
of Homer this feeling of pressure is absent. There
was nothing to force the Greek communities, as the
Hebrews were forced in the time of Saul, to submit
to a government common to them all. In Hebrew
writings the ocean is noticed but little. In Homer it
dominates everything with its strange paradoxical
power to divide and connect. The village communities of Greece on the shores of a sea dotted with
islands, though self-contained, are in constant touch
with each other. As their products are readily ex-
changed they are less dependent than the Hebrews
on agriculture. They speak the same language and
follow the same habits of life. They appear as a
nation except in this, that they have not achieved a
national government. The idea of the state is confined to the village communities and develops within
those limits.

The Homeric poems were probably composed by
minstrels and placed on record at a later age. They
show us what Greece was at the time when David
was ruler of Israel. When four centuries later the
Greek world can be seen once more in the pages of
Herodotus, a change has occurred of which the
Greeks themselves were unconscious.

The village meeting has already been noticed as
a natural product of village life. In a village the
heads of families can gather to discuss their common
affairs, in the hope that discussion may lead to agreement. But conference seldom leads to agreement
when the parties are more than two or three. So long
as a general agreement is assumed to be necessary
it cannot develop as a means of creating or establishing order or of enforcing justice, and it cannot, therefore, compete with any form of autocracy.

So far as we are able to judge from the poems of
Homer, the village assemblies of that age in Greece
were no exceptions to this rule. When the pages of

accurate history open we find that Greek assemblies
have in the interval hit on the novel device of taking
a vote, and also of accepting the decisions of majorities as binding. They have ceased to be mere gatherings for discussion and have grown into organs
capable of government.

In the Greek world as revealed in the pages of
Herodotus, the hereditary rule of kings like Aga-
memnon, Menelaus, Achilles or Odysseus has almost
vanished. The kind of government which has grown
out of village meetings varies according to circumstances. The villages have grown into city-states, a
growth aided by other causes than birth-rate, by
captives in war reduced to slavery and by immigra-
tion from neighbouring states. The families which
constituted the village community in the time of
Homer are now in the position of an aristocracy
surrounded by a larger number of inferior people.
In some cases the heads of those families which
formed the original village meeting have succeeded
in reserving the government to themselves. In others,
they have had in various degrees and by varying
means to admit the newer and larger populace to a
share in the government.

The inland cities were most dependent on agriculture for subsistence and on military organisation
for defence. The older families were thus able to
retain the power in their own hands. In coastal cities
it was otherwise. Subsisting largely on trade, they
attracted immigrants in larger numbers. For the
purpose of defence the seafaring citizens were at
least as important as the soldiers supplied by the
landed families. These coastal communities were
largely Ionian, a product of the mixture in which the
versatile Mediterranean stock prevailed. The Dorian
race, more largely derived from the northern invaders, prevailed in the inland communities. So in
Dorian states political power was generally limited

to the few. The bolder development of popular government was achieved in Ionian cities.

No system of government can be based on a meeting until it has learned the art of reaching decisions by taking a vote. A system in which decisions are made by a single autocrat is always far easier to work. In Greek communities the failure of experiments in popular government often led to a seizure of power by one leader supported by an organised party of armed followers. Such a government, based on force, with no sanction in custom or law, was described as a 'tyranny'. The idea of a monarchy based on divine right had no hold on the Greeks of that age. To them a tyranny was a government devoid of all moral foundations.

Such, in brief, were political conditions in the age when the Greek communities began to experience that pressure from without which had tortured Israel for centuries. The great riverine monarchies which oppressed Israel were now themselves conquered and absorbed by the Persian Empire. The pressure on the country between these monarchies was thus relieved. A remnant of Jews was restored to its home, and their heritage of thought, the fruit of long anguish, was saved for mankind. But in Hebrew monotheism the God of purity and righteousness, of mercy and truth, was also conceived as the King of Kings. It implied no threat to the principle of monarchy. With Greece it was otherwise. The ideas which inspired their civilisation were a challenge to the monarchy which had now united in one vast empire the countries known to the Greeks as Asia.

CHAPTER VII

As Herodotus tells us in his opening paragraph, the theme of his history is the conflict of Europe with Asia. By Europe he means Greece and her civilisation; by Asia the kingdoms which Cyrus had absorbed in the vast empire of Persia.

For Asia, with all the various tribes of barbarians that inhabit it, is regarded by the Persians as their own; but Europe and the Greek race they look on as distinct and separate.[1]

The conflict was not in reality racial. The issue at stake arose from a struggle between two systems of society, which is still in progress and cannot be ended till one of them has completely destroyed the other. The first of these systems came from Asia, the second from Europe. But the secular struggle of Europe with Asia is blurred by the fact that the principle of monarchy, first developed in Asia, for ages mastered Europe itself, whilst the principle of the commonwealth which first sprang from Greece is now profoundly affecting Asia.

In Chapter II. we have seen how the first need of the village community based on agriculture was security. A village meeting where nothing was decided till all were agreed was powerless to meet this need. It was no match for the military conqueror, who found that it paid him to provide some security for the conquered villages, and inevitably based his right to rule on a claim to divine authority. Kingship based on religious sanctions in fact provided a degree of security for life and property much in advance of any security possible in a merely village or tribal society. It thus made possible a definite advance in arts and crafts, and finally led to the all-important invention of writing. With a system of record it was possible for rulers to organise states on a firmer basis and for larger areas. So recorded history opens with the story of great monarchies and greater empires in Egypt and Asia.

The theory of divine right enabled men to obey some motive higher than their own desires, and to this extent was based on reality. To this element of truth is due the contribution which monarchy has made to human progress. To its vast unrealities is traceable its ultimate failure to keep men moving along that path. For the ruler who thinks of himself as clothed with divine knowledge as well as authority is likely to lose his sense of proportion. The belief that his own ideas are inspired tempts him to reject the counsels of experienced advisers. His personal will, mistaken for divine intuition, is of more importance than the manifest wishes of his subjects. He becomes a prey to passion and caprice and learns to regard the people as well as the land he governs as his personal estate. In India to-day there are princes of native states who frankly adopt that view. The word 'state' is a remnant of this notion in royal minds. The monarch comes to think of his dominions, however vast, as the appanage of his throne rather than of the throne as their administrative axis. Crowns felt to be worn by right unfit the wearers for the duties they impose. Decadence is the ultimate trend of hereditary rule.

The mark of a sound political system is capacity to renew its own vigour, or else to render itself unnecessary. Autocracy is wanting in both these qualities. The doctrine of divine right disposes the minds of rulers and subjects alike to regard power over

others as a good in itself, indeed as the object of
human existence. It mistakes a necessary means for
an end, and so directs human endeavour to a false
destination, which proves when it is reached not
worth the effort to attain it. A ruler who believes
that his power is of God, because it is power, regards
its extension as an act of piety. The subjects added
to his rule by conquest come to accept his power to
govern them as proof of his claim. Time and space
are the only limiting factors, the amount of business
which one human being can transact, and the
physical difficulty of controlling his officers at a
distance.

Of greater importance is the effect of this principle of authority on the people to whom it is applied.
In a village community no progress is possible without some external protection for life and property.
In the Greek communities the mountains and seas
afforded security sufficient for the purpose; but this
was a very exceptional case. With nomadic tribes,
life is devoted to conquest or defence. In any case
the energies of a people are mainly absorbed in the
struggle for existence. The rule of a dynasty imposed upon village communities, until it becomes
wholly corrupted, relieves this pressure. The instinct
to decorate begins to have play, and a monarch
desires not only revenue to defray the costs of
government, but objects of beauty to grace his court
and excite idolatry of his person. But progress in
civilisation will sooner or later come to a standstill
where laws are regarded as based on divine authority, and not on experience of facts apprehended
and construed by human intelligence. The principles
which govern human relations come to be grasped
only when the task of adjusting them is thrown on
the shoulders of ordinary men. They must realise
that true knowledge is gained in the process of
handling the facts of nature and life by an effort of

mind. Creative thought is denied to those who believe only what they are told.

The idea of divine right thus presumes that the ordinary man is incapable of learning what is best for himself in public affairs. His whole duty is one of obedience to rulers to whom this knowledge is reserved. Independence of thought will tend to impair that spirit of obedience. A system of authority therefore tends to restrict freedom of choice not only in public but also in private matters. It does little to develop in those who live under it a skill in reading the meaning of facts, still less their sense of duty to each other. It stunts the growth of mind and character by accustoming men to lead their lives in accordance with fixed rules and prescribed ceremonies without examining the reasons which underlie them.

By enabling their village communities to reach decisions, the Greeks were destined to release mankind from this vicious circle. They were making it possible for ordinary men to read the lessons of experience in public life. Let us think, for a moment, how a man reads the lessons of experience in his private life. He deals with facts, makes decisions, acts upon them and in course of time sees the results. In the light of experience, though often unconsciously, he grasps the principles which govern the facts. It is for this reason that some men grow wiser as they grow older and develop a sense of responsibility. They have made decisions and acted upon them. A man artificially relieved from the necessity of making practical decisions remains with the mind of a child to the end. The mere physical growth of the brain is stunted for want of exercise, just as the muscles of a hand which is never used fail to develop. A certain amount can of course be learned from the experience of others, but only in so far as we are able to compare their experience with our own. Experience based on verified guesses lies at the root of all practical knowledge. It is thus that men learn to distinguish right from wrong in the actual cases which rise for decision. That suffering is not the ultimate punishment of error, but only a guide to wisdom, is a truth to be learned from the discipline of nature. In that school and in no other can its pupils discover that a preference for justice is the final good and a preference for injustice the absolute evil.

In a village community the heads of families begin to be faced by public questions which each cannot decide for himself, but which none the less call for decision. Where men have learned to grow most of their food in fields this situation becomes acute. There is only so much land within reach of the village, and no family can decide how much land to cultivate without affecting the welfare of others. Questions like these must be decided together, and may, for the purpose of mere village life, be decided by general agreement in a village meeting. But, as we have seen, communal development is arrested at a certain point when decisions are limited to those cases in which general agreement has proved possible. Such a polity is no match against a band of pastoral invaders who all accept the rapid decisions of a tribal chief. The villages are absorbed into a monarchy, in which political decisions are largely made over the heads of the people by an individual ruler, and come to be regarded as made by divine authority. In greater matters of public life the people are then too cowed to think, decide and act for themselves. The process of learning by experience, by mistakes which they themselves have made, is arrested. Nor do they come to regard the state as a living thing to which they themselves are imparting life.

The practice developed by some of the Greek

E

villages of accepting a majority vote enabled decisions to be reached whenever occasion called for decision. Laws have their origin in custom, and custom binds like a framework of iron where it cannot be changed, unless everyone, including the least progressive elements in the community, agrees to change it. But if ever a stage is reached when minorities are prepared to accept the decisions of majorities, the community will begin to grow like grass where a heavy stone has been lifted from the roots. Their decisions involve public discussion and, therefore, an appeal to reason. In the private decisions we have to make in our daily lives, we are conscious that reason will carry us to a certain point and no further. We have then to act, see what happens, and correct our methods by the results obtained. Life is one long process of correcting by trial the best guess we can make. Thought and action are alike indispensable, and success in life depends largely on a right adjustment of one to the other. And this also applies to a public assembly which is trying to compose matters too large for its individual members to decide for themselves. An assembly like the old Polish Diet, which can decide nothing until every member agrees, has no power of adjusting action to thought. The device of reaching decisions by a vote of the majority enables a public assembly to do what the individual does in his private life. By putting a period to argument, it enables hypothesis to be tested by action and wisdom to be drawn from experience of facts as gold from ore.

If these considerations were held in mind, less time might be wasted in debating the moral right of a majority to decide. *Vox populi vox Dei*, the favourite gibe of those who dislike popular government, is a covert appeal to the creed that guidance in public affairs is really a matter of divine inspiration. The principle of decision by counting heads is based on the fact that all decisions are essentially human and, as such, liable to error. No course of action can be said with certainty to be right or wrong until it has been tried and the people who have made the decision have experienced the results.

The principle of majority rule is justified by the fact that so and not otherwise can a public meeting function as an engine of government. But its operation in practice implies more than an intellectual capacity in the members of the meeting to recognise this fact. In a commonwealth a citizen often knows that some decision made in the general interest means ruin and possibly death to himself. If self-interest or self-preservation are the strongest instincts of human nature, what reason can the citizen have to accept and obey such decisions? In fact human nature is capable of responding to another and higher instinct; for members of free communities constantly accept and obey laws ruinous to themselves. Majority rule can operate only in so far as citizens have come to recognise the interests of the commonwealth as above their own, and in fact to treat that interest as their highest good. The axiom which explains all others, but cannot be explained, is this, that a man's highest good is to use himself for the benefit of others. Imperfect as they are, human beings are capable of loving their neighbours as themselves and will come to do so the more they are called upon to exercise this faculty. Such mutual devotion, which finds its expression in a sense of duty, is the ultimate bond which unites society. The end and object of all political measures should be to strengthen that bond.

The commonwealth is a state whose members have acquired the faculty of making decisions for themselves and obeying them as laws. Its essential feature is the sovereignty of law based on its own reading of facts. But citizens cannot be allowed to obey the laws only when each is willing to do so. There will always be those who fail to see their own interest in that of others. Unless they are constrained, the law will cease to operate at all, and the decisions upon which it rests lose their effect. If the commonwealth is to exist, it must call upon those who recognise their duty to obey it to enforce its decisions on those who do not. The basis of law is devotion, not force, but a commonwealth must use that devotion to enforce its law.

This does not mean that the whole duty of a citizen to the state is comprehended in obedience to law. The community is composed of human beings liable to error, even in the things which most concern themselves. A loyal citizen may find a law so fatal to his fellows who have passed it that in loyalty to them he must set it at naught. Beyond comparison such decisions are the gravest that a member of a commonwealth can be called upon to take. A man must indeed be sure of himself before he presumes to judge that the true interests of his fellow-citizens are best served by resisting their will and by breaking their laws. In the last resort, however, there is no external authority, not even that of a law made by general consent, which a man may accept as overriding his own conscience. The commonwealth rests on the principle that in the last resort each man must decide for himself between right and wrong. For its end and object is to render them fitter for such decisions.

In a commonwealth the safety of life and property, and the power of the state to secure such safety, are not treated as ends in themselves. They are necessary means to the ultimate end, which is a continuous growth in the characters and minds of the citizens, a continuous improvement in their sense of devotion to each other and also in capacity to judge rightly of measures which tend to the general welfare. It was this which the Greeks meant by saying that the state existed for the sake of goodness ; for by goodness they meant a growing excellence in the character of the citizens. They had grasped the profound truth that the growth of character and mind depends, not merely on individual nature, nor even on teaching as applied to that nature, but also on a form of society which calls on its members to exert their faculties in the public interest as well as in their own. They had seen this happening in the limited circle of their tiny commonwealths, states so small that all the citizens could meet in the market-place to elect officers, enact laws and make even executive decisions. To them it was inconceivable that a system based on the principle of the commonwealth could ever be applied to larger communities. They never arrived at the principle of representation, and a commonwealth embracing Greece as a whole was therefore impossible.

The principle of a commonwealth closely connects the citizens who compose it with the land they live in, more closely than the subjects of a despotism based on the theory of divine right. A commonwealth must coincide with a definite section of the earth's surface or else with the whole of it. A ruler who claims an authority based on divine right may also claim that his edicts operate without reference to particular territories. The importance of this will be seen in later chapters of this inquiry.

The city of Athens was the state in which the principle of the commonwealth reached its fullest expression in Greece. It was here that poets, historians and philosophers came to interpret its meaning. The civilisation of Greece reached its highest development in Athens. It was she by her leadership that saved that civilisation when Asia threatened to overwhelm it. The names of Europe and Asia stand for ideas as well as for continents. The vast territories which extend eastwards as far as the Pacific were destined in time to inherit the name of Asia. The world owes it to Athens that the name of Europe was preserved and extended to the shores of the Atlantic.

NOTE

[1] Herodotus, i. 4 (Rawlinson's translation).

CHAPTER VIII

THE PERSIAN WARS

HELLAS in all its political varieties was a model of
Europe, as we see it to-day, on a miniature scale. Its
numerous states, though deeply conscious of a civilisation common to them all, were acutely jealous of
their separate sovereignties. The Greek communities
were unable to achieve a national government for the
race as a whole. Some states were of course more
powerful than others, notably Sparta, which by
means of a highly militarised system based on con-
servative institutions had attained a recognised
primacy at the period when Cyrus was creating the
Persian Empire.

Athens, the leading Ionian city, was next in authority. The foundations of her constitutional government had been laid by Solon in the opening years of
the sixth century. In 560 B.C. the supreme power in
the state was seized by an able tyrant, Peisistratus.
In 510 B.C. the sons of Peisistratus were expelled by
Cleisthenes, who headed a popular revolution. Under
his leadership the people of Athens re-established
their commonwealth and carried the principle of
responsible government to limits which could only
be exceeded when centuries later the device of representation was conceived and applied in the British
Isles. As many citizens were admitted to the sovereign assembly as could gather in the great market
of Athens and listen before they voted to the arguments of their leaders.

> For forms of government let fools contest;
> Whate'er is best administered is best.

How different was the view taken by the father of history may be seen from his comments on these events:

Thus did the Athenians increase in strength. And it is plain enough, not from this instance only, but from many everywhere, that freedom is an excellent thing; since even the Athenians, who, while they continued under the rule of tyrants, were not a whit more valiant than any of their neighbours, no sooner shook off the yoke than they became decidedly the first of all. These things show that, while undergoing oppression, they let themselves be beaten, since then they worked for a master; but so soon as they got their freedom, each man was eager to do the best he could for himself. So fared it now with the Athenians.[1]

In his opening pages Herodotus tells us how Cyrus, at the head of his Persian army, conquered the whole of Asia Minor. The Ionian cities on its western shores were submerged in these conquests. Their free institutions were suppressed. They were placed under native tyrants, supported by Persian troops and tributary to the King of Kings. By 545 B.C. their subjugation was almost complete.

In 539 B.C. Babylon fell to the arms of Cyrus, and in 538 B.C. he allowed the Jews to return to Jerusalem. In 528 B.C. Cyrus was succeeded by his son Cambyses, who added Egypt to the Persian Empire.

Since the age of which Homer tells us, the Greeks had founded prosperous colonies in Sicily and the south of Italy, an extension afterwards known to the Romans as Magna Grecia. The Greek communities of Europe were now confronted by the greatest empire which Asia had yet produced, a despotism which controlled the resources not only of Persia and Asia Minor, of Mesopotamia and Egypt, but also the maritime power of Phoenicia.

In 521 B.C. Cambyses died by his own hand. A usurper who seized the throne was quickly removed and his place taken by Darius, who belonged to a younger branch of the family of Cyrus.

About 512 B.C. Darius crossed the Bosphorus with an army, conquered Thrace and Macedonia, and then, after bridging the Danube, attempted to subdue the tribes of the Russian steppes. Darius was the first to experience the perils which beset the would-be conquerors of Russia. He retreated in time, but only with the remnants of his vast army, to find his power in Asia Minor seriously shaken. In 499 B.C. the Ionic cities revolted and appealed to Sparta and Athens for support. Sparta 'abode in her breaches', but Athens came to their aid with ships. In a few years Darius had organised new armies from the obedient millions of his vast empire. The free cities of the mainland collapsed at their approach. The islands of the Aegean resisted so long as their ships were able to retain command of the sea against those of the Tyrian Semites who were subject to Persia. A Phoenician crew was no match for a ship manned by resourceful Greeks fighting for the freedom of their own city. But the ships from these numerous cities were unable to establish and recognise a united command for their fleet as a whole. In 494 B.C. they joined battle at Lade and collapsed before the combined tactics of the Tyrian admiral. The islands of the Aegean were swept by the troops of Darius and incorporated in his empire.

Darius was now in a position to prepare an attack on Athens herself. In 492 B.C. an army and fleet, led by his nephew Mardonius, were ordered to move on to Greece by way of the Thracian coast. In rounding the promontory of Mount Athos the fleet was destroyed by a storm. Mardonius and the army had then to retreat. Warned by this failure, Darius decided to send a fleet across the Aegean with an army on board to invade Attica from the sea. In 490 B.C. Datis and Artaphernes, who commanded this armament, succeeded in landing at Marathon, on the east coast of Attica, troops greatly outnumbering the

citizens of Athens who opposed their advance. They
were swept from the shore by one brilliant charge of
the civic militia led by Miltiades. The Persians hastened by sea to Athens, hoping to land their reserves
and seize the defenceless city. But Miltiades rapidly
crossed the peninsula, and the Persians reached
Piraeus to find ranged on the shore the same spears
which a few days before had heaped the sands of
Marathon with dead. They returned to Asia to report
their failure.

The defeat of his army in a land battle by one
puny Greek city was an insult which the Persian
despot could scarcely afford to accept. He determined
to mobilise the naval and military resources of his
empire for the destruction of Athens and the conquest of Greece. He planned therefore to invade
Greece by land with an army so large that it would
have to be fed by sea. His fleets were organised and
reserved for that purpose. He died, however, in
485 B.C. After some hesitation his son Xerxes resolved to persist in the enterprise. According to
Herodotus his motives were explained in the following words:

Once let us subdue this people, and those neighbours of
theirs who hold the land of Pelops the Phrygian, and we
shall extend the Persian territory as far as God's heaven
reaches. The sun will then shine on no land beyond our
borders; for I will pass through Europe from one end
to the other, and with your aid make of all the lands which
it contains one country. For thus, if what I hear be true,
affairs stand: The nations whereof I have spoken, once
swept away, there is no city, no country left in all the world,
which will venture so much as to withstand us in arms. By
this course then we shall bring all mankind under our yoke,
alike those who are guilty and those who are innocent of
doing us wrong.[2]

His plans for the conquest of all Greece were based
on a strategy widely conceived. He arranged (so it
seems) for Carthage to attack the Greek communities

in Sicily from the west, while the Persian army and
fleet were advancing on Greece from the east. For
this purpose was assembled an army, the largest
which had ever been mustered for a single campaign.
The Hellespont was bridged and the danger of
rounding Mount Athos avoided by cutting a canal
through the isthmus which joins it to the mainland.
In 480 B.C. the hosts of Xerxes crossed into Europe
and advanced down the coasts of Thrace, Macedon
and Thessaly, drawing their supplies from the
Persian fleets.

Sparta at length realised that the Peloponnesus
itself was doomed unless the advance of the Persian
host could be stayed. She despatched a force under
Leonidas to hold the narrow defile of Thermopylae,
between Mount Oeta and the Maliac Gulf, through
which the Persian host must pass before it could
deploy for battle in Boeotia, overrun Attica and
attack the isthmus of Corinth. The Persians, however, got round his flank and surrounded Leonidas.
At the head of three hundred Spartans he died, leaving a name for valour rather than generalship. The
Persian host swept through the pass, and occupied
Athens. The citizens took refuge on the island of
Salamis protected by their ships and those of their
allies. In the sea fight which followed the Persian
fleet was utterly destroyed.

On the same day (so runs the story) the rulers of Syracuse
and Agrigentum, Gelon and Theron, vanquished the im-
mense army of the Carthaginian general Hamilcar, son of
Mago, at Himera so completely, that the war was thereby
terminated, and the Phoenicians, who by no means cher-
ished at that time the project of subduing the whole of
Sicily on their own account, returned to their previous de-
fensive policy.[3]

With the Greeks in command of the sea the Persian hosts encamped in Attica could no longer be fed,
so Xerxes retired in haste to Asia, leaving behind

him in Greece a force small enough to live on the country. In 479 B.C. the Greeks, led by the Spartan Pausanias, destroyed this force at Plataea, together with its leader, Mardonius. In the meantime the Athenians had crossed the Aegean and landed in Asia Minor with a number of allies. On the same day that Plataea was fought they defeated a Persian army at Mycale. A number of Ionian cities in Asia were thus relieved from the Persian yoke.

NOTES

[1] Herodotus, v. 78.
[2] *Ibid*. vii. 8.
[3] Mommsen, *History of Rome*, vol. i. pp. 330-31.

CHAPTER IX

In the course of this struggle the Greeks had received more effective leadership from Athens than Sparta. For a little the victory of Plataea restored the Spartan prestige, and Pausanias was placed in command of the Greek fleets organised for the purpose of freeing the cities still subject to Persia. Athens supplied the largest contingent, in command of Cimon, son of Miltiades, the victor of Marathon, and of Aristeides, whose return from exile at a critical moment had largely contributed to the victory of Salamis.

In 478 B.C. Pausanias sailed in command of the Greek fleet to Cyprus, which lay opposite the coast of Phoenicia, upon which the naval power of Persia was based. The Greek cities of the island were freed from Persian control and re-established as outposts on the southern flank of the Greek world. Pausanias then left with the fleet to accomplish a similar task in the north. Passing through the Straits of the Hellespont into the sea of Marmora, he besieged Byzantium and took it.

Pausanias had now conceived the idea of achieving the mastery of Greece for himself, and offered to betray her cause to Xerxes in return for the hand of his daughter in marriage. The Ionians got wind of his purpose and secured his recall to Sparta. His proven treachery was a final blow to her waning prestige. The leadership of the fleets passed to the Athenian commanders.

Aristeides, who was recognised as the most disinterested man of his time, was entrusted with the task of organising a league to defend the states more immediately threatened by Persia, those on the islands and eastern coast of the Aegean. He devised a scheme under which the states, members of the league, should contribute men, ships and money to the common defence. A synod was then convened in the island of Delos, to which delegates to the number of at least two hundred were sent by the member states. The synod adopted his scheme and the cash contributions were lodged in the temple of Delos, in the hands of ten 'stewards of the Greeks' who were as a matter of fact Athenians. For some years the synod continued to meet and discuss the affairs of the league under the presidency of Athens. In the meantime the combined forces of the league completed the work of freeing the Greek cities from Persian rule, under the leadership of Cimon.

In opposition to the growing power of Athens a Peloponnesian league was formed under the leadership of Sparta which included most of the states on the mainland of Greece. Of these many had colonies on the islands and eastern coast of the Aegean which were now the unwilling subjects of Athens.

The numerous states of Hellas were thus ranged into two leagues. Those on the mainland of Greece, which were largely Dorian, followed the leadership of Sparta. Opposed to these were the island states, and those on the northern and eastern shores of the Aegean, whose normal communications with the mainland of Greece were across that sea. Behind the racial and military rivalry of Dorian land power and Ionian sea power was a deep political issue. In each city the older families were averse to sharing the government of the state with the growing population. Such growth was of course greatest in commercial and maritime cities, like Athens herself, and in those ranged under her leadership. In the mainland cities which followed Sparta political power was usually

confined to the older families, who guarded that
power by reserving to themselves the use of the
heavier armour and weapons. In Ionian cities which
followed Athens there were often a group of powerful citizens ready to side with Sparta, if ever she
were strong enough to establish them in power over
the populace. In Dorian states like Corcyra the populace was sometimes ready to enlist the aid and help
of Athenian forces in expelling a native oligarchy.
The league headed by Sparta thus stood for the
principle of confining political power to leading
citizens, while the league headed by Athens stood
for the principle of extending it to as many citizens
as possible, though not to women or children, aliens
or slaves.

By a paradox, strange as any in history, the city
of Athens, which stood for the principle of democracy, became the tyrant of Greece. As the Persian
menace receded, the members of the league turned
once more to domestic affairs and left the control of
its general policy to Athens. Chios, Lesbos and
Samos continued to furnish their quota of ships; but
the rest preferred to commute this arduous service
for payments of money. The delegates failed to
attend at Delos, the synod faded out of existence and
Athens remained in undisputed control. The league
forces were used to coerce Naxos and Thasos when
those states withheld their contributions and claimed
the right to secede. In 454 B.C., when the synod had
ceased to assemble in Delos, the treasury was removed to Athens for greater security from Persian
attack. Henceforward the revenues of the league
were spent not only on the fleet, but were also used
for adorning Athens and providing doles for her
sovereign voters. By imperceptible stages the confederacy of Delos had become the Empire of Athens.

CHAPTER X

THE GREEK COMMONWEALTH AS VIEWED BY
CONTEMPORARIES

IN 431 B.C., the mainland states led by Sparta determined to challenge the growing power of Athens.
In the long struggle known as the Peloponnesian
War nearly all the cities of Greece were involved.
It was ended in 405 B.C., when Athens, defeated at
sea, accepted the terms dictated by Sparta. Its story
is told by Thucydides, an Athenian general, who
was banished from Athens in 424 B.C. and devoted
his exile to writing the history of this war. In brief
and pregnant words he stated the point of view which
has since governed all genuine historical writing.

The absence of romance in my history will, I fear, de-
tract somewhat from its interest; but if it be judged useful
by those inquirers who desire an exact knowledge of the
past as an aid to the interpretation of the future, which in
the course of human things must resemble if it does not
reflect it, I shall be content. In fine, I have written my work,
not as an essay which is to win the applause of the moment,
but as a possession for all time.[1]

Like Herodotus before him, Thucydides saw the
characters of the combatants as profoundly influenced by their institutions. The Spartan and
Athenian characters are contrasted in a speech which
he puts into the mouth of Corinthian envoys who
were trying to persuade Sparta to declare war.

The Athenians are addicted to innovation, and their designs are characterised by swiftness alike in conception and
execution; you have a genius for keeping what you have
got, accompanied by a total want of invention, and when
forced to act you never go far enough. Again, they are ad-

venturous beyond their power, and daring beyond their judgment, and in danger they are sanguine; your wont is to attempt less than is justified by your power, to mistrust even what is sanctioned by your judgment, and to fancy that from danger there is no release. Further, there is promptitude on their side against procrastination on yours; they are never at home, you are never from it: for they hope by their absence to extend their acquisitions, you fear by your advance to endanger what you have left behind. They are swift to follow up a success, and slow to recoil from a reverse. Their bodies they spend ungrudgingly in their city's cause; their intellect they jealously husband to be employed in her service. A scheme unexecuted is with them a positive loss, a successful enterprise a comparative failure. The deficiency created by the miscarriage of an undertaking is soon filled up by fresh hopes; for they alone are enabled to call a thing hoped for a thing got, by the speed with which they act upon their resolutions. Thus they toil on in trouble and danger all the days of their life, with little opportunity for enjoying, being ever engaged in getting: their only idea of a holiday is to do what the occasion demands, and to them laborious occupation is less of a misfortune than the peace of a quiet life. To describe their character in a word, one might truly say that they were born into the world to take no rest themselves and to give none to others.[2]

This theme is more fully developed in the speech which Pericles, the greatest of Athenian statesmen, delivered at the burial of the first Athenians who lost their lives in the Peloponnesian War.

Our government is not copied from those of our neighbours: we are an example to them rather than they to us. Our constitution is named a democracy, because it is in the hands not of the few but of the many. But our laws secure equal justice for all in their private disputes, and our public opinion welcomes and honours talent in every branch of achievement, not for any sectional reason but on grounds of excellence alone. And as we give free play to all in our public life, so we carry the same spirit into our daily relations with one another. We have no black looks or angry words for our neighbour if he enjoys himself in his own way, and we abstain from the little acts of churlishness

F

which, though they leave no mark, yet cause annoyance to whoso notes them. Open and friendly in our private intercourse, in our public acts we keep strictly within the control of law. We acknowledge the restraint of reverence; we are obedient to whomsoever is set in authority, and to the laws, more especially to those which offer protection to the oppressed and those unwritten ordinances whose transgression brings admitted shame. . . .

We are lovers of beauty without extravagance, and lovers of wisdom without unmanliness. Wealth to us is not mere material for vainglory but an opportunity for achievement; and poverty we think it no disgrace to acknowledge but a real degradation to make no effort to overcome. Our citizens attend both to public and private duties, and do not allow absorption in their own various affairs to interfere with their knowledge of the city's. We differ from other states in regarding the man who holds aloof from public life not as 'quiet' but as useless; we decide or debate, carefully and in person, all matters of policy, holding, not that words and deeds go ill together, but that acts are foredoomed to failure when undertaken undiscussed. For we are noted for being at once most adventurous in action and most reflective beforehand. Other men are bold in ignorance, while reflection will stop their onset. But the bravest are surely those who have the clearest vision of what is before them, glory and danger alike, and yet notwithstanding go out to meet it. . . .

In a word I claim that our city as a whole is an education to Greece, and that her members yield to none, man by man, for independence of spirit, many-sidedness of attainment, and complete self-reliance in limbs and brain. . . .

Such then is the city for whom, lest they should lose her, the men whom we celebrate died a soldier's death: and it is but natural that all of us, who survive them, should wish to spend ourselves in her service. That, indeed, is why I have spent many words upon the city. I wished to show that we have more at stake than men who have no such inheritance, and to support my praise of the dead by making clear to you what they have done. For if I have chanted the glories of the city it was these men and their like who set hand to array her. . . .

We survivors may pray to be spared their bitter hour, but must disdain to meet the foe with a spirit less triumphant. Let us draw strength, not merely from twice-told arguments—how fair and noble a thing it is to show courage in battle—but from the busy spectacle of our great city's life as we have it before us day by day, falling in love with her as we see her, and remembering that all this greatness she owes to men with the fighter's daring, the wise man's understanding of his duty, and the good man's self-discipline in its performance—to men who, if they failed in any ordeal, disdained to deprive the city of their services, but sacrificed their lives as the best offerings on her behalf. So they gave their bodies to the commonwealth and received, each for his own memory, praise that will never die, and with it the grandest of all sepulchres, not that in which their mortal bones are laid, but a home in the minds of men, where their glory remains fresh to stir to speech or action as the occasion comes by. For the whole earth is the sepulchre of famous men; and their story is not graven only on stone over their native earth, but lives on far away, without visible symbol, woven into the stuff of other men's lives.[3]

We have here a picture of life actually lived on a plane which no community had before reached: and no one has questioned the substantial truth of the portrait. The object for which the Athenian had learned to feel this intense devotion was not some vague abstraction, nor yet the place in which he lived, but the fellow-citizens who dwelt in that place with himself. "The people not the buildings are the city." "Neither tower nor ship are anything apart from the people who live in them."[4]

Amongst those who listened to the statesman and poet was a man greater than either, who was able to see what this kind of devotion implied. Portraits of Socrates have been drawn by two of his disciples, Xenophon the soldier, and Plato the incomparable literary artist. Early in life he embraced poverty in order to devote himself wholly to the task of helping his fellow-citizens to live according to reason. This as he conceived was possible only in so far as they would use their minds to grasp the principles of right living. In Socrates the Greek instinct to leave nothing unquestioned is seen at its highest. Profoundly religious, he attacked the current theology which represented the gods as beings capable of immoral conduct. His conception of God as one spirit, all-knowing and wholly just, was contrary to the ideas of orthodox Greeks, who believed in a number of gods and goddesses. They readily interpreted his ideas as atheism. Perceiving that men must find in their own sense of duty the final criterion of private or public morality, he ruthlessly exposed the contradictions which underlie the accepted canons of conduct. To conventional minds he seemed to be attacking morality. Their self-content was irritated by his ceaseless questions: they voted the questioner a highbrow and a bore. The constructive principles of conduct and belief which came in view when the rubbish was cleared from their minds were revealed only to a band of disciples who hung on his words.

The expression of those principles in his own life and death was a factor which gave permanence to his teaching. As a soldier in many campaigns he showed in the highest degree the courage and endurance ascribed to Athenians by friends and foes. On two occasions he refused to become the agent of illegal proceedings at the risk of his life. The first was in 406 B.C., when in an official position he refused, in response to popular clamour, to submit, contrary to law, a motion for the execution of certain generals. Some two years later, when the Tyrants established by the Spartans in Athens proscribed their opponents and ordered Socrates to arrest one of their victims, he defied their orders.

In 399 B.C. he was brought to trial and condemned to death on the charge of not believing in the gods of the city and of corrupting the youth. By promising his judges to keep silence in future he might have avoided this sentence. He refused to give this undertaking on the ground that "an unexamined life is not worth living". The commonwealth and law have their root in truth, and when law is used to stifle the search for truth it may be the duty of a citizen to break the law. Dying as a rebel, Socrates proved his supreme loyalty to Athens. And yet at the moment of his death he placed the duty of obedience to law higher than it has ever been put before or since. His friends had arranged his escape from prison. The reasons he gave them for refusing to accept their good offices are recorded by Plato:

SOCRATES. Consider it this way. Suppose the laws and the commonwealth were to come and appear to me as I was preparing to run away (if that is the right phrase to describe my escape) and were to ask, "Tell us, Socrates, what have you in your mind to do? What do you mean by trying to escape, but to destroy us the laws, and the whole city, as far as in you lies? Do you think that a state can exist and not be overthrown, in which the decisions of law are of no force, and are disregarded and set at nought by private individuals?" How shall we answer questions like that, Crito? Much might be said, especially by an orator, in defence of the law which made judicial decisions supreme. Shall I reply, "But the state has injured me: it has decided my cause wrongly?" Shall we say that?

CRITO. Certainly we will, Socrates.

SOCRATES. And suppose the laws were to reply, "Was that our agreement? Or was it that you would submit to whatever judgements the state should pronounce?" And if we were to wonder at their words, perhaps they would say, "Socrates, wonder not at our words, but answer us; you yourself are accustomed to ask questions and to answer them. What complaint have you against us and the city, that you are trying to destroy us? Are we not, first, your parents? Through us your father took your mother and begat you. Tell us, have you any fault to find with those of us that are the laws of marriage?" "I have none", I should reply. "Or have you any fault to find with those of us that regulate the nurture and education of the child, which you, like others, received? Did we not do well in bidding your father educate you in music and gymnastic?" "You did", I should say. "Well, then, since you were brought into the world and nurtured and educated by us, how, in the first place, can you deny that you are our child and our slave, as your fathers were before you? And if this be so, do you think that your rights are on a level with ours? Do you think that you have a right to retaliate upon us if we should try to do anything to you? You had not the same rights that your father had, or that your master would have had, if you had been a slave. You have no right to retaliate upon them if they ill-treat you, or to answer them if they reviled you, or to strike them back if they struck you, or to repay them evil with evil in any way. And do you think that you may retaliate on your country and on its laws? If we try to destroy you, because we think it right, will you in return do all that you can to destroy us, the laws, and your country, and say that in so doing you are doing right, you, the man, who in truth thinks so much of virtue? Or are you too wise to see that your country is worthier, and more august, and more sacred, and holier, and held in higher honour both by the gods and by all men of understanding, than your father and your mother and all your other ancestors; and it is your bounden duty to reverence it, and to submit to it, and to approach it more humbly than you would approach your father, when it is angry with you; and either to do whatever it bids you to do or to persuade it to excuse you; and to obey it in silence if it orders you to endure stripes or imprisonment, or if it send you to battle to be wounded or to die? That is what is your duty. You must not give way, nor retreat, nor desert your post. In war, and in the court of justice, and everywhere, you must do whatever your city and your country bid you do, or you must convince them that their demands are unjust. But it is against the law of God to do violence to your father or to your mother; and much more so is it against the law of God to use violence to your country." [5]

In the speech of Pericles and the argument of Socrates begin to appear the qualities which distinguished the Greek commonwealth from anything which had gone before it. We see here a society based on the assumption that all its members are called upon to contribute to its well-being the whole of their faculties, and if necessary life itself. That society is so constituted as to call for the exercise of those faculties to the utmost, and so develop them in the process. It seeks to increase the devotion of each to all by making the utmost demands upon it. The task of making decisions is thrown as completely as possible on the citizens themselves. And those decisions reduced to law are the final authority in the state, an authority as binding on the citizens as the edicts of a Persian king on his subjects. But the laws are not unchangeable like those of the Medes and Persians. They are subject to revision in the light of experience; but the duty of reading the experience and making the change rests on the citizens themselves. Their faculty for doing these things is developed by exercise. The commonwealth is thus a system of society which is capable of continuous growth, because it develops the mind and character of the members of whom it is composed. It calls into constant and active expression the capacity in men for putting the interests of others before their own. And in doing so it stimulates their mental capacity for conceiving and initiating the means whereby each service can best be rendered.

The Greek word for a city is πόλις. To the Greeks that word also connoted a state. The political history of mankind may be said to open with the development of the commonwealth in its miniature form by the Greeks. Based on the duty of each to all, it was something which differed in kind from monarchies in which any number of subjects are united in a common duty of implicit obedience to one ruler claiming divine authority and also knowledge divinely inspired and beyond the reach of ordinary men. Monarchy and commonwealth are alike based on a moral principle, on belief in the spiritual basis of things. They differ in this that the commonwealth puts its trust in reason and therefore must in the end prevail. What the Greeks described as 'tyranny' is a form of government based on no moral principle at all, a government which treats the conception of right as a figment, and sees in force the only reality. Tyranny is the necessary outcome of materialism, of the view that ultimate reality is of the nature of our bodies and not of our minds and souls.

The question which distracted the Greek common-wealths, as to how far government was to rest in the hands of the few or the many, was one which commonwealths have always to face. The common-wealth is a polity which recognises that power should be shared not by all its members, but at any rate by those who are fit for the task. No commonwealth has ever existed in which the suffrage was universal. The vote has never been given to children, and seldom if ever to recognised criminals. The commonwealth in which political power is too widely extended ceases to have a government, ceases to be a state, and therefore ceases to be a commonwealth at all. The end and object of a commonwealth is to increase by exercise the sense of duty which each of its mem-bers feels to the body as a whole, and also to increase his capacity for discharging that duty. But a com-monwealth in which too many of the voters are de-ficient in their sense of this duty, or, like children, in the knowledge how to discharge it, falls into utter disorder. The more the voters, the greater the diffi-culty of practical government. Where those who exer-cise power are few it is for the moment easier to govern and maintain order. So those who recognise the vital importance of order are disposed to limit power to the few. But in doing so they are apt to forget that they leave unexercised and undeveloped the sense of devotion in the many to the state as a whole. The wise democrat is one ready to risk immediate order to a certain degree in order to cul-tivate in a larger number of citizens that loyalty and knowledge of public affairs upon which in the long run the structure of the state can alone rest in security.

We have dwelt here on the difference of principle which distinguished a commonwealth from a monarchy, and both from a tyranny; and also on the question which confronts each commonwealth as to how far it is safe to restrict or extend political power amongst the citizens, because those issues, which emerged in ancient Hellas, are exactly the same as those which mankind is now facing on the wider stage of the whole habitable earth.

The speech of Pericles is the earliest recorded expression of the principle of the commonwealth, clearer and simpler than anything we can quote from the literature of classical Greece. It is generally accepted that the thoughts recorded by Thucydides, in this particular speech, are those of Pericles himself, not those of the writer put into the mouth of the orator. It is likely that Thucydides listened to the speech, and even made notes of what Pericles said. Apart from this speech our ideas of the Greek commonwealth are largely derived from Plato and Aristotle, and from the history of Thucydides himself. Great as these masters of thought were, their minds were inevitably clouded by the ultimate victory of Sparta and the loss of her empire by Athens. We are some of us old enough to remember the respect which everything German commanded from 1872 to 1918. The speech of Pericles was delivered in an atmosphere as yet unclouded by disasters which might never have happened if he himself had survived to direct the counsels of Athens.

The theme of Thucydides is the failure of Athenian democracy to grasp the principles implicit in their own constitution, as expounded in the speech of Pericles, and apply them in the wider field of external relations. In dealing with the other cities of Greece and their own allies they relied on a doctrine, the negation of the principle of the commonwealth, the doctrine that society is founded on force, that might is right, that the weaker lies at the mercy of the stronger, that law is valid only where parties to a controversy are equals in strength.

NOTES

[1] Thucydides, i. 22 (Crawley's translation).
[2] *Ibid.* i. 70.
[3] Thucydides, ii. 37-43 (Zimmern's translation in his *Greek Commonwealth*, pp. 200-205).
[4] Sophocles, *Oedipus Tyrannus*, line 55.
[5] Plato, *The Crito* (Church's translation).

CHAPTER XI

In the earlier stages of the Peloponnesian War the advantage gained by Athens was such that, in 423 B.C., the Spartans asked for and obtained a truce, which was followed by a treaty of peace and indeed of alliance in the following year. This peace was never a reality. The fact that Sparta had sued for it led the Athenians to suppose that her power might now be safely ignored, and they dreamed of including the whole of Greece in their empire. One Dorian colony on the Island of Melos had throughout maintained a position of neutrality. In 416 B.C. the Athenians required them to join their confederacy and pay the tribute. The story is dramatised by Thucydides in the form of a dialogue between Athenian envoys and the Melian government.[1] One sentence from the argument of the Athenian envoys will suffice to reveal the moral and political philosophy which was now inspiring the policy of their state:

You know as well as we do that right, as the world goes, is only in question between equals in power, while the strong do what they can and the weak suffer what they must.

The Melians refused to accept this argument, and hoping for aid from Peloponnese, tried to defend their city. Their hopes were in vain:

some treachery taking place inside, the Melians surrendered at discretion to the Athenians, who put to death all the grown men whom they took, and sold the women and children for slaves, and subsequently sent out five hundred colonists and inhabited the place themselves.

Since the truce of 423 B.C. the Athenians had dreamed of mastering the Greek colonies of Sicily and Italy, and of then using the resources of the west for the conquest of the Peloponnese. In 415 B.C. the strongest expedition ever despatched by a Greek state was sent to attack Syracuse, a Corinthian colony and the largest city in Sicily. Another, but little inferior in strength, was despatched in the following year. In 413 B.C. these fleets and armies were captured and destroyed by the Syracusans led by a Spartan general Gylippus.

This enormous disaster encouraged the allies to revolt from Athens. She herself was distracted by revolution and at times fell under the control of an oligarchy. The marvel is that a city so stricken could continue the struggle for eight years after the loss of her armaments in Sicily. Eventually the Spartans made an alliance with Persia, and with foreign gold constructed fleets strong enough to challenge the power of Athens on the sea. In 405 B.C. the Spartans destroyed the last Athenian fleet in the Hellespont. Athens was then at her mercy. Her walls were dismantled, and her empire dissolved.

To the conquerors in this war we owe the idea crystallised in the adjective 'Spartan' and little besides in the field of ideas. To Athens our debt is beyond calculation, and indestructible. We owe her those things which perish only to yield an increasing harvest of life. That Athens could give to the world poets like Aeschylus, Sophocles or Euripides, an artist like Pheidias, a statesman like Pericles, a teacher like Socrates or a thinker like Plato, while victorious Sparta continued sterile, was no mere accident. This amazing originative power was, as her own historians felt, something released by a system which laid the tasks of government on the largest possible number of citizens, on the largest number then possible, and in doing so raised, not only their faculties, but also their sense of mutual devotion to a higher power than ever before. Amongst these faculties was the gift of expression in permanent literary form. Time and again nations will fail in the task of establishing order for themselves, yielding to monarchies which claim divine inspiration, or tyrannies which deny the validity of anything but organised force. But so long as the literature which sprang from Athens remains, so long will the sense of freedom survive, to develop once more a system of society based on the infinite duty of each to all.

How comes it, then, that in this protracted struggle the Athenians appear as exponents of the opposite doctrine that right is a figment "only in question between equals in power, while the strong do what they can and the weak suffer what they must"? In answering that question it will help us to remember that Hebrew literature leaves the impression of a people time and again reverting to the worship of idols and human sacrifice. Yet will anyone seriously question that the vision of one God as the spiritual essence of all goodness and love was the special gift of the Hebrew race to the world? So a visitor to Russia or China, to India, Ireland or even the self-governing Dominions might receive the impression that they find in England a standing opponent to the right each nation claims to manage its own affairs. Yet in history England will figure as the foremost champion of that right.

The essential achievement of Greece was the realisation of a state, however small, in which the unlimited duty of each to all was reduced to a practical system of government and so developed by continuous exercise. By accepting the vote of majorities as binding, the village meeting had acquired the faculty of reaching decisions, had become the genuine government of the village. So, even when the village had grown to a city, the citizens could gather to discuss its affairs, to vote taxes and express their will in the form of laws. Such a system, so Aristotle said, was possible only where all the citizens could listen to the voice of a single orator. In Athens, the greatest city of Greece, it had reached its limits. So far as the Greeks and the wisest amongst them were able to see, the principle of the commonwealth was capable of realisation only in cities. It was not capable of realisation on the national scale, even for Hellas with its common language and civilisation. Yet the time had arrived when the mountains and seas no longer afforded sufficient protection for Greece as a whole. Her own inventiveness in the arts of shipbuilding, which nations to the south and east had copied, had exposed her cities to maritime invasions. Intrinsic efficiency in her cities and their citizens, developed by the habit of governing themselves, had just enabled them to repel the onset of Asia. But to hold Asia at bay some authority which could organise the forces of Greece as a whole was clearly necessary. The confederacy of Delos was an effort in that direction. It was doubtless intended that the synod at Delos should direct its policy. We only know that the synod failed; but it is not difficult to conjecture the reason. It is fairly safe to assume that delegates refused to agree to necessary measures proposed without further instructions from the several cities. It thus was found impossible to obtain decisions when decisions were urgently necessary for the public safety. The leaders of Athens, as the dominant partner in the league, then took the decisions and, fearing the menace of Persia, the allied cities accepted the results. The proceedings of the synod lost their reality and presently its members ceased to attend. The allies, by leaving the initiative and control in the military and maritime field to Athens, were in time obliged to accept her decisions. Allies in name, they

became her subjects in fact, and as the menace of
Persia receded, developed the outlook of subjects and
hated their Athenian masters in spite of their kinship.
No device had been found for realising the principle
of the commonwealth in the wider field of the national
life. In maintaining some kind of government for
Greece, the Athenians, without realising it, were led
to act on its very negation, to adopt that negation
as the basis of their rule, and in doing so compassed
their own destruction.

NOTE

[1] Thucydides, v. 85-116.

CHAPTER XII

NOTHING in her history became Sparta so much as her clemency to Athens in the hour of victory. She refused to condone the proposal of her allies that the people of Athens should be treated as they themselves had treated the people of Melos. Her walls were demolished, but the people were suffered to remain in their city, and even when shorn of all military power retained their predominance in the field of ideas. Some fifteen years later the walls were rebuilt, and by 377 B.C. Athens had emerged once more at the head of a maritime league.

The military power of Sparta was now being challenged by Epaminondas, a soldier of genius, who was arming and organising the citizen forces of Thebes on a new model. His methods were studied by Philip, a Macedonian prince, who in 367 B.C. was sent as a hostage to Thebes. In the course of his sojourn in Greece Philip fell under the spell of Hellenic culture, the recognised focus of which was Athens. When called to the throne of Macedon in 359 B.C. he used and developed the methods he had learned from Epaminondas to organise a regular army strong enough to cope with the citizen forces of Greece. No effort was spared to assimilate his barbarous subjects to the culture of Hellas, except of course in the field of government. With this object in view he brought Aristotle from the schools of Athens to act as tutor to Alexander, his son by an Albanian mother. At the age of eighteen this youth was leading the left wing of his army when in 338 B.C. Philip broke the combined forces of Thebes and

Athens at Chaeronea. To Thebes he showed no mercy. Athens he treated with clemency as the centre of Greek civilisation. He then convened a conference at Corinth, which Sparta alone refused to attend, and there combined the rest of Greece in a league to settle the long-standing accounts of Hellas with Persia, with himself as its military leader.

In 336 B.C. Philip was murdered by one of his own guard and the throne of Macedon with the military leadership of Greece passed to his son Alexander at the age of twenty. In 334 B.C. Alexander crossed the Hellespont and freed the cities of Ionia, substituting popular governments in the place of the tyrants and oligarchies established by Persia. He next proceeded to conquer the whole coast of the Levant. In 333 B.C. he destroyed in Tyre the heart of the Persian sea power. He then occupied Palestine and, by settling Greek communities in the heart of Judaism, this daemonic youth set in train events destined to shake the world and change the course of human history, as the writer of Daniel dimly divined.[1]

Through Palestine Alexander hastened to the conquest of Egypt. On the coast west of the Delta he founded a city which he called after himself. It was peopled partly with Greek settlers, partly with 100,000 Jews brought from Palestine. By 331 B.C. the conquest of Egypt was completed. The Persian monarchy was thus deprived of the last strip of coast from which ships could be launched in Mediterranean waters. Alexander was now free to strike at its heart, and on September 20, 331 B.C., he attacked and destroyed the armies of Darius near Nineveh. Ascending the throne of the fallen monarch, he reduced to obedience the distant satrapies which Darius had ruled in name rather than in fact. In achieving this object he marched to the furthest boundaries of the Persian Empire as far north as the Caspian,

G

eastwards beyond the Jaxartes and past Kabul into the Punjab to the valley of the Indus. A mutiny of his troops in 326 B.C. alone prevented him from pushing his conquests further. On the Indus he built a fleet which carried part of his forces back to the Persian Gulf, he himself leading the rest by a route near the coast to Susa, which he reached in 324 B.C. His superhuman vitality, which a number of wounds must have impaired, was now reaching its limits. In 323 B.C. he died at Babylon.

His father and he had imposed on Hellas a unity never achieved since the struggle with Xerxes, and under his leadership the Greeks had conquered the Persian Empire to its utmost limits. His amazing capacity as a soldier was merely one side of a greatness revealed in the field of creative ideas.[2] In the view of his master Aristotle the world was made up of Greeks and barbarians, "the lesser breeds without the law". The essential feature of Greek civilisation was the state, through the medium of which the fullest development of human faculties was alone attainable. But in Aristotle's mind such a state must be limited to the people of one city. To the Greek, no less than the Jew, the way of life for which he stood was limited to people of his own race. There is little in history more astonishing than the fact that the youthful pupil of Aristotle was able to transcend limitations from which an intellect so powerful as that of his master was unable to escape. In his schemes for ordering the world he had mastered Alexander deliberately set himself to destroy the idea that Greeks and barbarians were divided by a gulf which could never be bridged. Centuries later St. Paul was to picture a social order in which "there cannot be Greek or Jew, circumcision and un-circumcision, barbarian, Scythian, bondman, free-man".[3] This river of thought, if traced to its springs, will bring us, in the Hebrew world, to the prophet

Jeremiah, in the Greek to the youthful conqueror of Persia.

The world over which Alexander had ruled was divided after his death by his Macedonian companions and their successors. Macedon and the leadership of Greece fell to the house of Antigonus, Egypt to the Ptolemies, and the rest of the Persian Empire to the house of Seleucus.

By the conquests of Alexander Greek civilisation was so thoroughly established on the east coast of the Mediterranean that it lasted for more than a thousand years. Its influence extended even to India, and to-day sculptures can be noticed in the gardens of Peshawar which would not look out of place in the Greek galleries of the British Museum. But the empires of Seleucus and Ptolemy rapidly moved from the political traditions of Greece to those of Asia. In the Greek settlements the citizens continued to control their municipal affairs, but, in matters wider than those, learned to obey dynasties of their own race, who none the less claimed to derive their authority from Heaven, as frankly as their Persian predecessors had done. Though Greek manners and thought survived in these regions for some generations, they had no permanent effect on the structure of eastern society. The political traditions of Asia were impressed on the Greek monarchies, infected the Roman Empire which absorbed them, and through that empire have profoundly influenced the political development of Europe.

By his conquest of Palestine and Egypt Alexander had brought the Greek and Jewish communities into sudden and intimate contact. In Palestine he and his successors planted a number of Greek colonies. In Egypt, as we have seen, he created at the mouth of the Nile an entirely new city which was colonised partly by Greeks and partly by Jews. Throughout the Mediterranean Jewish and

Greek civilisation flourished for centuries side by side in separate and coequal communities. Except in Judea and Mesopotamia, the Jews acquired the Greek language and forgot their own. So a Greek translation of the Hebrew Scriptures had to be prepared to meet their needs. The Jewish mind which regarded these Scriptures as the word of God in the literal and absolute sense had a craving to feel that the Greek word was no less inspired than the Hebrew original. A legend was presently developed to satisfy this craving. Centuries later it was placed on record by St. Augustine and is worth quoting at length because it shows how this Jewish idea as to the means by which the eternal verities can be known to men fastened itself on the Graeco-Roman Empire, and through that empire on the Christian world.

§ 42. By what dispensation of God's providence the sacred Scriptures of the Old Testament were translated out of Hebrew into Greek, that they might be made known to all the nations.

One of the Ptolemies, kings of Egypt, desired to know and have these sacred books. For, after Alexander of Macedon, who is also styled the Great, had by his most wonderful, but by no means enduring power, subdued the whole of Asia, yea, almost the whole world, partly by force of arms, partly by terror, and, among other kingdoms of the East, had entered and obtained Judea also, on his death his generals did not peaceably divide that most ample kingdom among them for a possession, but rather dissipated it, wasting all things by wars. Then Egypt began to have the Ptolemies as her kings. The first of them, the son of Lagus, carried many captive out of Judea into Egypt. But another Ptolemy, called Philadelphus, who succeeded him, permitted all whom he had brought under the yoke to return free; and, more than that, sent kingly gifts to the temple of God, and begged Eleazar, who was the high priest, to give him the Scriptures, which he had heard by report were truly divine, and therefore greatly desired to have in that most noble library he had made. When the high priest had sent them to him in Hebrew, he afterwards demanded interpreters of him, and there were given him seventy-two, out of each of the twelve tribes six men, most learned in both languages, to wit, the Hebrew and Greek; and their translation is now by custom called the Septuagint. It is reported, indeed, that there was an agreement in their words so wonderful, stupendous, and plainly divine, that when they had sat at this work, each one apart (for so it pleased Ptolemy to test their fidelity), they differed from each other in no word which had the same meaning and force, or in the order of the words; but, as if the translators had been one, so what all had translated was one, because in very deed the one Spirit had been in them all. And they received so wonderful a gift of God, in order that the authority of these Scriptures might be commended not as human but divine, as indeed it was, for the benefit of the nations who should at some time believe, as we now see them doing.[4]

It was through this translation that the Hebrew Scriptures came to exercise their influence on the Greek and Roman Empires.

NOTES

[1] Daniel xi. 2-4.
[2] Tarn, *Cambridge Ancient History*, vol. vi. p. 437.
[3] Colossians iii. 11.
[4] *De Civitate Dei*, Book XVIII.

CHAPTER XIII

THE intrusion of northern tribes on Mediterranean
society and its effect in producing a new system of
life had not been limited to the shores of the Aegean.
Somewhere north of the Alpine and Balkan ranges
the migratory hordes had thrown off a second stream
which eventually had made its way to the centre of
Italy. There, as in Greece, they imposed their language on the composite race into which they merged.
When, three centuries before the Christian era, their
descendants came into contact once more, a thousand
years of separation would amply serve to account
for the difference of Greek and Latin.

The Latin peoples more nearly resembled the
Dorian than the Ionian branch of the Greeks. It may
well be that in Italy, as in the Peloponnese, the proportion of northern invaders was larger than that
which came to stay in the village communities on
the shores of the Aegean. They were less versatile
than Ionian Greeks, slower to imagine and invent,
but more stable in character and patient of detail.
With a higher sense of discipline they knew better
how to administer a system than how to change or
interpret it. When Rome had become the centre
of government for the whole Mediterranean, vast
hordes of slaves were recruited from all its shores,
especially from those of Asia Minor and Syria. The
dark hair and complexion of the Latin races must
be due in part to a large and continuous movement from the Levant. It need not surprise us,
therefore, that the Romans on their first appearance should seem to resemble in character the

nations of northern Europe rather than those of the south.

The political development of the village communities was closely parallel to that of the Greeks. The resemblance alone is enough to prove the nearness of their kinship. About the same period they abolished the paternal government of chiefs or kings. When they first emerged in the light of history a hatred of dynastic rule was the strongest element in Roman tradition. The fact that their officers were elected and their laws approved in public assemblies showed that they, like the Greeks, had grasped and applied the principle of decision by majorities. The citizens assembled in the forum were the ultimate source of all authority, though they never applied it to the details of government to anything like the same extent as the people of Athens. On the other hand, they evolved two leading ideas to which they adhered with singular tenacity. The object of Roman devotion, as with the Greeks, was the whole body of fellow-citizens and their successors. The general welfare implied by the word *respublica* supplied the motive of their public conduct. Side by side with this idea was the conception contained in the words *majestas populi Romani*, the sovereign authority of the Roman people, to which the citizen felt his obedience was due. The Greek had no word for obedience other than one which meant that his reason had been convinced. To the Roman mind the duty of obeying the law was prior to his right to share in framing it. The Greek was prone to forget that government is a condition precedent to self-government. For centuries the government of Rome was directed by a senate of hereditary elders by whom the traditions of public policy were handed on from one generation to another. The general assembly of citizens was content to elect officers and ratify laws submitted by the senate.

As in Greek cities, a number of slaves acquired

their freedom, and immigrants were attracted in growing numbers. In course of time this newer population aspired to share in the government of the state. The older families who tried to resist this claim became a nobility. The republican history of Rome is a long series of struggles by more recent and numerous immigrants for inclusion in the privileged circle of citizens. The principle that all power resided in the people of Rome was never in doubt, though the question as to who were to count as the Roman people was always at issue. But the party worsted in these struggles more rarely than in Greece made cause with the enemies of their city. In the story of Coriolanus we see what Rome thought of political emigrants.

The thoroughness of the Romans in all practical matters was reflected in their military organisation. When Alexander died in 323 B.C. the Roman republic was the dominant power in central Italy, and in course of time mastered the whole peninsula. The sovereignty was still vested in the citizens who could gather in the Roman forum; but Rome could marshal the whole manhood of Italy. Her resources in war were thus greater than any other power in the Mediterranean. Her commerce competed with that of the Greeks and Phoenicians. In the western Mediterranean Greek traders had founded cities like that at Massilia; but Carthage was the dominant power. Since Tyre had been absorbed in the Persian Empire her colony in the west had become the leading centre of Phoenician enterprise. Through colonies of her own on the coasts of Spain and Africa she guarded the Straits of Gibraltar and preserved her monopoly of the Atlantic trade.

In Hebrew, Greek and Roman literature the Phoenicians appear as a people with minds set on the possession of wealth, and their gift for creating it by production and trade was highly developed.

In their civilisation ideas played a lesser part than with any of their neighbours in the Mediterranean world. Their manner of life, and therefore their civil and military policy, reveal a tendency to measure all things by material values.

Granting that it is right to have regard not only to merit but also to affluence as a means of securing leisure, we may still censure the arrangement by which at Carthage the highest offices of State, viz. the Kingship and Generalship, are put up to sale. The effect of such a law is that wealth is more highly esteemed than virtue, and the whole State is avaricious. Whenever the ruling class regards a thing as honourable, the opinion of the citizens generally is sure to follow suit.[1]

As appears in this passage, the Carthaginians of historical times had abolished hereditary kingship. When Aristotle wrote, their institutions were influenced by the Greek and Latin republics with which they traded rather than inspired by their spirit. Wealth was regarded as a better title to authority than devotion to the public interest. The genius of Hannibal failed to command the support which Rome readily accorded to leaders of greatly inferior talent. By the merchant princes of Carthage war was conceived as a branch of commerce. Their armies were mainly composed of contingents hired from subjects and allies. The idea that the gods themselves give nothing except in return for value received helps to explain their retention of human sacrifice when other civilised races had abandoned the practice. As men rise to genuine religion they realise that the relation of God to man contains no element of barter. The Phoenicians were still in the clutch of a gross and primitive superstition when they lost their name and vanished from history.

Phoenician enterprise, none the less, was the main factor by which the civilisation of the eastern Mediterranean had in the age of Alexander spread to the whole of its shores, and beyond to those of the Atlantic. The Greek, Roman and Phoenician world had grown to be one economic unit. The premature death of Alexander and the absorption of his successors in the task of maintaining their various dynasties left Rome and Carthage to decide this phase of the long struggle between eastern and western ideas. As in the previous struggle of Greece with Persia, the issue was really decided by the relative merits of the two social systems. In the Roman polity the idea that a citizen owed more to the public interest than to himself was still uppermost, and stronger even than the passion for individual wealth. When all was lost the Carthaginians rose to heights of heroism, and, true to the tradition of the Semite race, they fought like lions when driven to their lair. With the total destruction of Carthage in 146 B.C. Rome was left with no serious rival in the Mediterranean.

Some fifty years before this time Rome had come into collision with Philip, a successor of Alexander in his Macedonian kingdom. At Cynoscephale in Thessaly the Romans defeated Philip in 197 B.C., and next year at the Isthmian games proclaimed the freedom of Greece from the Macedonian dominion. Now, as ever, the Greek cities proved incapable of maintaining stable relations between themselves, and Rome ere long was compelled to assume the office of constable from which she had ejected the Macedonian monarch. Her relations to the Greeks were marred by acts of cruelty, of which the destruction of Corinth, due to the jealousy of Roman merchants, was the most conspicuous. But, generally speaking, the relations of Greeks and Romans were in marked contrast to the relations of either people to the Semitic races with whom they came in contact. To the Semites both reacted as aliens, to each other as closely kindred peoples. The instinct of the Romans was not only to preserve the life, institutions and

civilisation of the Greeks, so far as was compatible
with the maintenance of order, but even to make
them their own. The cities were left to govern themselves, though not of course to make war on each
other. The institutions of self-government were thus
reduced from the political to the municipal scale.
The historians and poets of Rome, who wrote in
Latin, followed the Greek models and metres; but
Greek was recognised as the language of culture.
The plastic arts of Greece were simply adopted by
Rome as they stood. The city of Athens was treated
with special tenderness and respect, and became the
university where young Romans completed their
training.

In less than a hundred years from the fall of
Carthage the Roman republic had mastered the
entire basin of the Mediterranean, the west of
Europe from the Rhine to the Atlantic, and the
whole Greek world including most of the conquests
of Alexander, that is to say, Egypt, Syria and Asia
as far as the Euphrates. The civilisation imposed on
this vast area was neither Greek nor Latin but a
fusion of both, Greek elements prevailing in the
east and Latin in the west.

After the Persian wars the Athenian commonwealth had organised the cities of the Aegean in one
political system by the simple expedient of rendering
them all subject to her sovereignty. In two generations the system collapsed, to the ruin of Athens. In
like manner the Roman commonwealth imposed its
will on the vast congeries of heterogeneous peoples
surrounding the Mediterranean. The system she
created lasted for centuries, long enough to enable
the principles of Graeco-Roman civilisation to take
permanent root in the life of mankind. How she
achieved so much and at what cost to her own institutions remained to be seen. The sovereignty of
Rome was exercised by the citizens assembled in the

forum, though the general transaction of business was left to the senate. The overmastering idea of *respublica*, the general interest, as something to which private ambitions and interests must in the last resort yield, enabled the illogical system to work for centuries. The hereditary capacity of the senators, and the continuous tradition of policy they maintained, enabled Rome first to conquer and then to master the whole shore of the Mediterranean. To the senate, however, the idea of the general interest was still that of the city of Rome, or rather of their own order. The popular assembly which met in the forum was largely composed of elements more recent than the senatorial families. The assembly, however, was really narrower in outlook than the senate, and interpreted the general interest as equivalent to its own. In early days the popular assembly which elected the officers and ratified laws was mainly composed of the same men who, enrolled in the legions, had marched from Rome for the conquest of Italy. But this was no longer possible when the armies were employed in long campaigns in Spain, Africa, Syria, Greece or Asia. And these armies were recruited to an ever-increasing degree from the fighting races outside Italy. They and the Roman generals who led them were little inclined to see their labours exploited either by the oligarchy which met in the senate house or the rabble which gathered in the forum at Rome.

When Rome had mastered the Mediterranean, the citizens who could gather in the forum represented the communities they controlled no more, and indeed less, than the citizens of Athens in the ecclesia represented the cities combined in the confederacy of Delos. They, like the people of Athens, failed to conceive the idea of representation. With their practical minds they disliked civil disorder more than the Greeks: so they solved the problem by entrusting the general interest to the one man able to maintain order, who could be no other than the leader whom the legions were willing to obey. When Rome had conquered the world the reality of power had passed from bodies which could gather in Rome to the conquering armies and the general they obeyed.

The long revolution which transformed Rome from a city republic to a world empire was consummated by Caesar. He was in fact a tyrant in the Greek sense of the word, in that he used force to destroy the existing forms of law. The selection of officers and the ratification of laws by popular vote ceased, except in form. Henceforward the official appointments were the choice and the laws enacted the edicts of a monarch. But these appointments and enactments were still influenced by the conception of the general interest extended from the city republic of Rome to include the whole of the people governed by the Empire. Emperors like Caligula were of course blind to the notion, but the marvellous succession of public-spirited rulers who administered the Empire in the course of three centuries, several of whom were not even Italian, attest the potency of the idea which the city republics had bequeathed to a society too large to be capable of direct government by its own citizens.

An essential feature in the principle of the commonwealth was the rule of law as the Greeks had divined. For this momentous discovery the Romans did what in our own time mechanicians, of whom Marconi is the greatest, have done in the realm of physics. In their laboratories researchers like Crooks had recognised the existence, apart from the air, of something they called ether through the medium of which waves of electric energy can be passed. Marconi and others used this discovery to construct mechanism by which signals could be sent through the ether, and finally the words of a human voice. So the Romans adopted the supremacy of law, as conceived by Pericles, Socrates and Plato, from their reading of Greek experience, and constructed a practical system of law, applicable to the Empire as a whole, by which the daily life of a great part of the modern world is now ordered. The despotic power of the emperors enabled them to do this; but the element which distinguishes Roman jurisprudence from any previous system of law was derived from the city-state, which conceived law as the reasoned experience of the people who obeyed it, and not as the edicts of a monarch divinely inspired.

To men like Caesar, Augustus, Trajan, Hadrian and the Antonines the general interest of the whole civilised world was the end and object of public policy. As things were, the only possible way to preserve it was to entrust its maintenance to the master of the legions. But then, as always, the minds of men refused to accept a theory of government based on nothing but physical force. Quickly the idea developed that the emperor wielded his power by divine right, and was in fact himself divine. In a world which accepted polytheism the idea presented no difficulties, and throughout the Empire temples rose and altars smoked to the genius of Caesar. The magistrates and officers of the Empire relied on the theory in much the same way as officials and lawyers of the British Commonwealth rely on the theory of sovereignty of the Crown. As Kitchener imposed the oath of allegiance to Edward VII. on Cape rebels as a test of loyalty, so Pliny in Asia Minor imposed on Christians the duty of sacrifice as a test of loyalty to Trajan. But Pliny mistook the man Trajan for a god no more than Kitchener supposed that King Edward was the actual ruler of the British Dominions.

To the masses of Asia conquered by Alexander, organised by Seleucus as an empire and annexed

by Rome, the idea of the emperor as divine was a
living reality. In these regions the western culture
imposed by the Greek conquerors was a veneer.
Asiatic ideas of divine right were accepted as fundamental. They gradually mastered the Roman Empire itself until, in its later stages, there was little to
distinguish it from the typical despotisms of Asia.
The Christian Church absorbed the idea from the
Empire, and Church and Empire together are
largely responsible for its survival in Europe to the
present age. Slowly but surely the idea of government by divine right destroyed the conception of the
general interest which the best of the Roman emperors inherited from the city republics of Rome and
Greece. The idea was the fruit of a system by which
the people of a village community had learned to
control their own public affairs, and in doing so had
contracted a sense of devotion to the public welfare
which was new to the world. The Roman Empire
afforded a breathing-space in which a system of law
and administration directed to the public interest
could be developed. But the principle of authority
which made this possible destroyed the springs from
which the sense of devotion in individuals to the
public interest had grown. Had migratory hordes
from the north not appeared to destroy it, the Roman
Empire would still have collapsed for lack of subjects with the public spirit to hold it together.

NOTE

[1] Aristotle, Book II. chap. xi. (trans. Welldon).

CHAPTER XIV

"IT was not the Romans that spred upon the World;
But it was the World, that spred upon the Romans:
And that was the sure way of Greatnesse."[1] The
world of ideas which spread itself on Rome was a
world created by Greek and Hebrew.

In the earlier records of Greece and Rome we
meet the Phoenician traders everywhere scattered
along the coasts of the Mediterranean. But after the
fall of Carthage they seem to fade from the pages of
history. Before the time of Caesar we meet the Jews
in every part of the Graeco-Roman world, filling the
place which the Phoenicians once occupied in the
commercial life of the Mediterranean. Paul in his
journeys finds a settlement of his countrymen in
almost every city which he visits.

The explanation is fairly obvious. So long as Carthage remained the greatest centre of Semitic life,
the mistress of Greek cities in Sicily and the formidable rival of Rome, the Phoenicians wherever they
lived and traded boasted their race and their name.
The splendour and wealth of Carthage covered the
monstrous religion of which she was the centre with a
cloak of respectability. But when Carthage was wiped
from the map the cloak fell off and the Phoenicians
in the Graeco-Roman world learned to be ashamed of
human sacrifice practised in its most revolting form.

Carthage fell in 146 B.C. It so happened that their
near kindred, the Jews, at that very moment had
reached a stage in their history which recalled the
days of the house of David.

In 175 B.C. Seleucus IV. was murdered by his minister Heliodorus, who hoped to govern in the name of his infant son. Antiochus, the brother of Seleucus, had for some years lived at Athens, and was indeed elected to the chief office in the city republic. He now managed to frustrate the designs of Heliodorus and seized the throne of his brother at Antioch.

With a natural bias in favour of Greek culture, he thought to unite the many and various races of the Seleucid Empire by a general adoption of Greek rites, manners and customs. Indeed he seems to have gone so far as to extend the self-governing powers of the leading cities on Greek lines. At this period Greek culture had acquired the same kind of prestige as European culture acquired in Bengal in the first half of the nineteenth century. His policy seems to have met with general acceptance outside Judea. But even in Jerusalem hellenisation, since the conquest of Alexander, had begun to exercise a marked influence, especially in priestly circles. Judea was by no means a rich country, but the Temple had become the repository of fabulous wealth annually furnished by the piety of the Jews, whose trading colonies now spread from Spain to Mesopotamia. Like the Vatican in the fifteenth century, the Levitical hierarchy of the Temple was tending to become rich, luxurious and sceptical and readily absorbed the fashionable side of Greek culture. There were noble exceptions, like the Maccabees and the sons of Zadok who seceded to Damascus in the time of Herod the Great and later on, in all probability, joined the Christians. But, generally speaking, the priests represented the pagan elements in Judaism and may be identified with the Sadducee party. In their view of a future existence they never advanced beyond the pagan idea of Sheol; religion was a question of securing the favour of Jehovah by appropriate ritual during men's lives.

H

The champions of the Jewish faith and law were drawn for the most part from the peasants and poorer classes. From these elements was formed about 200 B.C. a small sect called the Chasidim, who opposed the spread of Greek culture with the heroism and devotion of their race. The Epistle to the Hebrews refers to them as people who

were beaten to death, not accepting their deliverance; that they might obtain a better resurrection: and others had trial of mockings and scourgings, yea, moreover of bonds and imprisonment: they were stoned, they were sawn asunder, they were tempted, they were slain with the sword: they went about in sheepskins, in goatskins; being destitute, afflicted, evil entreated (of whom the world was not worthy), wandering in deserts and mountains and caves, and the holes of the earth.[2]

The history of the Chasidim bears an interesting resemblance to that of our own nonconformists. The religious developments of the two centuries before Christ described in the next chapter were mainly, if not entirely, their work.

The sect of the Pharisees, which was presently to play so important a part, was an offshoot of the Chasidim. Its organisation was far less close than that of the Sadducees to which it was opposed. They stood for resistance to foreign influence. The name Pharisee implies separation, devotion to the idea of a people separated from all others as the people of Jehovah. In accordance with the teaching of the prophet Jeremiah, they included in this people all who accepted the Law of Moses, irrespective of natural descent.

This explains the missionary activities of Judaism in the period between the exile and the destruction of Jerusalem in A.D. 70. Behind this anxiety of the Pharisees to make proselytes was the motive which inspires the Christian missions of to-day. They were also responsible for organising synagogues, which discharged the functions of both churches and schools.

Though ardent exponents of the Law, they held, at least in their earlier stage, that God's will must be read from the course of history. When numbers of faithful Jews were massacred by Antiochus, they drew the conclusion that these martyrs of righteousness would be raised to life in the day of judgement to take their place in the Kingdom of God. It was thus that they came to teach a doctrine denied by the Sadducees.

In the view of the Pharisees God was their real King. No human ruler was entitled to obedience except as the mouthpiece of God. While the Sadducees held that the books of the Law as they stood were sufficient, the Pharisee scribes undertook to interpret the Law. In course of time their logical deductions from the text developed a mass of minute provisions, which some of them treated as of higher importance than the Law itself. The denunciations of Jesus were directed against this legalism, which had grown more oppressive than the Law as administered by the priests. But the Pharisee movement as a whole is no more to be judged by these later developments than the Protestant movement is to be judged by the fundamentalists and the rigid deductions they have drawn from Scripture.

With these explanations we may now return to the thread of our narrative.

Antiochus IV. naturally supported the priestly party which favoured hellenisation. He appointed one Jesus or Joshua as high priest, and authorised him to convert Jerusalem into a Greek city. He changed his name from Joshua to Jason, as a Jew nowadays will change the name of Levi into Lewis. A Greek gymnasium was established, for which the priests forsook the Temple. The young priests adopted the garb of the Greeks. The Chasidim were driven into fierce opposition. They resented the athletics and hats of the Greeks, just as the Moslems of Afghanistan resented the western clothes and habits of King Amanullah.

The cultural aims of Antiochus IV. were reinforced by the desire to possess himself of the vast treasures accumulated in the Temple. In 170 B.C. he plundered the Temple, massacred numbers of Jews, ordered the nation to adopt the polytheistic rites of Greece, and sacrificed swine to Zeus on the altar sacred to Jehovah. The sanctuary was dedicated to Zeus Olympius, and the Samaritan shrine on Mount Gerizim to Zeus Xenius. The rites of Judaism and the observance of the Sabbath were proscribed, and the Greeks in Palestine ordered to enforce the proscription. An Athenian missionary was introduced to direct the ceremonies of Greek worship. The first book of the Maccabees tells how matters came to a head. The story may be summarised as follows. When the king's officers reached the city of Modin to insist on the performance of a pagan sacrifice, Mattathias, the descendant of one Hasmon, an aged priest, moved to frenzy by the sight of an apostate Jew performing the rites, cut him down and slew the king's officer. He then fled with his five sons to the mountains and raised a rebellion, which was joined by the Chasidim. The third son of Mattathias, Judas, proved himself a brilliant military leader and acquired the Aramaic title of 'Maggaba', or 'the Hammer' (like Charles Martel). The name was shared by his brothers, who came to be known as the Maccabees.

Antiochus IV. died in 164 B.C. After his death the Seleucid Empire was so weakened by internal dissensions that the Maccabees were able to establish the virtual independence of Judea. They entered into friendly relations with Rome, and were able to extend their dominions over regions wider than Solomon had ruled. In 143 B.C. Simon, the last of the brothers, was invested with the office of high priest and clothed with absolute powers as ruler of the nation. The combined offices of priest and ruler were declared to be hereditary in his family. Simon was murdered by his son-in-law Ptolemy in 135 B.C. But Simon's son, John Hyrcanus, succeeded in seizing the high priesthood and, in doing so, lost the support of the Chasidim. He extended his father's conquests and died in 104 B.C. His son Aristobulus assumed the title of king. The office of high priest and king were thus combined in his person. Aristobulus conquered Galilee, a region occupied at this period by the normal Syrian mixture of Phoenician, Philistine, Hittite and Greek elements,[3] a people who had not as yet adopted the Jewish faith. They were suffered to remain in Galilee only on condition of submitting to circumcision. The majority appear to have accepted the condition and so to have joined the Jewish community, which, unlike the Samaritan sect, looked to Jerusalem as its centre. But their non-Jewish origin explains the contempt with which Galilee was regarded in Judea.[4]

From the moment when Simon in 143 B.C. assumed the high priesthood the worship of Jehovah in the Temple and the rigid enforcement of the Mosaic law was once more observed. Jerusalem acquired the place from which Tyre and Carthage had both fallen as the leading centre of Semitic civilisation. The monotheistic worship of which it was the seat was as much above the level of Graeco-Roman polytheism as the worship of Baal was below that of Athens and Rome. The numerous colonies of Jews dispersed from Babylon to Spain proudly regarded Jerusalem as the centre of their faith. The aim and hope of every Jew was, at least once in his life, to visit Jerusalem, to say his prayers and offer his sacrifice at the altar of Jehovah. Vast revenues flowed to the treasury of the Temple in the form of voluntary offerings collected by the synagogues in every commercial centre from the shores of the Atlantic to those of the Persian Gulf.

The Jews proudly viewed themselves as the people to whom the God of the universe had chosen to reveal not only his nature but the ritual and law by which men ought to live. Believing this, it was natural that, under Pharisee influence, they should wish to convert others to their faith. Their readiness at this stage of their history 'to compass sea and land to make one proselyte' is a well-established historical fact. The edict of Hadrian forbidding circumcision, at least of proselytes, was needed to quench it. With Jerusalem in her glory and Carthage in ruins the scattered Phoenician traders with their close racial affinity to the Jews were likely to be the readiest converts. From the time of Plato a certain drift towards monotheism had begun to affect the thought of the Graeco-Roman world. The Greeks and Romans viewed the religion of Jehovah with involuntary respect, and until the fall of Jerusalem regular provision was made by Roman emperors for sacrifice to be offered in the Temple on their behalf. The Jewish communities in Rome and elsewhere were allowed to lead their separate life and accorded certain privileges. Except in Judea and Mesopotamia they had generally adopted the Greek language, and after the fall of Carthage the Phoenician traders no doubt followed suit. They had thus every motive as well as every facility for abandoning the worship of Baal, with its hideous and barbarous rites, for that of Jehovah and for merging themselves in the Jewish communities. The process was gradual, and we know from Tertullian that up to the time of Tiberius they were still suspected of reverting to the practice of child sacrifice.

The upshot was that after the fall of Carthage the

Jews replaced the Phoenicians as the champions of Semitic culture in opposition to Graeco-Roman civilisation. The issues were postponed by the fact that the Maccabees sought the protection of the Roman republic against the Seleucids and became involved in the struggles of Roman parties and generals which ended in the establishment of the Empire. When Pompey was organising the Roman ascendency in the east he was called upon to settle between two Hasmonean princes, Hyrcanus and Aristobulus, their claims to the throne and high priesthood of Jerusalem. Pompey decided in favour of Hyrcanus, who was guided by the counsels of Antipater, an Edomite. As the followers of his rival refused to accept the award, Pompey besieged them in the Temple, slew some 12,000, and forcing his way into the Holy of Holies was astounded to find no image of Jehovah. This was in 65 B.C. When after the battle of Pharsalus in 48 B.C. Pompey had fled to Egypt, Caesar, who followed hard in pursuit, arrived to find that Pompey had been murdered on landing. Lured by the charms of Queen Cleopatra, the conqueror of the world got involved in a squalid local embroglio, and found himself entrapped with a mere handful of his men in the fortress of Alexandria. Antipater was mainly instrumental in extricating Caesar from his predicament, by inducing the vast Jewish population to take his side, and by marshalling for his rescue large forces from Syria and Arabia. The Jews found their reward in the privileges which Caesar accorded to their colonies at Rome and elsewhere throughout the Roman dominions. The payment of tribute by Jewish colonies to the Temple was legalised. Judea was relieved of any obligation to pay taxes to Rome. Antipater was appointed as Procurator. His son, Herod the Great, became king of a powerful monarchy under Roman protection. The high priesthood was now separated from the kingship

and rendered subordinate to it. The high priests were
in fact appointed by the king.

NOTES

[1] Bacon, *The Greatnesse of Kingdomes.*
[2] Hebrews xi. 35-38.
[3] My authority for this statement is Col. Lawrence.
[4] Bevan, *The House of Seleucus*, vol. ii. p. 256.

CHAPTER XV

In an earlier chapter we have traced Jewish ideas as to their future and that of the Gentiles up to the period when a remnant returned from exile in Babylon, rebuilt the Temple in Jerusalem and re-established the Law of Moses in all its rigour. The writings of certain prophets as well as the books of the Law were recognised as divinely inspired. But the priests had endeavoured to end the disturbing influence of prophets by establishing the belief that the age of divine revelation was now terminated once for all. The prophecies of Amos, Hosea, Isaiah, Micah, Nahum, Habakkuk, Zephaniah, Jeremiah, Ezekiel, Haggai, Zechariah and Joel had been recorded in their own names. This obscure remnant of Israel was still to produce books like Daniel, Job, Jonah and Ecclesiastes, which remain as landmarks in literature. Some of them won their way into the canon with books previously recognised as inspired. But this was only because their real authors were able to pass them off as the work of historic or legendary prophets of an earlier age. To such devices we owe Daniel and many of the finest chapters in the prophecy of Isaiah. The first nineteen verses of Isaiah xxvi. are no earlier than the time of Alexander the Great. Messianic passages were freely interpolated in the older prophets. Many of the Psalms belong to this date. For a number of centuries the literature of the Jews was either anonymous or else given to the world under the names of men who had never existed or had died centuries before the books ascribed to them were written.

The old prophets were primarily interested in the future of Israel in this world. But the question of the future which awaited the individual, not merely the Israelite but also the Gentile, had been gradually forcing itself to the front. In the sufferings which Israel continued to endure after the exile some of the conclusions which follow from the postulate of one eternal, omnipotent and righteous God were dimly reached. Jewish thinkers had come to see that if Jehovah was indeed eternal, omnipotent and righteous, the life of the individual in God, that is to say the moral life, could not be limited to life in the flesh. The existence of the righteous must be eternal as that of the God by reason of whom all righteousness is. Life in God could not be ended by physical death.

A solution of the problem was attempted by combining into one picture the national restoration of Israel foretold by the prophets with the promise to righteous individuals of eternal life. In this picture 'the day of Jehovah', originally conceived as a day of battle, is now becoming a day of judgement. In that day God will appear as ruler of the universe to sift out the righteous from the wicked. His kingdom on earth will be constituted from the righteous in Israel. The thinkers who followed Jeremiah as opposed to Ezekiel did not exclude from this kingdom the Gentiles who turned to God. This kingdom would be everlasting, as the prophets had foretold. But leaders of thought who came after the exile had advanced beyond the prophets, and now held that the righteous included in the kingdom would live for ever. As noticed in Chapter V., this led them to ask what would happen to the righteous who had died on the earth before the day of the Lord had come? The answer to this question was supplied by the theory that they would rise from their graves on that day and live for ever in the Kingdom of God. The miracle required to produce this result presented no difficulty to the Jewish mind.

In the earlier conceptions the wicked are simply to perish; eternal blessedness in the kingdom is the proper reward of the righteous. The consummation of life for the individual was thus represented as inseparable from the consummation of life for the nation. By their own peculiar road these Jewish thinkers had arrived at a point little removed from that reached by Plato and Aristotle. To the Greek thinkers the state existed for the sake of goodness. A full development of goodness in the citizens was inconceivable apart from a full development of the state. So minds far removed from each other, who have groped their way to a truth, reach it and find themselves face to face.

In later Jewish conceptions the wicked as well as the righteous dead are to rise, and all the wicked are then adjudged to eternal punishment, often described as fiery torments. The vindictive side of the picture was accentuated by the miseries inflicted on the Jews by the persecution of Antiochus Epiphanes. In the last century before the Christian era the valley of Hinnom, or Gehenna, is fully developed as a place of torment for the wicked, where the worm dieth not and the fire is not quenched. In the *Assumption of Moses*, by an author contemporary with Jesus, the anguish of the wicked will serve to enhance the joys of the righteous: "and thou shalt look from on high and see thy enemies in Gehenna, and thou shalt recognise them and rejoice, and thou shalt give thanks and confess thy creator".[1] We shall presently find Tertullian preaching the same idea.

In the second century B.C., while the nation had leaders of genius in the first Maccabees, the yearning for a coming Messiah fell into the background. But when, in the next century, their successors began to oppress the Chasids, that yearning revived. By some of them Messiah was conceived as a supernatural being. But others who returned to the study of the Scriptures revived the idea that a son of David would appear to inaugurate the Kingdom of God.

In the gathering calamities of that age a further change took place in this compound of folk-lore with genuine philosophy. The Jewish quietists had begun to feel that no blessed future for the righteous was possible on this earth. According to chapters in the book of Enoch, composed between 94–64 B.C., Jehovah will appear and with him the Messiah, who is variously described as 'the Christ', 'the Righteous One', 'the Elect One', and 'the Son of Man'.[2]

The whole conception had thus reached the transcendental stage for those capable of such ideas. But a large proportion of the Jews reached these more spiritual conceptions with difficulty or not at all. To the Sadducee priesthood, who still adhered to the old pagan conception of Sheol, the transcendental view of the kingdom was of course impossible. To them the Kingdom of God could only mean what it meant to the old prophets, the restoration of an earthly kingdom. As a class their position was too comfortable to make them anxious to treat such projects as a question of immediate or practical politics. There were no such motives to curb the fanaticism of the proletariat which battened in the lanes of Jerusalem on the pilgrim traffic, or the proselyte ardour of the peasants who tilled the soil of Galilee and Judea.

Side by side with the spiritual conception of the Kingdom of Heaven, the crude nationalist idea that a day was at hand when God would send a scion of David to restore the kingdom to Israel maintained its hold on a large section of the people. As the project of a world empire came into view, the Jewish idea inevitably assumed wider proportions. From the moment that Pompey stormed Jerusalem and entered the Holy of Holies, there were Jews who kept in their hearts the dream of a day when a prince of the house of David, backed by the power of Jehovah, would transfer the dominion of the world from the Capitol to the Temple and teach the nations to exchange the laws of Rome for the laws of Moses.

It must always be held in mind that the great Jewish community settled in Mesopotamia was not at this time subject to Rome. In 248 B.C. the Parthian kingdom had broken off from the empire of Seleucus. The Romans themselves, after conquering that empire, had been unable to subdue the Parthians. In 53 B.C. these Iranian nomads had utterly destroyed Crassus and his army at the battle of Carrhae, after which Mesopotamia and Babylon remained in the hands of the Parthians till the time of Trajan. At the period with which we are now dealing this Parthian Empire was the spear-head of the Asiatic reaction against Graeco-Roman civilisation. Its frontiers were not very distant from Galilee and Judea and the famous disaster to Roman arms was vividly present to the minds of the Zealots.

We are here approaching the climax of history, when diverse materials of human experience smelted in a furnace were to yield elements of indestructible truth. A patient sifting of the ashes will for ever continue to uncover grains of gold which past generations have missed in their search. We must pause, therefore, to examine the forces which were seething in the human oven of which Jerusalem with its Temple was the mouth.

Masefield traces the catastrophes of Shakespeare to obsessions of the mind, to some blindness to truth, some passionate belief that things are thus when in fact they are otherwise. If so, then Shakespeare was handling the absolute stuff of human life, for obsession is the key to the tragedies of history. Apprehension of one truth so vivid as to make it appear as the whole and final truth is such an obsession. And round the luminous spot where the mind is focussed there presently gathers a cloud of phantasies. The conception of one righteous God which came to the people of Israel in the deserts of Sinai has appealed to the minds and consciences of men as a real intuition. But this intuition the people of Israel saw as a special revelation vouchsafed to themselves alone as the favourite people of God. The series of legends which purported to show how the ruler of the universe had made this special revelation to his chosen race were accepted as historical fact.

The conception of one righteous God raised their ideas of the conduct which ought to be expected of men. In time those ideas were reduced to a code which was in advance of the standards observed in that age by the rest of mankind. The code was reduced to writing, and ere long was believed to have been graven by God on tablets of stone. But the process did not stop there. The pagan rites by which they worshipped Jehovah, and the tedious and elaborate ceremonies developed during their settled life, were presently placed in the same category. The manuals in which their national customs and rites were recorded by the priesthood were believed to have been dictated by Jehovah himself and to have been taken down by Moses in the kloofs of Horeb. And so developed the creed that Jehovah was to be served only by their punctual observance.

None the less, the Hebrew gift of spiritual insight was from time to time revived from the deserts. 'Prophets arose' who dared to announce that Jehovah was not to be satisfied by burnt offerings, by elaborate washings and by the payment of dues to the priests, but rather by righteous dealing and mercy to the meek. Tradition tells that such prophets were fated to perish at Jerusalem, to die at the hands of priests and scribes whose profession it was to administer the rites and interpret the Law.

The same obsession coloured their view of history and determined their political outlook. Their minds dwelt on the brief period when the house of David had ruled from north of Damascus to the confines of Egypt. They thought of its founder as the chosen and anointed of God. Their Scriptures were saturated with prophecies that a scion of David's house, the Lord's anointed, was destined to be born and rule the whole earth in the name of Jehovah. This was the orthodox national belief of the Jewish communities throughout the world. Generally, no doubt, it was held as a dream to be kept in the background of their minds, but not permitted to interfere with the business of daily life. Not so with the poor and pious of Judea. There the belief possessed their minds and was one for which they were ready to die. The wealthy and cynical rulers of the Temple had always to reckon with it.

Twin are the gates to the impalpable land of dreams, these made from horn and those of ivory. Dreams that pass by the pale carven ivory are irony, cheats with a burden of vain hope: but every dream which comes to a man through the gate of horn forecasts the future truth.[3]

NOTES

[1] *Assumption of Moses*, x. 10 (Charles' translation).
[2] Charles, *Eschatology*, pp. 265-6.
[3] Homer, *Odyssey*, xix. 560 (trans. by Laurence).

CHAPTER XVI

THE IVORY GATE

On the death of Herod in 4 B.C. the Emperor Augustus divided his kingdom between three of his sons. Philip received the northern portion south of Damascus and west of the lake of Gennesareth, including the Greek cities of Decapolis, east of the Jordan. To Antipas was assigned Galilee and the regions east of the Jordan inhabited by Jews. To each was assigned the title of Tetrarch. Samaria, Judea and Idumaea (Edom, the native country of the Herods) were assigned to Archelaus, with the title of Ethnarch. The Herods, though conforming to Judaism, were in open sympathy with Greek culture, and the nationalist party of the Jews never forgot their Edomite origin. At the Passover following the death of Herod the Great the mob in Jerusalem clamoured for the Ethnarch to eject pagans from Jerusalem, and also to dismiss the high priest appointed by his father. Archelaus quelled the disorder in blood and started for Rome. The outraged Jews thereupon sent a deputation of fifty delegates after him to oppose his appointment as Ethnarch. Augustus received them in the temple of Apollo, to which they were escorted by 8000 of the Jewish colony in Rome. The deputation perhaps included the moderate leaders and also spokesmen of the priestly caste who preferred the rule of Rome from a distance to that of an Edomite prince on the spot.

While matters were still in suspense at Rome, the nationalists in Judea broke loose and attacked the Roman garrison. The whole country was in fact the scene of a dangerous rising, and the Roman legions had to be called out by Varus, the governor of Syria, to suppress it. Augustus decided in favour of Archelaus. He proved so worthless a ruler, however, that in A.D. 6 Augustus deposed him and Coponius was appointed to rule as procurator of a Roman province under Publius Sulpicius Quirinius, the Prefect of Syria. These officials were responsible for maintaining the peace; this of course involved the presence of a Roman garrison and the levying of taxes to meet the cost.

In Jerusalem a wide jurisdiction was allowed to the native authorities. The human agency through which Jehovah was supposed to regulate the affairs of his people had developed before the age of the Maccabees. Like the constitution of Carthage it was influenced by the form rather than by the spirit of Greek models. It consisted of a council of elders called the Sanhedrin, a Semitic form of the Greek συνέδριον.

The presidency in it was held by the high priest, whom each ruler of the land, if he was not possibly himself high priest, appointed for the time. To the college belonged the former high priests and esteemed experts in the law. This assembly, in which the aristocratic element preponderated, acted as the supreme spiritual representative of the whole body of Jews, and, so far as this was not to be separated from it, also as the secular representative in particular of the community of Jerusalem. It is only the later Rabbinism that has by a pious fiction transformed the Synhedrion of Jerusalem into a spiritual institute of Mosaic appointment. It corresponded essentially to the council of the Greek urban constitution, but certainly bore, as respected its composition as well as its sphere of working, a more spiritual character than belonged to the Greek representatives of the community. To this Synhedrion and its high priest, who was now nominated by the procurator as representative of the imperial suzerain, the Roman government left or committed that jurisdiction which in the Hellenic subject communities belonged to the urban authorities and the common councils. With indifferent shortsightedness it allowed to the

I

transcendental Messianism of the Pharisees free course, and
to the by no means transcendental land-consistory—acting
until the Messiah should arrive—tolerably free sway in
affairs of faith, of manners, and of law, where Roman interests were not directly affected thereby. This applied in
particular to the administration of justice. It is true that, as
far as Roman burgesses were concerned in the matter,
justice in civil as in criminal affairs must have been reserved
for the Roman tribunals even already before the annexation of the land. But civil justice over the Jews remained
even after that annexation chiefly with the local authority.
Criminal justice over them was exercised by the latter probably in general concurrently with the Roman procurator;
only sentences of death could not be executed by it otherwise than after confirmation by the imperial magistrate.[1]

From this account it is easy to see why the cynical
realists of the Temple hierarchy preferred the distant
rule of Rome to that of a local prince professing the
Jewish religion. To the people of Israel God was
their king and the Temple his dwelling. The hereditary caste which administered the Temple and
controlled the vast and increasing revenues which
poured into its coffers from all parts of the world
naturally aspired to rule in the name of the invisible
king. In their hearts they preferred the control of
Seleucid emperors to that of the Maccabees, even
though its founders were of their own order. A subordinate Roman official was easier to manage than
a Herod.

The recognised leader at this juncture was Annas,
a Sadducee who held the office of high priest. In
A.D. 7 he persuaded the Roman governor to re-
appoint him to that office. He held it for seven years
till the death of Augustus, but for long after was
usually able to secure the appointment either of one
of his sons or of some near relative like his son-in-
law Caiaphas. In fact the appointment was kept
in his family almost without interruption for fifty
years.

The struggles in which the Roman republic had foundered were finally closed at the battle of Actium in 31 B.C. From that moment the motive which governed the policy of Augustus and Tiberius was to tranquillise the provinces. Magnificent gifts were made to the Temple treasury, and the Emperor paid for the daily sacrifice of a bullock and two lambs to the 'Supreme God'. Detachments detailed for garrison service at Jerusalem were ordered to leave the effigies of the Emperor at Caesarea. The most sacred robes of the high priest, which the Romans had kept in the citadel, were now restored to the Temple. There is clear evidence that the government was concerned not only to conciliate the hierarchy, but also to remove whatever might excite the fanaticism of the people. There were things, however, which no government at Rome could accomplish. It tried to restrain, but could never wholly prevent, failures in tact, lack of patience, or even rapacity in its local officials. Still less could it wholly exempt a province directly subject to Roman rule from the payment of taxes to the central treasury. Such taxes were far lighter than those levied by native princes with courts to support. With the best of goodwill the Roman government in suppressing the rule of native princes could not have avoided this issue. But inevitably it brought a system based on realities into conflict with the fundamental Jewish obsession.

Quirinius proceeded to frame the assessments of property necessary for levying the taxes. The wealthy classes were with difficulty persuaded by the high priest himself to swallow their resentment. But there sprang into being a party beyond the control of the priests and propertied classes—a party which believed in nothing but physical force. Its founder was Judas of Gamala, a Galilean. He raised a rebellion which was quickly suppressed, and Judas was nailed to a cross. This execution was the first scene in a tragedy which in two generations reached a climax, the horrors of which make those which attended the fall of Carthage seem faint and pale.

From the ashes of Judas there sprang a sect known to the Jews as Zealots. By the Romans they were known as *sicarii* or men of the knife. In these days the word 'gunmen' would express the significance of the term. They are best described in the words of a contemporary, Josephus:

They said that God would not otherwise be assisting to them, than upon their joining with one another in such counsels as might be successful, and for their own advantage; and this especially, if they would set about great exploits, and not grow weary in executing the same; so men received what they said with pleasure, and this bold attempt proceeded to a great height. All sorts of misfortunes also sprang from these men, and the nation was infected with this doctrine to an incredible degree; one violent war came upon us after another, and we lost our friends, who used to alleviate our pain; there were also very great robberies and murders of our principal men. This was done in pretence indeed for the public welfare, but in reality for the hopes of gain to themselves; whence arose seditions, and from them murders of men, which sometimes fell on those of their own people, (by the madness of these men towards one another, while their desire was that none of the adverse party might be left,) and sometimes on their enemies; a famine also coming upon us, reduced us to the last degree of despair, as did also the taking and demolishing of cities; nay, the sedition at last increased so high, that the very temple of God was burnt down by their enemy's fire. Such were the consequences of this, that the customs of our fathers were altered, and such a change was made, as added a mighty weight toward bringing all to destruction, which these men occasioned by thus conspiring together; for Judas and Sadduc, who excited a fourth philosophic sect among us, and had a great many followers therein, filled our civil government with tumults at present, and laid the foundation of our future miseries, by this system of philosophy, which we were before unacquainted withal; concerning which I shall discourse a little, and this the rather, because the infection which spread thence among the younger sort,

who were zealous for it, brought the public to destruction. . . .

These men agree in all other things with the Pharisaic
notions; but they have an inviolable attachment to liberty;
and they say that God is to be their only Ruler and Lord.
They also do not value dying any kinds of death, nor indeed
do they heed the deaths of their relations and friends, nor
can any such fear make them call any man Lord; and since
this immovable resolution of theirs is well known to a great
many, I shall speak no further about that matter; nor am I
afraid that anything I have said of them should be disbe-
lieved, but rather fear, that what I have said is beneath the
resolution they shew when they undergo pain; and it was
in Gessius Florus's time that the nation began to grow mad
with this distemper, who was our procurator, and who occasioned the Jews to go wild with it by the abuse of his authority, and to make them revolt from the Romans.[2]

In countries ruled by foreigners whose views are
in fundamental conflict with those of their subjects,
political factions tend to develop on similar lines.
The rulers enter into relations with such of the native
race as are willing to act as their agents. They
naturally endeavour to make this section feel that
its interests are identical with their own, and, with
this object in view, often entrust them with extensive
powers. The people at large view with disfavour
those of their race who are helping the foreigner
to rule them. The native agents themselves regard
with suppressed dislike the foreigners whose authority it is their interest to maintain. The best
friends of the foreign authority are usually to be
found in the classes more interested in business than
politics. They fear disorders which any attempt to
eject the foreigner will necessitate. On the other hand,
they are chafed by the failures and abuses from
which no government is exempt. They seek reforms
without revolution, but are seldom satisfied with such
reforms as are actually made.

There is, also, the party mainly drawn from the
young and the poorer classes who, with little to lose

but their lives and with no experience of administrative problems, mistrust all measures for reform which are not based on physical force. If inseparable from the system there is some condition which continues to outrage their ideals, there comes a time when they are willing to kill and also to be killed rather than endure it. If once blood begins to flow, the line which separates fighting from murder, war from banditry, or resistance to authority from wholesale crime, begins to vanish. These exponents of physical force come to regard terror as the only bond which unites society. To maintain unity amongst themselves they resort to murdering one another.

These three typical groups existed in Judea, and there, as in other countries moving towards revolution, they overlapped, and were sometimes combined in action by a hatred of the foreigner common to them all. The disturbance in which Pilate slaughtered a number of Galileans is a case in point. The inflammatory state of Judea was partly the result of unhealthy social conditions. The districts surrounding Jerusalem were barren and incapable of supporting so large a city. Its wealth was in fact the product of the dispersion. In every commercial centre of the civilised world were Jews making proselytes, gathering wealth and pouring it into the coffers of the Temple. In the general prosperity created by Augustus these contributions must have increased by leaps and bounds. The hierarchy, to which Augustus in A.D. 6 conceded such wide powers, had vast revenues at their disposal, a portion of which no doubt found its way into their private purses. They were not disposed to deplete the treasury by embarking on public works, such as Herod had freely undertaken. But this rapidly growing resort of pilgrims was in need of an adequate supply of potable water. To the Roman official with his orderly western mind, like that of an Indian civil servant, the filth and insanitary condition of the town was intolerable. His budget upon which the garrisons and his own establishment were charged was not intended to meet the cost of municipal services. The need of water in the city was created by the hordes of pilgrims attracted to the Temple, and was therefore a proper charge on its treasury. And so, says Josephus:

Pilate undertook to bring a current of water to Jerusalem, and did it with the sacred money, and derived the origin of the stream from the distance of two hundred furlongs. However, the Jews were not pleased with what had been done about this water; and many ten thousands of the people got together, and made a clamour against him, and insisted that he should leave off that design. Some of them also used reproaches, and abused the man, as crowds of such people usually do. So he habited a great number of his soldiers in their habit, who carried daggers under their garments, and sent them to a place where they might surround them. So he bade the Jews himself go away; but they boldly casting reproaches upon him, he gave the soldiers that signal which had been beforehand agreed on; who laid upon them much greater blows than Pilate had commanded them, and equally punished those that were tumultuous, and those that were not, nor did they spare them in the least; and since the people were unarmed, and were caught by men were prepared for what they were about, there were a great number of them slain by this means, and others of them ran away wounded; and thus an end was put to this sedition.[3]

The construction of a great aqueduct must have meant the employment of numerous workmen and can scarcely have been an unpopular measure. The handful of wealthy priests were the only people who, on grounds of self-interest, were likely to resent the action of Pilate in challenging the exclusive right to control the wealth banked in the Temple. They had, as we have seen, material reasons for supporting the settlement made by Augustus. But some of them at any rate were unable to bridle their anger or resist the temptation to teach Pilate that the Temple treasure could not be touched with impunity. A hint of sacrilege spread through the whispering galleries of the great city would suffice to inflame the fanaticism of the Zealots. Men to whom human life was of no account were unlikely to consider the benefit done to a multitude of workers, still less the sanitary needs of the city. A handful of knife-men amongst the gangs could create a tumult and bring the works to a standstill. In the vain hope of composing the dispute, Pilate appeared on the spot with a guard dressed as civilians but with arms concealed beneath their cloaks. But the crowd, coerced by the knife-men, refused to take up their tools. The parley developed into a tumult. Pilate's suite drew their swords, and in the slaughter which followed there perished with the knife-men numbers of workers who would have been only too glad to have been left at peace to earn their wages.

The contributions which came from the trading communities were not the only or perhaps the largest stream of wealth which enriched Jerusalem. In the course of the year countless pilgrims came to pay their vows and offer their sacrifice. A bazaar where the offerings could be purchased was established in the courts of the Temple. And, as at Benares or Mecca, the performance of rites involved the payment of fees to priests. We have reason to know that the ceremonies attracted streams of pilgrims from Persia, Mesopotamia, Asia Minor, Egypt, Cyrene, Crete, Arabia and from Rome itself.[4]

Catering for pilgrims was the industry upon which Jerusalem had grown to affluence. A large proportion of the permanent residents no doubt lived by it. The political geography of the civilised world must have been as familiar in Jerusalem as in Athens or Rome. No man of intelligence interested in public affairs who lived in Judea at this period could have failed to know the outstanding facts of the Roman Empire. A great part of the known world was now subject to Rome. So much at least was familiar even to the peasants and bandits from whose ranks the Zealots were drawn. But by minds like these the facts of life were seen only through the coloured windows of the national legend. It was they who worshipped the one true God, whose chosen abode was the shrine at Jerusalem. The only authority they acknowledged was his, until he saw fit to send them a visible king of the lineage of David, anointed like him with the holy oil. But the days were long gone when the sovereignty of God could be limited to the narrow frontiers of David and Solomon. Not the Romans and their emperor, but the Jews and their king, were destined to govern the earth under the authority of Jehovah himself. The Kingdom of God was at hand. He was calling his chosen people to action, and whatever was lacking in organised force his miraculous power would supply.

A people whose mind is largely nourished with a legendary past are a grave menace to themselves and the world. Ideas are portable, and this fatal fanaticism could not be confined to the hotbed in which it was brewed. From a centre of pilgrimage like Jerusalem it was certain to spread to the Jewish settlements throughout the Empire. It infected even the Christian churches, and both Peter and Paul, in writing to churches in Rome and Asia, found it necessary to insist on the duty of civil obedience.[5]

Elsewhere in the Roman Empire troops were recruited from the local inhabitants. In Syria, Spain or Gaul, the most spirited youths were thus placed under strict discipline. Careers were opened to their talents which more than once led men of ability from the ranks to the throne. The discipline of a soldier's life was not compatible with the observance of the Sabbath, and one of the numerous privileges granted to the Jews was exemption from military service. Jews who were young, poor and ambitious were thus freed from discipline and also had closed to them military careers, open elsewhere to soldiers of ability and courage. The blood of Judas thus fell like seed on a soil peculiarly ready for its growth.

As imperial prestige declined in the hands of Caligula, Claudius and Nero, the growing unrest rapidly moved towards open revolution. But even so the hierarchy, which had everything to lose by rebellion, continued to play with fire. We have evidence of this from the pen of an eye-witness. In the year A.D. 57, Paul, a Pharisee by birth, had made up his mind to visit Jerusalem, where he was regarded as a dangerous schismatic. His friends at Caesarea besought him with tears to desist from his project; but he persevered, and his visit to the Temple led to a riot. Paul was with difficulty rescued by the officer in command of the Roman garrison, and was sent for trial heavily guarded before the Sanhedrin. There Paul dexterously raised the burning issue of the resurrection, and so enlisted the sympathy of the Pharisee members against the priests. So great was the uproar that the Roman officer removed him to the citadel. The knife-men approached the leaders of the priestly faction, who undertook to secure a further trial before their court, in the course of which these assassins were to overpower the guard and kill Paul. Claudius Lysias, the Roman officer, got wind of the plot and despatched Paul by night to be tried by Felix at Caesarea. The formidable nature of the plot is shown by the fact that the Roman commandant thought it necessary to provide an escort of 400 infantry and 70 cavalry.

Felix was succeeded by Porcius Festus, who died within two years of assuming office. He seems to have been the only honest and competent procurator appointed to Judea from the death of Tiberius till the siege of Jerusalem. The seat of Roman government was at Caesarea, where Greeks were as numerous as Jews. In Jerusalem the Roman authority was only represented by a garrison in the citadel under the command of a military officer. The rural districts were gradually abandoned to the knife-men, though during the brief period of his office Festus did what he could to round them up. The mass of the people, who wished only to be left alone, were terrorised by a handful of youthful fanatics. Their creed was war to the knife with Rome. Any Jew suspected of compromise on that point was marked for destruction at their hands. They seized whatever they needed in the national cause. The stage had been reached when everything which distinguished brigands and patriots had gone by the board.

The work begun by Festus was quickly undone by his two successors, Albinus and Florus. The friends of knife-men imprisoned by Festus secured their release by bribing Albinus. Florus seems to have found a speedier way to wealth by tapping the coffers of public corporations. His success on these lines in the north developed in his mind the dangerous ambition of seizing the fabled treasures of the Temple, and, with that object in view, he entered Jerusalem with a couple of cohorts. Such, however, was the fury of the populace that his courage failed him, and he retired, leaving one small detachment in the citadel of Antonia.

Agrippa, a prince of the house of Herod, at this juncture visited Jerusalem in the hope of allaying the popular excitement. He explained to the mob the strength of the Roman Empire, and argued that its power could not have been established except in accordance with the providence of God. Their belief that Jehovah would intervene to enable Jewish fanaticism to overcome Roman efficiency was a dangerous madness. His intervention seems to have restored the ascendency of the moderate party for the moment.

Florus, however, was supported by his senior officer Cestius Gallus, the Governor of Syria, who tried to bring home to the frivolous mind of Nero the formidable nature of the situation. In A.D. 65 he asked the priests, for the information of the Emperor, to compute the number of people collected in Jerusalem at the time of the Passover. The priests reported that there had been 256,500 Paschal suppers, at each of which at least ten persons would attend. From this they inferred that at least 2,700,200 were present at the suppers. But this did not include foreigners and persons debarred from attendance by ceremonial impurities. The arithmetic as reported by Josephus is confused, and the total incredible. It is difficult to see how 3,000,000 people could be fed in a place not open to water-borne traffic. It is clear, however, that vast multitudes were collected annually in this centre seething with religious fanaticism, and were recognised as a danger to the peace of the Empire.

Fanaticism, bred by a national obsession, is never confined to one class, and breaks out in the least expected quarters. It was suddenly realised that Eleazar, the son of the High Priest Ananias, had thrown in his lot with the revolution. As captain of the Temple he stopped the sacrifice endowed by Augustus which was daily offered on behalf of the Roman Empire. It was even as when Caesar ordered his army to cross the Rubicon, Washington decided on independence, or the mob of Paris stormed the Bastille. For the Jewish revolution was reserved a fate other than theirs. So devouring was the spirit of anarchy which possessed it, that its children consumed each other.

The high priests and moderate leaders withdrew their party to the upper city, and despatched mes-

sengers imploring Florus and Agrippa to send troops
to assist them in restoring order. The Zealots, however, stormed their stronghold, burned the houses
of Ananias and Agrippa, and besieged the Roman
garrison in the tower of Antonia. At this juncture
another band of Zealots led by Manahem, son of
Judas the founder of zealotry (two other of his sons
had been crucified by the Romans), entered the city
and joined the siege. Storming part of the citadel,
they allowed the party sent by Agrippa and others
who were Jews to depart. Three of the towers were
still held by a remnant of the Roman detachment.
Next day Ananias the father and Hezekiah the
brother of Eleazar fell into the hands of Manahem
and were butchered. Eleazar now turned on Manahem, defeated his band and tortured him to death.

Eleazar then promised to spare the Roman garrison if they would surrender their arms. They accepted the promise, but no sooner had the Zealots
taken their arms than they slaughtered them all with
the single exception of Metelius, the officer in command, who agreed to be circumcised. So was the
stage prepared for the long orgy of blood in which
Zealot bands divided their time between fighting
the Romans, massacring the starving people and
doing each other to death in and about the sanctuary
of God.

Jerusalem was thus overwhelmed by the anarchy
which had long reigned in the country districts. It
began to react on cities where the Greeks outnumbered the Jews. On the same day that the
Roman garrison was butchered (August 6, A.D. 66),
the Greeks in Caesarea rose and massacred the Jews.
The thirst for carnage then spread, till the towns of
the Levant from Antioch to Alexandria were run-
ning with blood.

The challenge thrown down by Eleazar could not
be ignored by the Roman governor of Syria. In

September he entered the outer walls of Jerusalem with an army of 20,000 legionaries and 13,000 auxiliary troops. The inner city, including the Temple and palace, was held by the Zealots. The moderates secretly offered to admit Cestius, but, mistrusting their overtures, he endeavoured to storm the walls. On the first failure of the assault he lost his nerve and determined to retreat to Caesarea. As the whole country rose around him the retreat became a rout. The baggage and artillery were abandoned, and the Roman army only escaped destruction by leaving its rearguard to be slaughtered.

The rebellion now spread through the whole country up to the regions where Greeks outnumbered the Jewish population. A few of the moderate leaders escaped to Caesarea. They were sent by Cestius to tell Nero what had happened and to throw the blame on Florus. Nero had gone to Greece to compete for prizes in a vast programme of public games. But the news from Judea convinced him that serious measures were needed, and he chose for the task the ablest of his generals, Titus Flavius Vespasianus, who had done good service in Britain and elsewhere. The old general was made of that stuff which so long enabled Rome to survive the rule of emperors like Nero. He had been in disfavour for not pretending to admire the Emperor's singing, and actually thought, when the imperial messengers were announced, that they came to order his execution. He instantly left for the east with his son Titus and Mucianus, who was sent to supersede Cestius Gallus.

Meanwhile the moderates who remained in Jerusalem lost their heads and threw in their lot with the revolution. For the moment the Zealots accepted the direction of men like Ananus, the son of Annas, who controlled the high priesthood in the days of Pilate. The notables were allowed to organise the defence of Judea and Galilee and administer the country.

In March A.D. 67 Vespasian set out with his legions from Antioch and proceeded to crush the rebellion in Galilee and Judea. Towns where Greeks or law-abiding Jews were able to open their gates were alone spared and left with garrisons to defend them. The wilder spirits escaped to Jerusalem, expecting to see from its walls the Angel of the Lord smite the legions, as according to Scripture he had once smitten the armies of Sennacherib. They were there joined by Edomite hordes from the south. Local leaders of various bands fought like wolves for the mastery of the city. The moderate leaders were incapable of controlling the situation. Their government collapsed like a house of cards. In the early days of A.D. 68 several of its leaders including Ananus were ruthlessly butchered. Burial was denied to the bodies, an outrage, in Jewish ideas, infinitely worse than murder itself. Fully apprised of this state of affairs, Vespasian decided to allow the defenders of Judaism leisure to massacre each other, and employed the time in reducing the cities and villages of Judea.

Events were in train elsewhere which postponed and enhanced the final catastrophe. The scandal of Nero's frivolities in Greece had finally destroyed his authority in the provinces. He reluctantly agreed to return to Rome, and on reaching Naples in March learned that Vindex had raised a revolt in northern Gaul. The revolt was crushed by the army on the Rhine, which, however, threw off its allegiance to Nero. In Spain the legions saluted Galba as Emperor, and the senate hastened to confirm the election. In June Nero put an end to his life. The news reached Vespasian just as he was marshalling his legions to advance on Jerusalem. He resolved to await events, and withdrew them to Caesarea. Civil war raged in the west. Galba and Otho—another candidate for the purple—perished in the struggle, and in January A.D. 69 Vitellius was placed on the throne by his German legions. This determined the army of Syria to propose for the purple a candidate of their own. At Caesarea in July A.D. 69 the Syrian legions proclaimed Vespasian as Emperor. Mucianus was sent to deal with Vitellius. The siege of Jerusalem was entrusted to Titus, while Vespasian watched and directed from Egypt. Vitellius was defeated and slain, and by July A.D. 70 Vespasian was ruling as Emperor in Rome.

In April A.D. 70 Titus and his army arrived before Jerusalem on the eve of the Passover. The doomed city was crowded with pilgrims to its utmost capacity. In the frightful convulsions which followed the fall of Nero, people in the east thought they were witnessing the death throes of Rome. To the Jewish mind it was clear that the Kingdom of God was at hand. It is likely that the pilgrimage of A.D. 70 was swelled by thousands who hoped to witness the long-expected appearance of Messiah.

Events conspired to prepare the stage for one of the great tragedies of history. Behind ramparts almost impregnable, three parties of Zealots fought with each other like wild beasts. The helpless masses huddled in the city were plundered and massacred by their own countrymen. The altars of the sanctuary smoked to God, and blood from the sacrifice ran down its steps mingled with that of the worshippers, while the Roman rams thundered against the walls. In one narrow circle were concentrated the worst horrors of a civil revolution and a foreign war. The Jewish historian who watched these events from the camp of Titus imputes to the Zealots every kind of depravity: greed, cruelty, treachery, dissension, murder and lust. But he does not conceal their implacable courage. To Roman science and discipline they opposed prodigies of valour.

Titus combined the method of circumvallation

with that of assault. His offers to spare the city, its people and defenders, were met, first by treachery, and then with derision. As provisions failed, the Zealots ravened like dogs through the city, seizing for themselves whatever remained. In this reign of terror multitudes were butchered and left unburied. Still larger numbers perished of hunger, till the streets and houses were piled with corpses. Some thousands who tried to escape through the gates were caught by the Romans and nailed to crosses in sight of the walls, till trees and the space in which to plant them were both exhausted. In the end the walls were breached and the battle raged through the precincts of the Temple till it reached the Holy of Holies. By this time the infuriated soldiers had fired the cedar roofs, and a fabric, gorgeous as any that human hands have raised, vanished in a welter of blood and flame. Overwhelmed in this furnace, there perished a crowd which had flocked to the Temple, impelled by the belief that Jehovah would wait till his enemies had entered his shrine to destroy them. A whole people were led to their ruin by prophecies fatal as those of the witches who hailed Macbeth on the blasted heath.

To reduce the city and collect the captives was now only a matter of days. By September 8, A.D. 70, the struggle was over. Of the prisoners many were slaughtered, the greater part were sold into slavery, some, more unhappy than the rest, were distributed throughout the cities of the Empire, to be burned or torn by beasts as a spectacle in the theatres. So vast was the treasure seized in the Temple that gold fell to half its normal value in Syria. The veil of the Temple, its golden vessels and ornaments were re-served for the triumph of Titus. The famous candle-stick with its seven lights may be seen sculptured on the Arch of Titus to-day. The city itself was de-molished and the walls surrounding it, all but three

K

towers. A legion was left encamped on the site to prevent resettlement. The focus of Jewish theocracy was finally destroyed. That tribute which the clemency of Caesar had allowed the priesthood to collect from the Jewish communities they were now ordered to remit to Rome for the service of Jupiter. In order to extinguish the line a sentence of death was announced against every Jew claiming descent from David. The story is told how certain great-nephews of Jesus who had settled east of the Jordan were arrested and brought to Domitian. The Emperor spared them when he saw what simple and mystic folk they were.

The conflict of Jewish theocracy with Graeco-Roman civilisation was renewed in the next generation. In A.D. 116, in the reign of Trajan, the Jews rose in Cyprus and Egypt to expel the Romans and Greeks. The Gentiles were massacred wholesale. The rising spread to the banks of the Euphrates, and required two of the ablest generals of the Empire to suppress it.

Thereafter Hadrian, who had governed Syria under Trajan and succeeded him as Emperor, went so far as to forbid the practice of circumcision. Judaism, threatened with extinction, prepared itself for one final struggle for existence. In A.D. 130 Hadrian visited Palestine and ordered a Roman city to be built from the ruins of Jerusalem under the name of Aelia Capitolina, which no Jew was permitted to enter under pain of death. A furious rebellion broke out in Judea headed by a priest Eleazar and one Simon, surnamed Bar-Kokeba ('Son of the Star of Messianic prophecy'), who claimed to be the anointed of God. The Jews defended a large number of subterranean strongholds. The Romans stormed as many as fifty of these. More than half a million Jews are said to have perished in the struggle. Nearly every village in

Judea had to be occupied by troops. When order was at length restored, the name of the country was changed to Syria Palestina (the land of the Philistines), and for close on eighteen centuries Judaism was deprived of its local habitation. In the end, the edict forbidding circumcision was confined to proselytes, and Judaism, accepting the compromise, became the least propagandist of all religions which have since been practised in Europe. The vision of a monarch sprung from the root of Jesse, administering to a Gentile world the laws given by Jehovah to Moses, was lost to the Jews in the dark ages. It had entered their dreams through the ivory gate.

NOTES

[1] Mommsen, *The Provinces of the Roman Empire*, vol. ii. pp. 187-8.
[2] Josephus, *Antiquities of the Jews*, Book XVIII. chap. i. (Whiston's translation), pp. 376-7.
[3] Josephus, *op. cit.* Book XVIII. chap. iii. p. 379.
[4] Acts ii. 9, 10.
[5] 1 Peter ii. 13-17; Romans xiii. 1-7.

CHAPTER XVII

CONTACT OF JEWISH AND GREEK IDEAS IN PALESTINE

As our minds dwell on the tragedy described in the previous chapter we are apt to forget how small was the theatre in which it was staged. The southeastern portion of England from Hull in the north to Brighton in the south, and from Oxford, Leicester and Nottingham east to the North Sea, represents an area approximately equal to that covered by Galilee, Samaria and Judea. To the north was Syria, in which Greek civilisation was firmly established with its centre at Antioch. Jerusalem with the country surrounding it was the fortress of Judaism. In and about Galilee Greek and Semitic civilisation intermingled and overlapped. Like Ireland or the Balkans in modern times, this region was fertile in militant movements. West of the lake of Gennesareth was a population forcibly converted to Judaism by the Maccabees a century before the Christian era, who had come to regard their adopted religion with the zeal of proselytes. The shores of the lake were dotted by Greek colonies. East and south of it were the cities of Decapolis.

This term denoted, not a homogeneous stretch of country, but a league of Greek cities. Each of these had its own territory, stretching in some cases over a considerable area; each its own constitution, its rights, and privileges. Their boundaries would be settled by tradition or by definite deed and grants. They might have acquired, by treaty, rights of water or pasturage. They were associated with one another by common interests and obligations. But the different cities did not necessarily march with one another, and they were separated by territory which belonged to the tetrarchy.

The majority of these cities had been founded in the early days of the Macedonian conquest, they had suffered from the religious zeal of the Maccabees, and they most of them owed their freedom to Pompey, from whose expedition they dated their era. A league of Greek cities in the midst of a barbarian and unsympathetic population, they were bound together by their common Hellenism, by Hellenic culture, life, and religion.

The cities of the Decapolis were Scythopolis, the ancient Bethshan on the western side of the Jordan, guarding the entrance to the Plain of Esdraelon; on the eastern side Hippus, Gadara, and Pella, whose territories were contiguous; on the road which ran south from Pella were Dium, Gerasa, and Philadelphia—the ancient Rabbath Ammon; on the road west from Gadara, Raphana and Kanatha, which lay at the foot of the Jebel Hauran; finally, to the north was Damascus.

The sites of these cities are remarkable at the present day for the striking ruins of the empire that they preserve. Their theatres, their amphitheatres, their temples still stand in ruined magnificence; their aqueducts stretch for miles across the country; their bridges and their roads survive as memorials of a past when the country was civilized; their great columned streets may still be traced; at Gerasa there are still 200 columns standing. One may wander still among the side streets, and see the remains of shop and store and private dwelling-place.

They were strongholds of Hellenism in a Jewish land. Their gods were Greek—Zeus and Pallas, Heracles, Dionysus, Artemis; their language was Greek; they were the homes of men famous in Greek literature. From Gadara came Philodemus the epicurean, Meleager the epigrammatist, Menippus the satirist, Theodorus the rhetorician. Galilee, says Josephus, was surrounded by foreign nations. It is not without significance that within sight of the Sea of Galilee, on the hills above the valley of the Jordan, might be seen the signs of the religion and culture of the Greek world, and that Greek language and thought were permeating even Jewish life.[1]

From Scythopolis or Gadara to Nazareth, near the centre of Galilee, the distance is about twenty miles, less than from Oxford to Reading. Hippus is ten miles from Capernaum. From that town or from Tiberias a boat could reach the Greek city in an afternoon. Another comparison from the British Isles will help us to keep the topography in mind. Make a transparent tracing of Ireland and super-impose it on Palestine, with Lough Neagh exactly over Gennesareth. The Lough will fit the lake like an oblong frame round an oval mirror. Tyrone will rest on the hills of Galilee, while Antrim and Down will roughly cover the region of Decapolis. The name of Dublin will be read about ten miles south of Jerusalem. The one is eighty miles south of Lough Neagh, the other seventy miles south of Gennesareth.

The Zealot movement had sprung from Galilee. Its founder Judas had aspired to emulate his name-sake 'the Hammer', and Jesus was old enough to remember his death on the cross. His blood, like that of the Maccabees, had nourished the seeds of the revolt; and as Jesus grew to manhood, the Zealot movement was fermenting in and about Nazareth. 'The Kingdom of God' was its whispered watch-word. Amongst his friends were in all probability youths who hoped to see it accomplished, or at least to suffer and die for the cause. We know that a Zealot called Simon was converted by Jesus to peace-ful ways and numbered amongst the apostles.

Greek culture and paganism, protected by Rome on the shores of Gennesareth, was a constant irritant to the Jews of Galilee, and they to the Greeks. A region where opposite systems of life are approach-ing their conflict is a hotbed of ideas. In such a society first principles are eagerly canvassed by young and old, and by all classes. A typical dis-cussion of this kind was in 1891 published by Pro-fessor Firth under the auspices of the Camden Society. It consists of the shorthand notes of a debate held at Putney on October 25, 1647, between

Ireton, Cromwell and the Levellers of the Puritan army. It is worth consulting by a reader who does not happen to have listened to ordinary men discussing the first principles of society in the crisis of a revolution.[2]

We are safe in assuming that the principles and merits of Jewish and Greek civilisation were the chief subject of discussion in Galilee during the first thirty years of the Christian era. Conventional pictures of Jesus, calmly maturing his thoughts in the quiet and retirement of rustic seclusion, are at variance with obvious facts. Such conditions could no more exist in the Galilee of that time than they could in our own, in Tyrone or Fermanagh. From the rising of Judas to the fall of Jerusalem the valleys where Jesus spent his youth were a furnace of revolution. He analysed life and studied its elements in a crucible white with heat.

"And in those days cometh John the Baptist, preaching in the wilderness of Judea, saying, Repent ye; for the Kingdom of Heaven is at hand." A typical ascetic of the East, John "had his raiment of camel's hair and a leathern girdle about his loins; and his food was locusts and wild honey". According to Josephus, John

was a good man, and commanded the Jews to exercise virtue, both as to righteousness towards one another, and piety towards God, and so to come to baptism; for that the washing would be acceptable to him, if they made use of it, not in order to the putting away, of some sins but for the purification of the body: supposing still that the soul was thoroughly purified beforehand by righteousness. Now when others came to crowd about him, for they were greatly moved by hearing his words, Herod, who feared lest the great influence John had over the people might put it into his power and inclination to raise a rebellion, (for they seemed ready to do anything he should advise,) thought it best, by putting him to death, to prevent any mischief he might cause, and not bring himself into difficulties, by sparing a man who might make him repent of it when it should be too late.[3]

In the Gospel narratives we find nothing to justify the fears and suspicions of Herod. Like the prophets before him, John was preaching a moral and spiritual reform. The divine kingdom was not to be realised by priests exploiting a costly ritual or by bandits committing the wildest excesses in the name of God. His own mission, he announced, was limited to these preparatory reforms. The nation when reformed would be led to its goal by another.

"The voice crying in the wilderness" drew Jesus from his home in Galilee to the Jordan valley, and the prophet saw in his young disciple the leader for whom he was looking. The son of a humble mechanic was presented by the teacher of his choice, and the foremost man of his time, to followers drawn from the finest elements in the country, as the leader pre-destined to fulfil the promise of ages.

In discussing first principles with friends of his age it is likely that Jesus had grown to be conscious of his own exceptional powers. He had probably realised his own capacity for handling the revolu-tionary movement, if he chose to do so, a genius for leadership which his calm, cheerful and balanced nature had perhaps obscured from his own family. A time had now come when he felt himself called to tasks other than those of a joiner. But with know-ledge of his own powers was coupled an unusual sense of responsibility as to their use. Before adopting the rôle of leader his mind was intent on defining the cause to which he would ask others as well as himself to devote their lives. To one who saw no virtue in hatred the Kingdom of God, as conceived by men destined to involve the whole nation in ruin, might well give pause. That subterranean fire was to end by choking its own crater in ashes. The ardour which Jesus brought to his task was calm as sunlight and as pregnant with life. He was none the less of an age when a man's passions and intellect, both fully developed, raise his ambitions to the spring tide. He knew himself able to make the most of the career opening before him. A time was to come when John felt some doubts on the subject. While perceiving the greatness of his young disciple, the ascetic did not perhaps understand the depths of a nature which could leave nothing unquestioned. To a mind so constituted it was necessary to know the end and be sure of knowing it before concerting the means. The end in truth must determine the means. So Jesus withdrew to the desert to consider in communion with God what course to pursue—to face the crisis of a great decision. "And straightway", writes our oldest authority, Mark, "the Spirit driveth him forth into the wilderness and he was in the wilderness forty days tempted of Satan; and he was with the wild beasts; and the angels ministered unto him".[4]

NOTES

[1] Headlam, *Life and Teaching of Jesus Christ*, pp. 73-5.
[2] Quoted by A. D. Lindsay, LL.D., Master of Balliol, in *The Essentials of Democracy*, pp. 11, 12.
[3] Josephus, *Antiquities of the Jews*, Book XVIII. chap. v. § 2.
[4] Mark i. 12, 13.

CHAPTER XVIII

THE evangelist Matthew, who was not satisfied with
the highly abbreviated narrative of Mark, has re-
produced the version quoted at the end of the previous
chapter; but before the last words he inserted a story
which he evidently felt must also be placed on
record:

> Then was Jesus led up of the Spirit into the wilderness
> to be tempted of the devil. And when he had fasted forty
> days and forty nights, he afterward hungered. And the
> tempter came and said unto him, If thou art the Son of
> God, command that these stones become bread. But he
> answered and said, It is written, Man shall not live by
> bread alone, but by every word that proceedeth out of the
> mouth of God. Then the devil taketh him into the holy city;
> and he set him on the pinnacle of the temple, and saith unto
> him, If thou art the Son of God, cast thyself down: for it is
> written, He shall give his angels charge concerning thee:
> And on their hands they shall bear thee up, Lest haply thou
> dash thy foot against a stone. Jesus said unto him, Again
> it is written, Thou shalt not tempt the Lord thy God.
> Again, the devil taketh him unto an exceeding high moun-
> tain, and sheweth him all the kingdoms of the world, and
> the glory of them; and he said unto him, All these things
> will I give thee, if thou wilt fall down and worship me.
> Then saith Jesus unto him, Get thee hence, Satan: for it is
> written, Thou shalt worship the Lord thy God, and him
> only shalt thou serve. Then the devil leaveth him; and
> behold, angels came and ministered unto him.[1]

It is now recognised by scholars that we have in
this story, as recorded by Matthew and again by
Luke, a parable in which Jesus had tried to convey
to his followers the nature of the spiritual conflict
through which he had passed in these weeks of retire-

ment. To himself and his hearers Satan was a very real person, and indeed continued as such to Christians till far on in the nineteenth century. So the parable was long accepted as a record of a real adventure which had taken place between Satan and Jesus in the hungry desert. When its real character is recognised as a parable, in which Jesus was trying to explain a spiritual conflict, and when we hold in mind the political conditions, described in the previous chapters, in which that conflict was taking place, we shall see in this story material for genuine biography.

Jesus had grown to manhood in Galilee in the heart of the Zealot movement, in frequent contact with fanatics who believed with all the ardour of youth that their people were destined to rule the world. Some of them had died, and more were willing to die, for that cause. He thought of the kingdoms of the world and the glory of them, all united in subjection to Romans and Greeks. He had always been taught to regard them as 'lesser breeds without the law', usurping the heritage destined by God for his chosen people, but denied them as yet by reason of their sins. Judea was only the nucleus of a race spread through the whole Empire, with vast financial resources and powerful allies beyond its confines. The elements of a great movement were there ready for a leader to combine and direct them; but Israel had produced no leader of its own since the days of the Maccabees. The carpenter's son was conscious of gifts higher than theirs. He must have reflected that the founder of the dynasty which inspired the hopes of his people had tended sheep on the hills of Judea.

Humility is a question of knowing the truth about oneself, and history has proved that the estimate made by this humblest of men of his own powers was right. His judgement of himself is final proof of this amazing capacity which Jesus had of seeing things as they really are.

Gifts like these devoted to leading the Jewish revolt against Graeco-Roman civilisation would have changed the current of history—how far we can only conjecture. The relations of Europe and Asia to each other and the rest of the world would be other than they now are. In the forty years which had yet to pass till Jerusalem lay a heap of ruins and Judea desolate of her people, some massacred by the Romans, more by each other, the survivors deported to the cities of the Empire as slaves on the public works, as prostitutes in the stews, as victims for slaughter in the amphitheatres, the Jewish revolution was not destined to produce anyone deserving the name of leader. No one appeared who was capable of realising the latent resources of Judaism, in the counsels of state or the field of war. With a single exception the actors in this tragedy are known only by students of history. If the name of Josephus the apostate is more widely remembered, it is only because it was blown through the great trumpet which he himself made for that purpose. The qualities conspicuously lacking in the bandits whose violence worked the ruin of their cause, and in priests, whose right hands ministered to Rome while their left trafficked with the Zealots, were exactly those which distinguished the character of Jesus—a freedom from superstition amazing in that age, a sense of realities, the knowledge that faith is wiser than treachery, that love is a bond stronger than fear; intuition, with that coolness of judgement which together mean rapid and right decision; a perfect control of his own passions; inexhaustible patience, and infinite capacity for loyalty to a cause. His courage was finer than that of the Zealots: with lesser gifts Hannibal had shaken the foundations of Rome; and Jerusalem enshrined ideals higher than those of Carthage. It offered an ideal centre from which to organise a people whose colonies had penetrated the civilised world from east to west.

The great temptation is no idle phantasm, but a picture of the truth drawn by the hand of an artist. The conflict fought in that hungry waste was great as the mind which faced and settled it. Its positive issues were destined in time to affect the whole development of human reason. But that is not all. The negative issues, the great refusal to lead the impending revolution, vitally affected the events of history from that moment.

What enabled this young Galilean to reject a career which was noble as measured by every standard of his time, which the world would still feel was heroic, which Napoleon would have chosen without any struggle? We can only infer that his mind was endowed with a sense of values finer than that given to anyone else who, before or since, has been called to play so great a part in human affairs. He evidently asked himself what end would in fact be achieved, even if the forces of Jewish enthusiasm, disciplined and directed by himself, succeeded in imposing orthodox Judaism on civilised society. In declaring the unity of God, Judaism had given the world the most vital of truths. It was now telling the world that the will of God could only be fulfilled by the observance of an ever-increasing system of rules and rites, a routine which deadened the conscience and blinded the soul. It presented God in a false relation to men, and did little to suggest the vital importance of human relations, of the attitude of men one to another. They were taught to think of these rules and this ritual as instituted and ordained by divine authority. Men had yet to realise that each has for himself in his conscience a continuous revelation of the will of God, of right and wrong, which is dulled by neglect and brightened by exercise. Human nature, to grow to its fullness, must learn to draw on its own resources. The priests and Pharisees were for ever elaborating new rules and binding on men burdens too grievous to be borne. To call upon men to discard these rules and to begin thinking and acting for themselves was the task to which Jesus decided to devote his powers. He felt himself able to enunciate the principles upon which any order of society which really deserved to be called the Kingdom of God must be based.

From the parable recorded by Matthew and Luke it is clear that Jesus had in his youth felt himself drawn to throw in his lot with the Zealot movement. The story also records his deliberate and final renouncement of that idea. The Kingdom of God on earth as conceived by the Zealots was a nightmare from which he awoke. He also had dreams, dreams which had entered his brain through the gate of horn, that common material which in Homer's mind had stood for realities and sober sense.

NOTE

[1] Matthew iv. 1-11.

CHAPTER XIX

THE GATE OF HORN (*continued*)

THE story suggests another and no less amazing renouncement. Jesus of Nazareth moved in a world which assumed that original truths are divinely revealed and cannot be found for itself by the human mind. The Mosaic law derived its authority from the unquestioned belief that its actual words had been learned by Moses from the lips of God. The prophets were inspired. The truths they uttered were breathed into their minds. The underlying assumption was that vital truths could only be known in the first instance by supernatural means. It was natural to suppose, therefore, that God would also employ supernatural signs to indicate the messengers of his choice. They must be expected to show their credentials by affording ocular proof of miraculous powers. The working of miracles was a necessary credential.

In discussing this all-important matter, I must be at pains to show what I mean by the word 'miracle' even at the cost of a lengthy digression. A miracle implies an effect produced by mind on matter beyond the limits of normal experience. The mind can set in motion the limbs of the body and direct their action. We know that in doing this it acts through the brain, nerves and muscles. But how that spiritual reality, the mind, acts on the matter of the brain we can never know till mind is able to explain itself, which is in the nature of things impossible. From the point at which the matter of the brain receives the spiritual impulse and transmits it through the nerves to the muscles, the process is one susceptible of study and inquiry. Cause and effect appear to operate as in physical nature. By studying these causes and effects the spirit of man has altered the state of this earth to what it now is, as contrasted from what it would be if it did not contain animals capable of reasoned thought.

This effect of spirit on the matter of the brain is not described as a miracle because, though it cannot be explained, we know by experience that it happens. We also know the limits within which it occurs, and whatever is outside those limits is described as a miracle. I know by experience that if my mind so wills, my hand can remove a molehill. I also know that large hills, if not actual mountains, have been removed at will by the use of explosives and machinery, agencies designed and created for the purpose through knowledge acquired by long study of cause and effect. The thing may be seen happening in American towns like Seattle, where large hills have been bodily removed and thrown into the neighbouring sea. But if one individual had accomplished their removal by a mere exercise of will, such as enables him to move his hand, the removal would properly be described as miraculous.

In an age when the causes of physical phenomena, earthquakes and storms, eclipses and plagues, were not understood, it was natural to suppose that God acted in this way upon nature. It was equally natural to suppose that he conferred on his human agents powers of acting on matter by a mere exercise of the will, and, indeed, would do so to mark them as such. One has merely to recall one's own childhood to realise the extent to which ideas of this order fascinate the natural mind. A modern child in his day-dreams weaves plans for building cities, creating fleets of ships, driving tunnels or erecting bridges, and thinks of prodigious results brought to pass by a mere exercise of will more easily than he makes a castle on the sand with his hands. In the same way the author of the Apocalypse sees vast cosmic forces set in motion merely by an exercise of will, without the slightest idea of interposing between the thing as willed and accomplished a laborious chain of cause and effect.

Before men acquired the habit of studying the facts of nature, the occurrence of miracles was accepted as a matter of course, and still is where that habit has not been acquired or is simply ignored. The further nature is studied the more does its course seem to follow a sequence of cause and effect. To such an extent has this happened that the whole system of civilised society is now based on the assumption that miracles do not in fact occur. If a court were asked by a witness to accept some occurrence as a miracle and therefore by nature beyond explanation, the judge would refuse to believe him, or if he believed him would be superseded by higher authority as unfit for his office. To an ever-increasing extent our existence is based on the assumption that, given certain conditions, gas, heat or electric current will behave in a certain way, and yield constant results. An accident arising from apparent failure in those results is accepted as proof of some variation in the previous conditions. Inquiry is instituted as to what the variation was and how it occurred, with the practical object of controlling its recurrence. The intricate machinery, by virtue of which alone masses of men now work and eat their daily bread, is the fruit of an infinite number of such inquiries all based on the assumption that nature follows a regular sequence of cause and effect.

So vast is the cumulative evidence on this matter that the onus of proving a miracle must rest on those who believe it to have happened. In dealing with miracles recorded in all sincerity by an ancient writer, the historian observes the same principles as the judge in a modern court. He may use it as

L

evidence of something normal which really happened, as when Rawlinson attributes the destruction
of Sennacherib's army before Jerusalem to an out-
break of plague. He may quote it to explain a view
taken by the author or by the actors in the events he
describes. He would never allow that something had
happened outside or contrary to the order of nature.
He applies to ancient events exactly the same standards as are used by judges in analysing evidence of
recent events.

The practice of methodical inquiry which has
led to this attitude of mind originated with the
Greeks. It had, however, made little impression on
the Jewish society in which Jesus moved. When the
nature of his teaching was realised in its fatal effect
on current belief, his opponents instantly claimed
that he should prove his authority by working a
miracle.

And the Pharisees and Sadducees came, and tempting
him asked him to shew them a sign from heaven. But he
answered and said unto them, When it is evening, ye say,
It will be fair weather: for the heaven is red. And in the
morning, It will be foul weather to-day: for the heaven is
red and lowring. Ye know how to discern the face of the
heaven; but ye cannot discern the signs of the times. An
evil and adulterous generation seeketh after a sign; and
there shall no sign be given unto it, but the sign of Jonah.[1]

i.e. As Jonah preached repentance to the Gentiles with
success, so a time will come when the Gentiles will hear and
accept the Gospel, while Israel will reject it.[2]

These beliefs, however, were not confined to the
hierarchy. They were so universal and engrained
in the minds of all about him that his followers continued to assume that the validity of his teaching
must be attested by wondrous works. The records
from which we have now to discover what the real
nature of that teaching was were preserved and
collected by people whose minds were saturated with

these views. They perceived in their hearts, as we also perceive, that here was one uttering priceless truths. They assumed, however, as we have no right to assume, that he must as a matter of course have miraculous powers.

It is clear that the person of Jesus commanded in those not biased by prejudice or interest against his teaching an unparalleled measure of devotion and reverence. Unlike Socrates, he impressed, not only a small circle of disciples, but whole multitudes in this way, and to such an extent that the enthusiasm they showed often endangered his safety with the civil authorities. To-day in the east, a teacher who makes this kind of impression not seldom acquires a reputation for miraculous power without desiring to do so. Indeed a teacher in whom was combined profound wisdom and purity of life with all the magnetic gifts of a leader would find himself power-less to arrest the growth of such legends. The writer has seen the thing happen to the saintliest woman it was ever his privilege to meet. Her story was told me by her son, a gifted and cultured Indian with whom I had formed an intimate friendship in the western hemisphere. For some time after her marriage his mother had remained childless. At length, in the anguish of her mind she recalled a picture of the crucified Christ circulated by Jesuit missionaries, which she happened to have seen. It occurred to her mind that a suffering God might grant what her own deities had denied, so she prayed to this unknown deity that a child might be given her, vowing that if her prayers were answered, the child should be dedicated to his service. Presently my friend was born, and she found herself faced by the question in what manner to fulfil her vow, cut off as she was from the world by all the restrictions that surround a high-caste woman in purdah. So determined, however, was the lady that her vow should not go unfulfilled that one day, in the absence of her husband, she escaped with the child in her arms, and made her way alone into the house of a Methodist missionary who lived in the English lines. The mental anguish involved in such a proceeding can only be understood by those who know what the restrictions of purdah in Indian families mean.

The missionary, to whom she explained her case, properly hesitated to baptize the child without the knowledge and consent of his father. But such was the urgency of the mother that at length he yielded, and baptized the child in his own house. The mother then wrote to her husband confessing what she had done. On receiving her letter, he instantly returned from a great distance and employed Brahmins to perform the elaborate and expensive ceremonies which were necessary to restore his son to the caste destroyed by initiation to another religion.

His mother, however, felt that her vow must be kept in the spirit as well as the letter. As the child grew she taught him to regard himself as dedicated to the God of suffering, and herself adopted the Christian religion. By the sheer force of her own conviction she eventually converted her husband. So my friend's brothers and sisters were also brought up in the Christian faith.

Some years after my friend had told me this story, I joined him in India at the place where he then lived with his family. I had to face with him a highly distasteful task, and as we set out to keep our appointment he told me that his mother was devoting the day to prayer that our work might be fruitful of good. When the task upon which we were bent was done he took me to his home, where I met his mother, for the first and only time, together with her husband and the rest of the family. In the few hours that I spent with them she was mainly busied with graceful duties of hospitality, but none the less she created an

impression that here was a soul in continuous communion with God. When the time came for me to go,
she signified the wish that I should go to a room
apart with herself and her son for prayer.

Some months later, when a guest at the house
of the Metropolitan, I found myself sitting next a
bishop of one of those ancient Syrian churches in
southern India which look to St. Thomas himself
as their founder, a striking figure in a simple cassock
of pure white. I addressed him with respect, and he
soon impressed me as a person of great culture and
profound sincerity. It presently appeared that the
lady referred to in the last paragraph was well known
to him. After emphasising the sanctity of her character he added quite simply, "She performs miracles,
as you doubtless know". I replied that I had not
heard this, and he then told me that some religious
friends had happened to wait on her when by chance
there was no food in the house. Quite undisturbed
by the fact, she placed a pot on the coals, and when
it boiled and the lid was removed it was found to
be filled with rice ready to be eaten. This gifted and
cultivated Indian bishop had no more doubts on the
subject than Mark when he first recorded the story
of the loaves and fishes as told him by Peter.

I have not published this story without submitting
the proofs to my Indian friend. On reading the
proofs he assured me with invincible sincerity that
the Indian bishop was perfectly right. "We often
had no food in the house; but my mother was never
perturbed. She simply filled a vessel with water, put
it on the fire, and when it had boiled and the lid was
removed, food for her family was there." My own
explanation of his statement is that the lady was
always careful to keep reserves unknown to the
family. When the time for the meal arrived her
children found food in the pot though they knew of
none in the house and ascribed to their wonderful

mother miraculous powers without her knowing that they thought she had worked a miracle.

Such anecdotes could be multiplied to any extent from the experiences of those who have sojourned in Asia. They show how absurd it is to impute conscious invention or fraud to those who ascribe miraculous acts to teachers they love and revere. We have only to turn to the New Testament books to see such stories in course of development. As compared with the other evangelists, Mark, the earliest of the four, seems to attach more importance to the miracles than to the teaching of Jesus. The story of how Jesus sent two disciples to prepare for the last supper is told in a manner which suggests that he had supernatural knowledge.[3] The author of Matthew's gospel, in copying Mark's narrative, omits all such suggestions.[4] More striking still is the story of Eutychus as told by Luke,[5] because here the writer was himself an eye-witness of the incident he relates. Eutychus fell from a window, and when he was picked up came to his senses in the arms of Paul. But Luke is so sure that the great apostle is a worker of miracles that he says that Eutychus was actually dead. With naïve fidelity to truth he records that when Eutychus opened his eyes Paul said, " Make ye no more ado; for his life is in him". And so in the story of the shipwreck, when the snake leapt out of a bundle of sticks and seized Paul by the hand, the natives assumed that he must presently swell and fall down dead. But when he shook the snake off into the fire and took no hurt they presently thought he was a god. The habits of the snake described by Luke are exactly those of the coronella, a tree snake which lurks in bundles of sticks. Though perfectly harmless it has the terrifying habit of leaping from its lair and seizing the hands of people who are gathering firewood. It is well known in the New Forest, and is found in Malta.

Like country folk elsewhere the natives of Malta believed all snakes to be venomous.

In recent years medical science has come to recognise how largely the physical health of a patient is
affected by the state of his mind. A power which
some great physicians have of influencing the minds
of their patients is regarded as a side of their professional equipment. There are recognised practi-
tioners who specialise in the treatment of health by
working on the mind. There are people with strong
serene personalities who have the faculty of improv-
ing health by influencing sufferers to forget themselves and ailments which are not really organic, but
which might become so if a state of distress were
allowed to continue. The cures undoubtedly worked
in cases of this kind by M. Coué, a simple and kindly
French apothecary, if done in the east, would
quickly breed a whole cycle of legends. It is clear
from the records that Jesus had a power of self-control, a calmness of mind and a joy in life and sympathy with others developed in marked contrast to
the tragic and high-strung people amongst whom
he moved. They always thought of his teaching as
a gospel, that is to say, good news, and as they
listened to it forgot their ailments, and thought
themselves healed by miraculous power. Such stories
would grow by leaps and bounds as they passed
from mouth to mouth, till wide circles came to believe that he had given sight to men born blind and
restored the dead to life.

It is usual to draw a sharp distinction between
miracles ascribed to Jesus, and acts of magic such
as that told of Elisha when he is said to have made
iron to float, and so reversed the evident physical
law that a body must sink so long as its weight is
greater than the body of water it displaces. The
story of Jesus walking on the water involves a re-
versal of natural laws equally great. And so do the

stories of raising the dead to life. It is possible to
restore life when the lungs and even the heart have
ceased to act, if an impulse sufficient to restart their
action can be given in time. But unless this is done
quickly the arteries empty and the blood solidifies in
the veins which connect them with the heart. The restoration to life of a man who has really died several
hours before, involves magical changes in physical
conditions just as crude as the floating of iron in
water, but more multifarious.

When in plain and gracious words Jesus expressed
truths which went to the root of human problems,
multitudes of simple folk felt them as such. So
ordinary men recognise poetry and music in so far as
they themselves are in a measure poets and musicians.
The divine intuitions of Jesus were seen to be such,
because in the minds of average men is implanted
a sense of divine intuition. Their hearts were stirred
as the strings of an instrument vibrate to the tones
of a mighty voice. But they could not escape the
traditional belief that as truths so striking could only
be revealed to a teacher by supernatural means, he
must be expected to display supernatural powers.
They remarked the amazing influence that he exercised on others, especially in calming troubled and
disordered minds, and related them as miracles of
healing. As they passed from mouth to mouth such
stories grew beyond all recognition, and the same
process applied to striking examples of practical
ability and foresight, such as Jesus showed when he
thoughtfully provided for the feeding of crowds who
had followed him to a lonely place to listen to his
teaching.

The idea that a spiritual truth can be proved by
a physical miracle was itself the deepest and most
comprehensive of all superstitions, and one which
persists to our own time. That right differs from
wrong, the most fundamental of all truths, involves

the hypothesis that the souls of men exist independent of time and space and are indestructible as matter itself. That belief is implicit in the teaching of Jesus. He said that the return of one from the dead would not of itself avail to convince the world of such truths. A little reflection will show that the return to life of any number of dead men would in no way prove the immortality of the soul. An age which knows that this earth will in time be unable to support any form of life has less excuse for persisting in such beliefs.

The story of the temptation shows that Jesus, before he embarked on his public career, had consciously made up his mind to resist the ingrained belief of his hearers that the truths he taught must be proved by miracles. From first to last the appeal that he made was to the conscience of ordinary men and to that alone. The theory of Renan that in practice he found it necessary to establish his position by conscious pandering to the current belief that he worked miracles, in fact by a few conjuring tricks, is contrary to evidence contained in the records. His public career was amazingly brief and covered at most some two and a half years. Its events and his sayings were not written down as we now have them till some thirty-five years after his death; for his followers believed that he had promised to return to them during their lives. The stories were told and retold till a whole generation had passed without his return. The circle of those interested in his life and teaching vastly increased, while those who had seen and heard him dwindled in number. A demand naturally developed for some record, and Mark, who shared to the full the predisposition of his race and age to believe in miracles, reduced to writing his own understanding of what Peter had told him. His gospel was probably written at Rome. When his work was read in the churches of Syria it was realised that Mark had omitted a great body of teaching which was there remembered. This teaching was added, and in order to make room for it in a roll of papyrus of the usual length, the stories of Mark were freely condensed. And so appeared the gospel issued under the name of Matthew. Luke, who had met the apostles at Jerusalem, and had spent two years at Caesarea with Paul, repeated the process. He used the writings of Mark and Matthew, but added a large body of tradition collected by himself from other sources. The fourth gospel was composed at or near Ephesus, on the lowest computation not earlier than two generations after the death of Jesus, a work in which dramatic and poetic elements are uppermost, and narrative is subordinated to the doctrines which the evangelist is writing to establish.

Earlier even than Mark are fragmentary statements contained in the epistles of Paul. Not one of these writers, not even Paul, one of the greatest of thinkers, was able to escape from the prepossession of the age in which they lived, or to see, as their Master had seen, that conceptions of ultimate truth cannot be supported by ocular proof, that they are of the nature of postulates, hypotheses necessary to account for our sense of the worth and meaning of life, that they are of the nature of faith which proves itself by practical effect.

Yet no one can read these records without realising how perfectly sincere not only the writers were, but also those whose memories had preserved the things they wrote. The best proof of this is the constant recurrence of sayings which they did not realise were contrary to beliefs so deeply imbedded in their own minds that they could not help imputing them to their great teacher. They repeatedly tell us how Jesus adjured those whom his influence had brought to a better state of health not to publish the fact abroad. If he really agreed with his followers that his mission was proved by his mighty works, it was

surely his duty and theirs that these works should
'shine before men'. But when we remember the story
of the temptation, which must have been told them
by himself, and his condemnation of the demand
that he should prove his mission by signs, his in-
junctions of silence can be only interpreted as a conscious effort on his part to prevent the good he was
able to do to the health of overwrought followers
from being noised abroad and exaggerated into
stories that he proved his teaching by an exercise
of magical powers. We know that he failed, and his
early death, and its circumstances, clearly contributed to the failure.

I have no doubt in my own mind that Jesus believed, not only in miracles, but in his own power to
cure the sick by miraculous means. In that age it
could scarcely be otherwise. His refusal to prove his
mission by 'signs' shows that he had seen that moral
truths cannot be proved like physical truths by any
phenomena. Such truths can only be recognised by
each for himself in his own conscience. The belief
that our choice between right and wrong is fraught
with consequences which have no limit, that the
world of spirit is indestructible and exists outside the
limits of time, in a word, that souls are immortal,
cannot be proved by evidence that a man has risen
from the dead. Such evidence can prove only that
the human spirit can continue in time for some
period after the body is dead. By the irony of fate
his followers believed that the doctrine of immortality
could only be proved by a man rising from his grave
or in some way convincing the senses of living
friends that his personality was still in existence. A
great body of Christians are to this day in the clutch
of that fallacy.

I read the story of the temptation as recorded by
Matthew and Luke as meaning that Jesus, believing
in miracles and in his own power to work them, had

felt himself tempted to appeal to these powers as proving the truths which he had to utter. The parable of his struggle with Satan in the desert records his conquest of that temptation.

NOTES

[1] Matthew xvi. 1-4.
[2] *A New Commentary on Holy Scripture*. Note on Matthew xii. 39.
[3] Mark xiv. 13-16.
[4] Matthew xxvi. 18, 19.
[5] Acts xx. 9, 10.

CHAPTER XX

THE COMMONWEALTH OF GOD

AMONG them that are born of women there hath not
arisen a greater than John the Baptist: yet he that is but
little in the kingdom of heaven is greater than he. And
from the days of John the Baptist until now the kingdom
of heaven suffereth violence, and men of violence take it
by force.[1]

We have seen how the Jewish world in the time
of Jesus was possessed by the notion that the Kingdom of God was at hand. We have also seen how
differently the nature of this kingdom was conceived.
The Zealots were looking for subversion of the
Roman Empire by physical force, aided perhaps by
a miracle, and the final establishment of Judaism as
a world power. Herod, misled by his own fears, had
seen in John a possible leader for this dangerous
movement. The words we have quoted above suggest that the Zealot idea of a kingdom to be won by
physical force was gaining ground.

It is also clear from these words that the Kingdom
of Heaven, as conceived by Jesus, was something
different from the Kingdom of Heaven as conceived
by John, and that Jesus was now aware of this difference. We know that John and his followers were also
aware of this difference. Like the Essenes they
taught and practised asceticism,[2] a practice which
Jesus openly renounced. He was seen enjoying the
pleasures of life with all sorts and conditions of men.
He said of himself that he "came eating and drinking", while John had abstained even from bread and
wine. This was probably the reason why John had
sent two of his disciples to ask Jesus, "Art thou he

that should come, or do we look for another?" [3] He consciously and deliberately discarded the asceticism practised by John, and in so doing rejected the whole system of thought which regards matter, and therefore the sense of matter, and pleasure in things of sense as evil. The notion that merit can be earned merely by suffering pain is the necessary consequence of that view. Indifference to pain endured by others is a further corollary. He rejected in terms the belief that things material, whether touched or tasted, could of themselves defile the soul. Such teaching was an open challenge to the Jewish law which governed the intimate details of life.

Without some time spent in the east it is difficult to realise how deeply the view that matter and sense are evil permeates thought in those regions. In adopting a life contrary to that view Jesus was erecting the most stubborn of obstacles to his own acceptance in eastern society as a teacher of truth. More than any other thing that we know of him it shows how great was his courage and capacity for original thought. As one of his own race has said in these days, "a greater than Aristotle" is here. [4] So much importance was attached in his mind to this view that he ended by making the simple act of breaking bread and drinking wine the only ordinance which he asked his followers to observe. Food was the substance of flesh, drink of the blood which flowed in the veins. He bade his followers revere their bodies as good in themselves, as the temple of God.

Things of the sense are for enjoyment; yet such is the paradox of life that the happiness open to men is largely frustrated by regarding these things as its object. The joy of living is marred by over-anxiety about them—a thought clothed in words destined to give us the most perfect sentence in English prose:

Consider the lilies of the field, how they grow; they toil not, neither do they spin: and yet I say unto you, that even Solomon in all his glory was not arrayed like one of these.[5]

Food, clothing, home, whatever makes for loveliness and joy would 'be added' if men but learned to seek first the Kingdom of God. They must realise the nature of God in order to know what his kingdom is.

The idea of God which he placed before them was the purified essence of Hebrew thought. The Jews had first given to the world their idea of the one and only God who is also perfectly righteous. They had first seen his relation to men as that of a king to his subjects. Hosea and Jeremiah had seen it as that of a father to sons. But even they still thought of Jehovah as the god of retributive justice. The Jewish conception of God as a father was still limited by the thought of themselves as the children of God, of the Gentiles as somewhere outside that relation. By Jesus God was conceived as a father whose love for his children had no limits. It included the Gentiles as well as the Jews, and indeed all sentient creatures:

Are not two sparrows sold for a farthing? and not one of them shall fall on the ground without your Father.[6]

The essential bond of society which unites men to each other and God is not primarily righteousness, as the prophets had taught, or justice, as Plato had assumed, but the love which results in righteousness and justice. To speak of God as a father, and of men as his children and therefore brethren, was the best image he could draw from physical life to express a spiritual truth. As letters of the alphabet are in origin pictures, so words are images chosen to convey ideas. Our tendency is to overlook the ideas, to dwell on the symbols and reason from them. By so doing, theology has spun the intricate webs which now make it so hard for us to see the significance of the images chosen by Jesus to convey his thoughts.

There is no evidence in our records that Jesus consciously attempted to harmonise eastern with western ideas. In fact he did it by force of an insight which perceived the truths implicit in both; for truths are by their nature consistent. Questioned by one of the scribes:

> What commandment is the first of all? Jesus answered, The first is, Hear, O Israel; The Lord our God, the Lord is one; and thou shalt love the Lord thy God with all thy heart, and with all thy soul, and with all thy mind, and with all thy strength. The second is this, Thou shalt love thy neighbour as thyself. There is none other commandment greater than these.[7]

Our word 'love', as used in this context, is somewhat spoiled by its sentimental associations. The attitude of God to men as conceived by Jesus is as an infinite desire to do them good. Of this the most perfect image he could find in nature is the feeling that a parent should have for his own children, and they to him and to one another. An infinite desire to serve God was the attitude proper to men, and this they could only attain by serving each other, by desiring to render such service and placing that desire before all others. In order to develop this desire, men must first see what God is, and also what their neighbour is in his eyes. To love beauty, goodness and truth, is to love God and become like him. In so doing the Kingdom of God will be realised and his will fulfilled. The two ideas are inseparably linked in the prayer he taught his followers: "Thy kingdom come, thy will be done on earth as it is in heaven". This Kingdom of God is a definite system of society to be realised on earth. He did not profess to originate or invent it.

Being asked by the Pharisees, when the kingdom of God cometh, he answered them and said, The kingdom of God cometh not with observation: neither shall they say, Lo, here! or, There! for lo, the kingdom of God is in the midst of you.[8]

The desire of men to serve each other was already existent and capable of infinite expansion. "Ye therefore shall be perfect, as your heavenly Father is perfect."[9] This presumption of the infinite duty owed by men to each other was no idle illusion. He saw it as destined to be realised and made the operative principle of human society. That vital principle, partially realised in the minds of a limited number, is in fact what enables civilised society to exist at all. He compared it to leaven, the tiny ingredient which transforms masses of dough into wholesome bread, or to salt which preserves meat from corruption. Hence the importance that such minorities should be careful to keep their intrinsic property. Let them look to quality and ignore quantity.

On the other hand, the few inspired by these principles must never think of the divine commonwealth as something confined to themselves. For

the kingdom of heaven is like unto a net, that was cast into the sea, and gathered of every kind: which, when it was filled, they drew up on the beach; and they sat down, and gathered the good into vessels, but the bad they cast away.[10]

And he adds, "So shall it be in the consummation of the age". The principle of the commonwealth by its own operation sorts out the good from the bad, preserves the one and discards the other. Trust to experience. Let survival of the fittest operate in the sphere of human institutions. The same idea is reflected in the parable of the wheat and the tares. Beware of thinking that we can at the first glance distinguish the good from the bad. Cast the net, drive the plough, scatter the seed, be tireless in pro-

M

duction. In the last resort the good and useful in men and things will survive by its own virtue, and the evil and useless will perish by its own vice and futility. To be tireless in service is also to be patient of results. Over-anxiety for the future, as to whether the work in hand is of permanent value, is expense of spirit and a waste of strength. Serenity is the temper which begets the finest quality in action. The Kingdom of Heaven in its small beginnings has the property of life which spreads without limit.

It is like a grain of mustard seed, which, when it is sown upon the earth, though it be less than all the seeds that are upon the earth, yet when it is sown, groweth up, and becometh greater than all the herbs, and putteth out great branches; so that the birds of the heaven can lodge under the shadow thereof.[11]

It is also a cause to which men will desire to give themselves wholly as they come to realise its nature.

The kingdom of heaven is like unto a treasure hidden in the field; which a man found, and hid; and in his joy he goeth and selleth all that he hath, and buyeth that field,[12]

and

Again, the kingdom of heaven is like unto a man that is a merchant seeking goodly pearls: and having found one pearl of great price, he went and sold all that he had, and bought it.[13]

This theory of an infinite obligation owed by each to all as the bond which unites human society and makes it a living thing, even when realised in part by the few, has nothing in common with the social contract of Hobbes and Rousseau. Attempts to exhibit society as held together by a balance of interests could only succeed if society were static. But in fact it lives and moves; the interests change and the balance is destroyed. To seek your own good is to miss it. As in the system propounded by

Socrates, the rights of men have here no place. But the thoughts of Jesus were conceived at a spot on the map of human society which was in certain respects more central than Athens or Rome. The infinite duty which Socrates conceived as due from himself to his city-state and its members, Jesus conceived as due to a society which included all classes and races of men, to the weak and the young, to the poor and also the rich, to the beggars, outcasts and criminals, to Gentiles no less than Jews:

> They shall come from the east and west, and from the north and south, and shall sit down in the kingdom of God.[14]

And the rules by which their lives are to be ordered are not to be gathered from laws, precedents and traditions, interpreted by kings or priests, regarded as channels of truth divinely ordained. Essential truth is revealed only to those who approach it with minds fresh and receptive as a child's, and as free from preconceived ideas. To be sure that you know is a fatal bar to the growth of knowledge. The real leaders are those who serve and are not afraid to make mistakes by which others as well as themselves will learn. They cannot rule in the Kingdom of God who shrink from responsibility for action; for the truth is only discovered in action and by contact with facts, and when discovered prevails.

The Kingdom of Heaven as Jesus conceived it consisted of men serving God by serving each other, the desire to serve increasing by exercise,[15] and depending for guidance on experience of facts interpreted by reason and conscience. For so and not otherwise could reason and conscience be made to grow, and with their growth the inclusion of all men in one society would become possible. These were the principles which Jesus propounded in the course of a public career which led to his death at the age of thirty. It is idle to speculate as to what he would have said if another thirty years had been given him in which to expound what these principles would mean when applied to the political structure of human society. The profitable task is to see for ourselves, in the light of all the experience gained since his time, how the structure of society must be designed if the principles he stated are to operate in practice. There are certain observations which will help us in this task. We can see, to begin with, that a community, a sufficient proportion of whose members had realised to a certain degree a capacity for putting the interest of others on a level with their own, could govern itself. A community consisting of people all clever as Iago could never govern themselves so long as they maintained his attitude to others. A convict settlement ruled by a governor with the powers of an autocrat would alone restrain them from mutual destruction. On the other hand, an island peopled by Humphry Clinkers would begin by governing themselves, and would quickly advance in culture and intelligence. Self-government is primarily a question of character, and the ultimate problem of politics is how to develop that character. A commonwealth is simply the sermon on the mount translated into political terms.

A further observation may be added. A community in which the goodness necessary for self-government is sufficiently developed will lose that goodness unless its structure is organised on the principle of the commonwealth. If forced to submit to autocracy its virtue will decay. This certainly is a lesson of history which points to a practical conclusion. The members of such a society must labour to change its structure to that of a commonwealth. Under real autocracy a society may advance for a time, but will presently come to a standstill, and finally begin to decline. A continuous advance in the welfare of society depends upon a continuous increase of responsibility assumed by its members for controlling their mutual relations. The effect of institutions on those who live under them is immeasurable. Religious and secular teachers have their part to play, and it is an important part. But the claim of churches and schools to be answerable in the first degree for forming the character of a people, a claim supported not seldom by politicians and public officials, is a dangerous fallacy. The most potent factor in raising or lowering the character of a people, in increasing or diminishing their sense of duty to each other, is the structure of the society in which they live. Politics is the art of so adapting that structure as to raise the sense of duty in each to all. All policies and all measures, however commonplace, can be ultimately tested by this criterion. To engender in men a desire to serve each other is the end and object of human existence. Teaching and preaching are necessary to the process, but they yield in the end a harvest of cynicism unless the actual power of men to serve each other is continuously increased as they can bear it.

The application of this criterion cannot be limited to politics in the stricter sense of the term. We have reached an age when human welfare depends as directly on industrial and commercial combinations as on those of the state. At the moment efficiency seems to depend on confining their control to a handful of directors. But we have to remember how recent and novel these combinations are, when viewed in comparison with the ages through which society has come to be what it is. Their permanence and stability will depend upon how far the whole mass of workers can be rendered answerable to society for the services they render. To compass this in the field of commerce and industry is a far more difficult task than to extend responsibility in the field of politics. In the end it will prove to be no less vital; for though personal hope of gain may help to hold together the members of these combinations, it cannot avail to keep them in stable relations to each other or to the whole society of which they are organs. Freedom is in fact the social product of a capacity in individual men to control their desires and direct their conduct to unselfish ends in every aspect of life. The world's problem is how to increase that self-control. Its solution can in fact be found by patient and continuous study of human experience. "Seek, and ye shall find; knock, and it shall be opened unto you." [16] "The price of freedom is eternal vigilance."

The principles of society which Jesus propounded on the hills of Galilee were those of a commonwealth, not of a kingdom. From the nature of the case he had nothing to say as to the mechanism by which those principles had been applied in the past, or might again be applied in the future. A language, moreover, is limited by the ideas of those who use it, and the Jews like other races in the east had no idea what a commonwealth meant. An eminent scholar, the late Dr. Cowley, has informed the writer that the only word to express 'the state' in Aramaic, the language Jesus used, is the equivalent of a 'kingdom', *malkutha*. (The root is the same as in Moloch and also in Malek Rik, the name by which Richard Cœur de Lion was known to the Saracens.) When, some decades after the death of Jesus, the oral traditions which preserved his teaching were recorded in Greek, the Aramaic *malkutha* was translated into the Greek βασιλεία, which also means kingdom. But the kind of state which Jesus described would have been properly rendered by the word πόλις, of which *civitas* is the Latin equivalent. It was so rendered by St. Augustine in the title of his great treatise *De Civitate Dei*, which was taken as an argument in favour of assimilating the Empire to the Church. Just as in eastern language equivalents of the word *kingdom* had to be used to express a commonwealth, so, under the Roman Empire, *civitas* came to be used to express an autocracy. If regard be had to the meaning which Jesus sought to convey, the words used in our own version of the gospels should be rendered 'the Commonwealth of God'.

The world has agreed to accept Jesus as the founder of a religion with a highly developed theology. In our records of the teaching which was clearly his, his religion is implicit rather than expressed, and is too simple and profound to form the basis of a theological system. His interest centred on men not only in themselves, but in their relations to one another. To him, as to the Greeks, life was a thing of surpassing beauty and value. The key to that value he drew from the faith of his own race. It explained the relation of brotherhood which men were destined to realise. It also supplied a basis for the permanence of life, of its indestructible quality, without which we cannot account for a sense of its worth. In discerning the principles upon which it was based the intuitive perception of Jesus was greater than any mind has ever possessed. So complete was his sense of life as a whole that he never parcelled it out into ethics, politics and religion. He was merely concerned to consider how men should live. The principles he enunciated were on that plane which cannot alter with time or place. And no one will ever succeed in reconciling that teaching with authority, which seeks to balance society like a pyramid on its apex. Society, as conceived by Jesus, is made to stand with its base on the ground of experience as interpreted by the mind and conscience of man, with its point to heaven.

NOTES

[1] Matthew xi. 11, 12.
[2] Mark ii. 18.
[3] Matthew xi. 1-3.

[4] Simkhovitch, *Towards the Understanding of Jesus*, p. 58.
[5] Matthew vi. 28, 29.
[6] Matthew x. 29.
[7] Mark xii. 28-31.
[8] Luke xvii. 20, 21. Marginal reading.
[9] Matthew v. 48.
[10] Matthew xiii. 47, 48.
[11] Mark iv. 31, 32.
[12] Matthew xiii. 44.
[13] Matthew xiii. 45, 46.
[14] Luke xiii. 29.
[15] Matthew xxv. 14-30. The parable of the Talents.
[16] Matthew vii. 7.

CHAPTER XXI

JESUS IN CONFLICT WITH JUDAISM

ACCOUNTS of the new teaching and of its popular reception in the north reached Jerusalem and occasioned uneasiness in official circles. Emissaries sent to look into the matter reported to the Sanhedrin that the young reformer was challenging the authority of the scribes and indeed that of Moses himself. He was questioning principles which to Pharisees and Sadducees alike were the basis of Judaism. The Sadducee priests were opposed to all popular movements which might threaten to disturb the existing regime; for it gave them more power than they could hope to enjoy under any king, whether native or foreign. As things were going it looked as though Jesus would soon have the people behind him and come into collision with the Roman authorities. A member of the Sanhedrin had evidently said that means must be found to 'remove' him. Some scruples were expressed, but the High Priest brushed them aside with the remark that it was better that one man should die than that the whole people should perish, as they would, if led into conflict with the Roman power.

The object which Jesus had in view was to purify Judaism and, through Judaism, the larger society in which it was everywhere intermingled. There was everything to lose and nothing to gain by provoking a controversy between Judaism and the Roman Empire. Such a project was practical, though it called for infinite patience and self-command. The Jewish conception of one righteous God was attracting converts in growing numbers. But the force of this great conception was maimed by the limiting doctrine that God was interested in Israel only. The stubborn adherence of its spiritual leaders to tradition and authority, and the vested interests which the priesthood had developed at its centre, were a fatal bar to any real conquest by Judaism of the Graeco-Roman world. If once the relations of God to man as seen by the Jews had been based by them on conscience and reason, on the principles enunciated in the teaching of Jesus, Graeco-Roman society would have spread on such Judaism as the world had spread on Greece and Rome.[1]

With this object in view Jesus was bound to respond to the crowds in Galilee who were calling on him to accept the position of national leader, however little they might understand what that position meant to himself. He could only lead them in the right direction by accepting their wish to follow him. In order to effect his purpose he would have to challenge not only the hierarchy, but also the authority of the scribes and Pharisees as the national teachers. With such far-reaching objects in view he could do no less than claim for himself the position of national leader. Nay, rather he must claim the position of that supreme leader of whom his people had dreamed, and claim it, not merely in Galilee and Judea, but from that greater body of Israelites dispersed throughout the civilised world. But this could only be done by challenging the established authorities at Jerusalem at a time when the great annual feast had drawn to that centre pilgrims from every Jewish community in Europe and Asia. This, as he well knew, would be done at imminent risk to his own safety. But the movement could make no further advance unless he was ready to take that risk.

As was afterwards shown in the case of Paul, the priests were capable of employing assassins. So, avoiding the main stream of the pilgrimage, he ap-

proached Jerusalem by a route east of the Jordan,
with a mere handful of intimate followers. They
knew of his intentions but misunderstood them, and
were beside themselves with grief when he warned
them of the fate which might overtake him. The
notion that somehow or other he must make himself
king possessed their minds. A legend that he sprang
from the lineage of David had created itself. He had
openly combated the idea, arguing that David himself could not have thought that the Messiah would
spring from his own family.² So great is the power
of a fixed idea that his own disciples failed to grasp
the significance of words which they faithfully trans-
mitted. In the same gospels which record them were
inserted genealogies tracing his descent from David
through Joseph, though elsewhere they affirm that
Joseph was not his physical father. In the mind of
Paul his lineage from David was a fixed belief.³

In sight of Jerusalem he disclosed his presence to
the stream of pilgrims arriving from Galilee. By
them he was hailed as the national leader and
publicly escorted through the gates of the city to the
Temple. At the time of the feast the Procurator
moved his quarters from Caesarea to the palace of
Herod at Jerusalem to watch for and deal with any
disturbance. That Pilate had seen nothing to fear
in the conduct of Jesus on his public entry is plain
from his attitude at the subsequent trial. Escorted
by his followers he entered the Temple. No one
building has ever counted for so much to a people
as the Temple at Jerusalem to the Jews. Though
prayer and worship might reach Jehovah at a distance, the offerings due from his people must be
brought to the Temple. The priests had reason to
regard as a mortal enemy anyone who called these
ideas in question. From the story of his talk with the
woman of Samaria it would seem that Jesus had
openly challenged them.

The hour cometh, when neither in this mountain (Geri-zim), nor in Jerusalem, shall ye worship the Father. . . . But the hour cometh, and now is, when the true worshippers shall worship the Father in spirit and truth: for such doth the Father seek to be his worshippers. God is spirit: and they that worship him must worship in spirit and truth.[4]

A leaf from the pages of a German scholar enables us to picture the kind of scenes in the Temple which Jesus witnessed in the course of that day:

But copious as those *public sacrifices* no doubt were, they still seem but few when compared with the multitudes of *private* offerings and sacrifices that were offered. It was the vast number of these latter—so vast in fact as to be well-nigh inconceivable—that gave its peculiar stamp to the worship at Jerusalem. Here day after day whole crowds of victims were slaughtered and whole masses of flesh burnt; and when any of the high festivals came round, there was such a host of sacrifices to dispose of that it was scarcely possible to attend to them all notwithstanding the fact that there were thousands of priests officiating on the occasion. But the people of Israel saw in the punctilious observance of this worship the principal means of securing for them-selves the favour of their God.[5]

The inner courts where this wholesale slaughter went on must for all their marble and gilt have had the appearance of a knacker's yard. The idea that men could worship God by killing countless oxen and sheep, offering him their blood and by burning their fat, can only have repelled a mind that dwelt on the lilies of the field and loved to consider how they grew. But whatever pity he felt was turned into wrath by the things which he saw in the outer courts. In the precincts of the Temple itself dealers were licensed to sell the victims and in various ways to exploit the wealth which the pilgrims brought to Jerusalem:

And when he had looked round about upon all things, it being now eventide, he went out unto Bethany with the twelve.[6]

In the course of this night he seems to have resolved on an act which would bring home to the
world of Judaism the degrading character of the
priestly regime. Like the modern Vatican this vast
establishment had guards of its own.

According to Philo, there were keepers in his day not
only at the entrances to the inner court, but likewise at the
gates of the outer one as well, one of their principal duties
being to see that the prohibition in question was rigidly
complied with. In addition to these there were watchmen
patrolling all round by night and by day to make sure that
nothing of an unseemly character was going on anywhere.[7]

When Jesus appeared in the Temple next morning
and assumed the right to control what went on there,
the priests and their guards must have seen that the
vast concourse of pilgrims were ready to support
him in anything he did. Resistance, however, was
shown by the traders, and some force had to be used
in clearing them out. We are told that

he made a scourge of cords, and cast all out of the temple,
both the sheep and the oxen; and he poured out the
changers' money, and overthrew their tables; and to them
that sold the doves he said, Take these things hence; make
not my Father's house a house of merchandise.[8]

He would not suffer that any man should carry a vessel
through the temple. And he taught, and said unto them, Is
it not written, My house shall be called a house of prayer
for all the nations? but ye have made it a den of robbers.
And the chief priests and the scribes heard it, and sought
how they might destroy him: for they feared him, for all the
multitude was astonished at his teaching.[9]

There was symbolism in his act. The bazaar was
established in the court of the Gentiles, the only
part of the Temple to which the world at large was
admitted. This also, to him, was an integral part of
the house of God, no less than the inner sanctuaries.
We know the effect which the growing abuses at

Rome came to have in the Middle Ages on the minds of pilgrims from northern Europe. Had Wycliffe or Luther appeared there at the head of a following strong enough to have purged the Vatican, they would probably have perished, but from their blood the Reformation would have drawn a wider momentum than it actually acquired. For the next few days Jesus was able to use the Temple as a centre from which to attack the whole fabric of orthodox Judaism. Unlike Paul thirty years later, he refrained from any attempt to conciliate the Pharisees or enlist their support in his struggle with the priests. Their blind attachment to the principle of authority and the rigid legalism of their scribes was a worse, because less obvious, evil than the greed and corruption of the hierarchy. They were stifling the growth of conscience and reason by leading men to think that life, whether private or public, must be governed by rules. The Sadducees at any rate were content with those embodied in the law which Moses was held to have received from God. But the Pharisee scribes had deduced from the written code a body of minute and trivial rules, which people were taught to regard as their necessary guide in every detail of life. The system is one which destroys all power of initiative and capacity for accepting responsibility in those who live under it. Its effects can be studied to-day in the sphere of public administration, especially in the east. In our Indian administration duties assigned to subordinate officers are governed by volumes of rules which seek to specify in all circumstances what the officer is to do and to leave nothing to his own judgement. With little justice we tax native officials trained in this way for backwardness in accepting responsibility. The effect of this system in depriving soldiers of initiative is common knowledge. By the Pharisee it was extended to the whole sphere of conduct and life. The rules they formulated were as frivolous in kind as they were infinite in number. They were treated as of greater importance than the written law, and the fact that these rules existed only in the memory of the scribes enhanced the position of their order. Jesus attacked these legalists in terms more scathing than any he used of the priests. Both Pharisees and Sadducees saw that their prestige would be permanently shaken unless they could either discredit or destroy him before the pilgrims dispersed.

Counting on Pharisee support the priests took the initiative. Their first idea was to undermine his influence with the crowd by making him show his hand on the burning political issue of the day. Not wishing to be openly involved in such controversies they arranged for some Pharisees and members of Herod's party to ask him in the presence of his followers whether he thought that tribute should be paid to Rome. It was difficult to see how he could frame an answer to this question which would neither involve his immediate arrest by the Pro-curator nor arouse the nationalist fury of the Galileans and turn his own followers against him. But the answer he gave them shows how far they had underrated the hold he had got on the popular party. He made his questioners show him a coin and then asked them:

Whose is this image and superscription? And they said unto him, Caesar's. And Jesus said unto them, Render unto Caesar the things that are Caesar's, and unto God the things that are God's. And they marvelled greatly at him.[10]

He thus boldly advised the paying of tribute, openly renouncing the most certain appeal which any leader could make to the passions of Judaism. His opponents had failed, as politicians so often fail, to realise the part which moral courage and sincerity play in the leadership of men. The latter part of the answer was a reference to the tribute which the pilgrims brought at the Passover from the distant Jewish communities. It raised the dangerous question how far these vast revenues really accrued to the service of God in the hands of the priests.

This failure to alienate the affection of the people for their leader had to be recognised. The priests now set themselves to discover where he spent the night outside the walls, in order to arrest him while the pilgrims slept. They succeeded in corrupting Judas, one of his immediate followers, who guided their police to a garden to which Jesus had withdrawn for prayer together with Peter, James and John and some other disciples, who were all seized with panic and fled when the temple guards arrested him. He was then led to Jerusalem to the house of Annas,[11] the real head of the hierarchy, who had managed to keep the high priesthood in the hands of his own family for a series of years. Meanwhile his son-in-law, Caiaphas, had the members of the Sanhedrin roused and collected at his own house. In the small hours of the morning the prisoner was brought to them for trial.

These movements were watched in the darkness by Peter, who, trying to master his terror, had managed to mix with the throng when it entered the gates of Caiaphas. Challenged by a servant and betrayed by his northern brogue, Peter's courage again failed him. He escaped by denying all connection with Jesus, a denial which tortured his mind till the day of his death.

The charge formulated against Jesus was clear and accurately stated the matter at issue between the heads of the Jewish polity and the popular leader:

And there stood up certain, and bare false witness against him, saying, We heard him say, I will destroy this temple that is made with hands, and in three days I will build another made without hands. And not even so did their witness agree together.[12]

As to the exact words which a prisoner has used witnesses seldom agree, unless they have taken short-hand notes. The principles enunciated by Jesus led to a practical conclusion clearly expressed in the statement made by the witnesses. He had boldly declared his intention of destroying the institutions of which the Temple was the pivot, in order to clear the ground for a system based on the verities of life. The thought was his, though his own followers were unable to face its full implications. The evangelists were less near to the truth than the evidence they branded as false.

No attempt was made by Jesus to deny the charge. He refused to plead, and in fact treated the Sanhedrin, as he had treated the classes from which they were drawn when he met them in the Temple, as rulers who had forfeited the right to rule. Secretly arrested when his followers were asleep and deprived of their protection, he still confronted the Sanhedrin as the real national leader. By unanimous consent of those present Caiaphas pronounced the sentence of death.

To execute the sentence was not in their power. That lay with the Procurator, who had to be convinced that the prisoner had deserved it. The Sanhedrin realised that the reasons for which they had sentenced Jesus were scarcely likely to appeal to Pilate. When day dawned a further meeting was held to decide how best they could handle the matter in the Procurator's court where they must appear not as judges but as accusers. Their best plan lay in the open assertion made by Jesus of his claim to the position of national leader. They hoped to persuade Pilate that this implied a seditious intention, as it had done in the case of Judas the Zealot. Against this was the stand he had taken in the Temple against

N

the Zealot movement and in favour of tribute. But men like Annas and Caiaphas, who had kept the appointment of the high priesthood in their family for years, knew how to apply political pressure. The position of Pilate, stubborn as he was, must have been permanently weakened when he was forced to remove the standards from his own palace to Caesarea.

Pilate must have known about Jesus long before he saw him in court; for the first duty of a Roman governor was to keep an eye on popular movements. He had evidently seen that Jesus was turning the mind of his countrymen from the dangerous dream of a rupture with Rome to the wholesome and practical project of setting their own household in order. He must have felt that sympathy with the movement which an English administrator cannot help feeling for the non-Brahmin movement in India.

It is equally clear that Jesus had read the character of his judge and had made up his mind that Pilate's goodwill to himself would yield to the persistence of the hierarchy the sacrifice of justice which their interests required. He stood before Pilate as the national leader well knowing that the Governor saw in his position no menace to the *pax Romana*. The Sanhedrin spoiled their case by asserting that Jesus had not only claimed the position of national leader (which was true), but had ordered the public to refuse the tribute to Rome (which was false). After questioning the prisoner, Pilate bluntly rejected the second charge and told the Sanhedrin that they had no case upon which to proceed in his court. He evidently knew that Jesus had openly enjoined the payment of tribute since he came to Jerusalem. His accusers tried to counter this by asserting that in Galilee he had preached sedition. This gave Pilate a possible loophole; for Galilee was outside his jurisdiction. It so happened that the native prince who ruled there had come to Jerusalem for the feast, just as Hindu princes go to Benares on similar occasions. So he sent him to Herod, who accepted the compliment, but was far too astute to incur the hostility of the Jewish hierarchy. He ridiculed Jesus as a pretentious impostor and returned him as such to the Procurator. Pilate tried to act on this view of the matter by first flogging Jesus and then telling the Sanhedrin that after inflicting this punishment he proposed to release him. The hierarchy evidently knew that if Jesus once came back into personal contact with the pilgrims their own position would be finally ruined. The ill-treatment he had met at their hands and at those of Herod and Pilate would merely enhance his influence. So they angrily protested against Pilate's decision by concentrating on the fact that the crowds had hailed him as Messiah and insisting that Jesus, in accepting this position, was assuming the political status of a king.

Pilate, though deeply alarmed, still shrank from judicial murder and thought of a way in which he might turn the tables against those who were hinting disloyalty against himself.

In the east it is customary for rulers to signalise great occasions by granting their subjects a boon, and the Romans had been in the habit of showing their clemency at this feast by pardoning a political prisoner. A certain Barabbas, who had taken part in some insurrection, had been chosen for the purpose.

It occurred to Pilate as an excellent plan to execute a man convicted of murder and sedition, and release in his stead a leader from whom the hierarchy had everything and the Romans nothing to fear. He might certainly have effected the exchange on his own authority. But he could not resist the temptation of turning the tables on the priests, who had openly

hinted a charge of disloyalty against himself. For if
they demanded the release of Barabbas it would not
afterwards lie in their mouths to accuse the Governor
of favouring a rebel. So he chose to allow the crowd
in his court to say whether Jesus or Barabbas should
be pardoned and released. In all these hurried proceedings the initiative lay with the priests, who had
certainly seen that Pilate's court should be filled with
their own supporters. The traders and other para-
sites of the Temple were available for the purpose.
A court, even in the open air, would not contain the
mass of pilgrims, whose presence in the Temple on
previous days had helped and protected Jesus. So
when Pilate made his proposal, it was met with a
violent outcry for Barabbas, with renewed suggestions that Pilate was trying to protect a rival to the
throne of his imperial master. His courage and re-
source finally failed him and he sent Jesus to be
crucified with a couple of criminals already condemned.

In one direction, at any rate, the Romans had followed the example of Carthage rather than of Greece.
They had studied the practice of cruelty in the
terrible school of the Punic wars. The Phoenicians
had invented crucifixion as a punishment for slaves.
They were thought of as 'hands', and the nailing of
hands to a cross was meant to express that the slave
had finally failed in the only function for which he
existed. In suppressing the revolt of Spartacus,
Crassus had crucified thousands of his followers.
Roman governors were expected to provide gladia-
tors for the games, and had found it easier to obtain
recruits when criminals realised that crucifixion was
the only alternative.

To this fearful and lingering death Jesus was now
legally condemned, in the hands of a Roman guard
and beyond the reach of popular rescue. The real
situation is revealed by the fact that Pilate thought

it necessary to order the entire garrison, a whole cohort of five hundred men under a centurion, to escort the prisoner to the place of execution outside the walls.[13] "And there followed him a great multitude of the people, and of women who bewailed and lamented him."[14]

It is clear that the officer in command of the guard had seen in the verdict and sentence a gross miscarriage of justice. What little he could do to lighten its severity he did. The timber to be used in the execution was usually carried by the victim himself. The centurion saw that Jesus, exhausted by mental anguish and torn by the scourge, was unequal to the burden, and requisitioned one Simon, a pilgrim from Cyrene, to carry the cross. His sons Alexander and Rufus were evidently known to Mark and the readers for whom he wrote as members of the Christian community. When the place of execution was reached a potion of wine drugged with myrrh was offered to Jesus and refused. He was then nailed to the cross, and the cross planted in the ground with those of the bandits on either side of him.

It is known that crucified men often survived the slow process of exhaustion for several days. All the authorities agree in stating that Jesus succumbed at the end of six hours. It is natural to suppose that he passed to unconsciousness through a state of delirium, in which words are the mere reflex of physical conditions. In response to his cry of thirst one of the soldiers in mercy saturated a sponge with drink and held it to his mouth at the end of a stick. We are then told that Jesus having drunk the wine in the sponge "gave up the ghost".

NOTES

[1] See note 1 to Chapter XIV.
[2] Mark xii. 35-37.
[3] Romans i. 3.
[4] John iv. 21-24.

⁵ Schürer, *The Jewish People in the Time of Jesus Christ*, Division ii. vol. i. p. 298.

Upon this description a distinguished Indian civilian has written the following comment: "This description of the temple reminds me of the Hindu temple to Devi at ——, and the priests must have been just as big scoundrels as the pandits who officiated and still officiate at ——. Once when inspecting officially I had to wade ankle deep in buffalo and goats' blood while in the precincts dealers were licensed to sell the victims and exploit the wealth of the pilgrims."

⁶ Mark xi. 11.

⁷ Schürer, Division ii. vol. i. p. 266.

⁸ John ii. 15-16.

⁹ Mark xi. 16-18.

¹⁰ Mark xii. 16, 17.

¹¹ Streeter, *The Four Gospels*, pp. 381-2.

¹² Mark xiv. 57-59.

¹³ Mark xv. 16.

¹⁴ Luke xxiii. 27.

CHAPTER XXII

THE STORY OF THE RESURRECTION

WE have here to do with events which more than all others have affected the course of human affairs. The writers who tell us about them certainly believed what they wrote, but do not agree in their various accounts of the miracles they relate. We have, therefore, to think for ourselves what probably happened, in the light which modern research has thrown on these records.[1]

The death of Jesus in six hours on the eve of the Sabbath confronted the priests with a difficulty they had not foreseen. In the law it was written:

And if a man have committed a sin worthy of death, and he be put to death, and thou hang him on a tree; his body shall not remain all night upon the tree, but thou shalt surely bury him the same day; for he that is hanged is accursed of God; that thou defile not thy land which the Lord thy God giveth thee for an inheritance.[2]

On hearing that Jesus was dead, members of the Sanhedrin hurried to Pilate and urged him to authorise the immediate burial of the corpse. Their demand naturally raised the question as to what should be done with the two criminals who still survived, but might also die before the Sabbath was over. So the cruel suggestion was made that their legs should be broken to prevent all chance of escape. It is difficult to avoid the idea that this was preliminary to removing them dead or alive to their graves, though it must be remembered that burial alive was perhaps less painful than a lingering death on the cross.

According to Mark, Joseph of Arimathea, a member of the Sanhedrin, had a tomb prepared for his own burial in the rocks not far from the place where the crosses were planted. His offer to remove the body of Jesus to this tomb, before the Sabbath began with sunset, was accepted.

It is safe to assume that members of the Sanhedrin took no further step in the matter before the Sabbath was ended at sunset on the following day. That a special place was reserved for the bodies of executed criminals we know. It is possible, therefore, and indeed probable, that the Sanhedrin intended to remove the body of their victim to the less honourable place of burial when the Sabbath was over. As to whether they did so in fact we have no information.

Simon Peter and the other Galileans who had been with their Lord at Gethsemane had fled from Jerusalem. Peter, we know, was tortured by the sense of his own cowardice in refusing to admit any knowledge of his master, when challenged on the subject in the hall of Caiaphas. In their homes round the Lake of Gennesareth they presently recovered from the panic and despair which had overtaken them in the murderous atmosphere of Jerusalem. Those exquisite shores must have recalled to their minds the words at once powerful and tranquil by which they were drawn to Jesus in the earlier days of his ministry. The love which his person had inspired was refreshed, and with it the faith in his mission which his sudden and violent fate had almost destroyed. Their minds rejected the idea of his life as ended and done with, which indeed it was not. They recalled his attitude to physical death as a necessary step in the spiritual life. He had constantly dwelt on the soul in God as immune from decay. To the Sadducees he had said that God is not the God of the dead, but of the living. He had asked his disciples to believe

that his death would not end the reality of his presence amongst them. "Lo, I am with you alway even
unto the end of the world." So vivid were these
memories to Peter and so powerful the emotions
they awaked, that he saw in a vision the glorified
presence of his Lord.

From the Gospel of Mark we know that Peter
believed that he had seen Jesus during his lifetime
on a lonely mountain "transfigured . . . his raiment
. . . shining, exceeding white as snow; so as no fuller
on earth can white them",[3] talking with Moses and
Elijah. As to the vision of Jesus which Peter saw
after his death we have evidence which is even more
trustworthy. In after-years Peter was intimate with
Paul, and the statement written by Paul to the Church
in Corinth may be taken to represent what Peter
himself believed and had told him.

For I delivered unto you first of all that which also I
received, how that Christ died for our sins according to the
scriptures; and that he was buried; and that he hath been
raised on the third day according to the scriptures; and
that he appeared to Cephas; then to the twelve; then he
appeared to above five hundred brethren at once, of whom
the greater part remain until now, but some are fallen
asleep; then he appeared to James; then to all the apostles;
and last of all, as unto one born out of due time, he appeared to me also.[4]

As to the vision which Paul himself had seen we have
here the statement of the writer himself. In the Acts
we have fuller accounts of this vision recorded by
Luke, who must often have listened to the story as
told by Paul.

In this the earliest and most authentic account
of the resurrection the appearances seen by Peter,
by the other apostles, by more than five hundred
disciples and also by James are placed on exactly
the same footing as the vision seen by the writer
himself. There is no suggestion that the body of

Jesus emerged from the tomb to eat and drink with his followers, and even to be touched by their loving hands.

That rational men and women, whose emotions have been deeply aroused, have believed that they saw and conversed with supernatural beings is a fact entirely beyond dispute. The most critical student of history can find no difficulty in thinking that Peter believed that his Lord had appeared to him in Galilee, or that this belief had revived his courage and inspired the thought that his master had returned to convince his followers that death meant change to a higher life, at any rate for those who accepted his message and followed his teaching. The revival of Peter's faith spread to the other disciples in Galilee. They shared his emotions and passed through the same religious experience. A number of them also came to believe as firmly as Peter himself that the person of their Lord had been made known to them in visible shape. Together they resolved to return to Jerusalem, to brave its perils, and discharge the task which their Lord had bequeathed to them of conveying his message to the world.

On reaching Jerusalem they told their story to the followers of Jesus in that city. Amongst them were women who had also a story to tell. On the morning of the third day, the day, that is, after the Sabbath, which followed the day of the crucifixion, they had sought the tomb where Jesus was laid, in the hope of giving to his body the rites of an honourable burial. They had gone to the sepulchre which they thought was his and found it open. Within was a young man who told them that the body of Jesus was not there. They were so overwhelmed by this failure that they had told no one about it, until they met Peter and his friends and had heard the marvellous and inspiring story of the visions they had seen in Galilee.

It is natural to suppose that as soon as the Sabbath

was over the Sanhedrin had lost no time in removing
the body from the tomb which Joseph of Arimathea
had made for himself to the common grave allotted
to criminals. It is also possible that the women had
hit on the wrong grave in the cemetery, a slope in
the limestone formation honeycombed with tombs.
A young man, working in the tomb, had simply told
them that the body they were looking for was not
there. Discouraged by this failure these distracted
women had then abandoned the search.

The story told by Peter and his friends, coupled
with that told by the women, gave rise to a new train
of ideas. The doctrine which Jesus had preached to
them, that human personality survived the fact of
physical death, had been preached by the Chasidim.
In Chapter XV. we have seen how the Pharisees had
taught that the bodies of the righteous would rise
from their graves to live once more in this world.
These two ideas, though entirely distinct, were
capable of confusion in an age when this physical
world about us was thought to be permanent, however subject to change by supernatural means. If the
actual facts were somewhat as those outlined above,
a belief was certain to develop that the body of Jesus
itself had risen, and issued from the tomb in some
glorified shape, and in that shape had appeared to
his followers.

A comparison of the earliest account, which is
given by Mark, of the visit to the tomb by the women
with later accounts given by Matthew, Luke and
John, and also the story of the ascension given in
the Acts, will show how the legend developed in
response to various motives. Men readily believe
what they wish to believe. The idea, conceived by
the Pharisees and denied by the Sadducees, that the
righteous would rise in the flesh from their graves,
made it easy to believe that the body of Jesus had so
risen. The young man who had told the women that

the body was not in the tomb was the nucleus of the story of one or more angels, messengers of God, sent to announce that the Son of Man had risen from the dead. The legend of his final ascension to heaven grew up to explain why his corporate presence was no longer amongst them. They saw in Jesus the Messiah foretold by the prophets, and especially the suffering servant of Isaiah. So grew belief in his lineage from David, in miracles connected with his birth and in the story told by John how the soldiers pierced his side. "They shall look on him whom they pierced."[5]

These accounts, it is further suggested, were influenced by one of the earliest controversies which distracted the Christian Church. The Docetists were teaching that the Christ, the Messiah of prophecy, was a being who existed through all eternity. This supernatural being had been somehow immanent in the man Jesus during his lifetime on earth. The man Jesus had died on the cross, but not the immanent Christ.[6] The idea that the body of Jesus had risen from the tomb was thus contrary to the teaching of Docetists who held that the Christ had appeared to his followers after the crucifixion, but not the man Jesus who had died on the cross. The opponents of this doctrine had thus a motive for asserting that the actual body of Jesus had risen in the flesh. In the heat of the controversy they came to believe that Jesus had eaten and drunk with his followers. In time the story developed how the doubts of Thomas were removed by seeing the wounds in the risen body of his Lord. Such stories, readily believed by those who denied the Docetist doctrine, were incorporated in the later gospels, to become the foundation of the orthodox creed. It is easy to see how the visions recorded by Paul led the followers of Jesus to see in him the Messiah promised to their race by the prophets of old, the ruler descended from David and clothed with supernatural powers. Belief in his resurrection was of itself enough to create the atmosphere in which stories of the miracles he had wrought in his lifetime came to be told and widely accepted.

By his Jewish followers Jesus was thus recognised as the Christ foretold by their Scriptures. Presently, as their teaching spread beyond Palestine, it began to absorb ideas which, as modern research has shown, were deeply embedded in the folk-lore of the races inhabiting the eastern Mediterranean. In Egypt, in Asia Minor and Greece were primeval legends of a god incarnate in human form who after meeting a violent death would return to life as the destined saviour of suffering humanity. In Egypt this naturalistic idea was expressed in the legend of Isis and Osiris. In Greek mythology it is traceable in the stories of Adonis and Hyacinth. In all probability such ideas had their source in the commonest facts of nature, in the beauty of flowers scorched and withered by the sun, in their seed falling, to lie in the earth for a season and to blossom once more in the following spring. The light of the moon obscured for three days before the new crescent begins to appear is perhaps another element in this folk-lore. The idea of the god returning to life on the third day is traced to this source. The belief that Jesus had risen from his grave was in the course of years inevitably seen through the medium of primitive legends like these.

The belief that God could be pleased by the slaying of animals and birds, and by offerings of their flesh and their blood, had clearly no place in the mind of Jesus. Christianity broke once for all with sanctified butchery, a habit of paganism to which Judaism clung till the Romans destroyed the Temple in which it was practised. Yet so deeply was the sacrificial idea ingrained in the minds of the disciples that they came to regard the death of their master on the cross as a sacrifice to God superseding all others. The Mosaic ritual of the scapegoat, and the pagan ideas of a slaughtered god returning to life and redeeming humanity from its fate, combined to develop a body of doctrine in which genuine religion and growing accretions from pagan folk-lore were closely mingled. These ideas were transferred to the meal which Jesus had instituted as expressing the attitude which man should assume to material comforts, to things of the sense. This meal from its first institution was connected with the Passover ceremony and therefore the sacrifice of a lamb. They thought of their slaughtered master as the lamb. As the wine of the last supper suggested his blood, the bread was taken as a symbol of his flesh. In course of time a belief developed that, by a continuing miracle, the wine became his blood and the bread his flesh. These were transmuted materials through which the nature of Jesus entered the souls of his followers through their bodies. The eucharist was regarded not merely as a sacrifice but also as a meal, at which worshippers partook of the actual blood and body of God.

So rapidly sprung the weeds of paganism in fields which Jesus had sown with truth and enriched with his blood. The tares and the wheat were for ordinary mortals hard to distinguish till they yielded their fruit. In the time of harvest let reapers gather first the tares, and bind them in bundles to burn them: "but gather the wheat into my barn".[7] Already the fields are white for the harvest.

.

NOTES

[1] In this chapter the reverent and scholarly analysis of the evidence made by Professor Kirsopp Lake, M.A.(Oxon), Professor of New Testament Exegesis and Early Christian Literature in the University of

Leiden, has been largely followed. His book, *The Historical Evidence for the Resurrection of Jesus Christ*, is published by Williams and Norgate in the Crown Theological Library.

[2] Deut. xxi. 22, 23.
[3] Mark ix. 1-10.
[4] I Corinthians xv. 3-8.
[5] Ps. xxii. 16, 17; Zech. xii. 10.
[6] Kirsopp Lake, pp. 155-6.
[7] Matthew xiii. 30.

CHAPTER XXIII

THE living contact of Jesus with his followers was a short one. As to how far he would have succeeded in purging their minds of the pagan ideas which infected Judaism, if sufficient time had been given him for the task, must always remain a matter of conjecture. With two vital aspects of his teaching they were seized. He had taught them to regard life as an episode of eternity. Now for the first time in history the idea that life must be lived as a phase of experience not to be ended by death began to influence increasing multitudes of ordinary men and women. He had further got into the minds of his followers the idea that the Father of all men must be served by the manner of life which his children adopted in relation to each other, as well as to himself. People from the lowest strata of society were inspired to practise the standards of personal conduct which Jesus had enunciated in the sermon on the mount. In eating and drinking, and above all in sexual relations, they learned to regard their bodies and those of others with the reverence due to temples where dwelt the spirit of God. They were taught to render not merely justice to each other, but an active solicitude, a desire in each to meet the needs of his fellows rather than his own.

It is safe to say that no person in history has ever so changed the current of human affairs by his life and death as Jesus of Nazareth. It is equally certain that the startling rapidity of this change was due to the belief in the minds of his followers that Jesus himself had risen from the grave, had conquered death, and that those who followed his teaching would share with their master eternal life. Every book in the New Testament shows that the impetus which enabled a movement, beginning in the humblest orders of society, presently to absorb the structure of the Roman Empire itself was a fervent belief in this miracle. It certainly enabled masses of people to grasp, in a form however crude, the essential conception which Jesus had taught of life on this earth, of the attitude of mind in which it should be led. But none the less, this belief that Jesus had returned from the grave to revive the faith of his followers obscured other aspects of his teaching which were no less important. "If they hear not Moses and the prophets, neither will they be persuaded, if one rise from the dead."[1] It is difficult to read these words without feeling that an intellect of the first order had at last transcended desires and superstitions deeply embedded in the human mind, and revealed to men the essential nature of spiritual truth. Ultimate verities cannot be proved by manifestations in the world of phenomena. Intercourse with the dead may convince us that the spirit is capable of surviving the flesh: as to whether the spirit is still indestructible it offers no proof. It cannot convince us that the issues of right and wrong affect an existence which has no limits in time or space. To us who know, as we now know, that experience of life on this earth, though extended by millions of years, must sooner or later be wiped out by physical forces, it matters little how many the millions be. Nothing less than permanence, apart from physical change, can satisfy the instinct that tells us that the difference of right conduct from wrong is a difference of infinite importance. That instinct, if genuine, drives us back on the view that the universe is of the nature of our minds rather than

o

of our bodies, and that personality is not subject to the utter destruction which sooner or later overtakes the form of all bodily things. But, if this be so, the resurrection, even in the visions recorded by Paul, is no more necessary to faith in the message of Jesus than the virgin birth which former generations have held as a dogma. Insistence on belief in a supernatural event as necessary to prove the teaching of Jesus is in fact fatal to the principle of faith in the true sense of that word.

If supernatural events are really a necessary basis of belief in doctrines of fundamental importance, why then should the Father of men have left his children any reason to doubt that such supernatural events have occurred. He must surely have so ordered such events that their actual occurrence would have been beyond question, not only by men at the time when they happened, but also by all men in ages to come. The claims of authority, however tremendous, must always submit in the last resort to the judgement of the individual conscience and mind.

This belief that Jesus had returned from the grave and been manifest to the senses of his followers had the effect of throwing them back on the basis of authority from which he had been trying to reclaim their minds. The effect of this on the growth of the Church will be seen in the subsequent chapters of this inquiry. It led his followers to forget the special conception he had tried to convey in his use of the term 'Kingdom of Heaven'. His ultimate aim was, beyond question, the perfection of human character. "Be ye perfect as your father also is perfect." In order to attain this perfection his followers must think of God as their Father, and of all men as brethren. The importance of personal religion and conduct he emphasised to the full, so fully indeed that it is now almost a heresy to suggest that the teaching of Jesus had political aspects. But the growth of character depends upon more than religious observance and instruction in personal conduct. It depends to an even greater extent on environment. As the Greeks had divined, the most important aspect of environment is the structure of society in which the life of its members is led. Our Lord had realised that the souls of men cannot grow to perfection unless the structure of society itself is ordered in accordance with the laws of God, that is to say, founded on verities. To him the ultimate verity was goodness personified—God, whose nature is expressed, however imperfectly, in his creatures. The cardinal factor in human nature, as he saw it, was the instinct in men to serve each other. By strengthening that instinct, and not otherwise, was it possible to develop the nature of God in men. He realised that in ordinary men this instinct will develop only in so far as it is exercised and that men's relations one to another must be so organised as to prompt them to exercise this sense of duty in the highest possible degree. Such a system could not be founded on authority, on some revelation of divine direction expressed through a supernatural medium or attested by a miracle in the physical world. It must in the last resort depend on the revelation which God has implanted in the conscience and mind of all his children. The task he entrusted to men was that of ordering their mutual relations in such manner as to exercise to the utmost their sense of duty one to another, and also their minds in learning from experience how that sense of duty could best be rendered. I believe that he said, "The Kingdom of Heaven is within you". I believe that he also said, "The Kingdom of Heaven is amongst you".

These two aspects of truth, the divine nature as realised in each member of society and also in the structure of society which governs our relations one

to another, are equally true, and inseparable, therefore, the one from the other.

The belief that their master had returned from the
grave to attest the verity of his teaching, and that
this miracle was the final proof of its verity, could
scarcely do otherwise than swing back the minds
of his followers to the basis of authority to which
human nature instinctively clings. He was taken
from them before he had had time to conquer their
prepossessions. There was in the structure of the
Roman Empire, as then developed, especially in its
eastern regions, so little to exemplify what he meant.
With us it is different in a world which has since done
something to show how society can be made to rest
on the mind and conscience of ordinary men. Happily
for us, his followers remembered sayings and parables
in which Jesus was expressing ideas less intelligible
to them than they are to us in the light of our longer
experience. In loving reverence they preserved many
of his words much as he uttered them and, in their
simplicity of mind, failed to perceive that these
genuine truths could not be reconciled with much
else that they came to attribute to Jesus and in all
sincerity believed that he had said and done. The
legend of his miraculous birth and of all the wonders
he had wrought in his life was thus the natural
corollary of the belief in the great miracle which had
closed his career on earth.

The power of this idea was the greater because it
led them to fit their master into the great national
tradition and to see in his career the fulfilment of
prophecy. In their belief he had lain dead in the
grave for more than twenty-four hours, had returned
to life and, after staying amongst them long enough
to inspire them with unquenchable hopes, had withdrawn from their sight. They were comforted for his
absence by remembering how he had told them that
he would always be with them, though no longer

visible to their eyes. These impressions shaped their ideas. His body having died and come to life again was no longer subject to death. Exempted from all the laws of matter and no longer subject to age and decay, he had withdrawn for a time to heaven, which they pictured almost as a place in the physical universe. But presently he would appear again in his glorified body, no longer as the humble mechanic and preacher, but in such manner as would render his sovereign power and position clear beyond all dispute. When he came again it would be as the ruler of the world. He would have no need to appeal to physical force. One side of their master's teaching had entered their minds so deeply as to render them immune from the madness of the Zealots. When Christ returned to rule the world as heavenly king, his power would be such that all men would recognise and obey him. He would put an end to sin and death. Those who had loved him and believed on him would lose all desire to sin. They would cease like him to be subject to death, and enjoy the presence of their master for ever. But those who had refused to recognise him and had rejected his teaching would be driven from his presence. The belief quickly developed that the most terrible miseries awaited them, miseries which included physical tortures without end. They could not escape the idea of reward and punishment deeply embedded in the human mind, which pervaded the religions of Jew and Gentile alike. But to earn the rewards it was necessary to believe not only on Christ, but also to live, as he himself had lived, in accordance with his teaching. So his followers formed themselves into societies, the members of which were to live the life which he had prescribed, and to persuade others to do so in preparation for his second coming. Their view was insensibly coloured by the Jewish tradition in which they were bred. His death on the cross they interpreted as a supreme sacrifice, superseding and ending the necessity for sacrifice in the Temple. His escape from death was the sure promise of immortal life for themselves. Their master had left them the task of warning all men that the Kingdom of God was at hand, and bidding them prepare to inherit its blessings. The master himself would return to inaugurate the kingdom by a miracle as great as that which had happened in the first creation of the world. The wicked would then be banished from his kingdom for ever. The meek alone would inherit the earth, and Christ at his second coming would inaugurate a regime in which evil would have no place and righteousness would wholly prevail. The conception of Jesus as the Messiah who had actually come, who was with them still and would presently establish the Kingdom of Heaven on earth, occupied their minds. He had come to fulfil and not to destroy the Law and the prophets. They still thought of God as mainly, if not exclusively, interested in the Jewish race. Before Gentiles could be included in the promised kingdom they must, as a matter of course, be circumcised as well as baptized.

NOTE

[1] Luke xvi. 31.

CHAPTER XXIV

JUDAISM FREED FROM ITS LIMITATIONS

THE doctrine that Messiah had actually come in the person of Jesus was an insult to orthodox Judaism. Its leaders who had planned and accomplished his death were presently aware that his followers had recovered their courage and enthusiasm. The movement centred in Jerusalem, where its members had copied the communistic ideas of the Essenes. We are told in the Gospels that the family of Jesus had not been in sympathy with his teaching. After his death one of his brothers, James, had come to believe in him, and presently appears as a kind of caliph at the head of the Church in Jerusalem.

The Sanhedrin did not again attempt the difficult task of persuading the Roman authorities to execute the leaders, but at times availed themselves of the violence of the mob. The stoning of Stephen was a case in point. In these proceedings their chief agent was Saul, a zealous and able young Pharisee, born and bred amongst Greek surroundings at Tarsus, a centre of those Greek mystery religions, the language of which is clearly reflected in his letters. He found, however, that his efforts to suppress the sect in Jerusalem were driving its members to distant cities where they made converts and created schisms in the local synagogues. So he furnished himself with letters from the high priest to the rulers of the synagogue in Damascus, and set out to suppress the sect in the north. We can scarcely doubt that the future author of the Epistles had argued at length with his prisoners, especially Stephen, and that what they had said to him haunted his mind. On the way to Damascus he passed through some great mental experience. What happened is best described by himself.

For I make known to you, brethren, as touching the gospel which was preached by me, that it is not after man. For neither did I receive it from man, nor was I taught it, but it came to me through revelation of Jesus Christ. For ye have heard of my manner of life in time past in the Jews' religion, how that beyond measure I persecuted the church of God, and made havock of it: and I advanced in the Jews' religion beyond many of mine own age among my country-men, being more exceedingly zealous for the traditions of my fathers. But when it was the good pleasure of God, who separated me, even from my mother's womb, and called me through his grace, to reveal his Son in me, that I might preach him among the Gentiles; immediately I conferred not with flesh and blood: neither went I up to Jerusalem to them which were apostles before me: but I went away into Arabia; and again I returned unto Damascus. Then after three years I went up to Jerusalem to visit Cephas, and tarried with him fifteen days. But other of the apostles saw I none, save James the Lord's brother. Now touching the things which I write unto you, behold, before God, I lie not. Then I came into the regions of Syria and Cilicia. And I was still unknown by face unto the churches of Judaea which were in Christ: but they only heard say, He that once persecuted us now preacheth the faith of which he once made havock; and they glorified God in me. Then after the space of fourteen years I went up again to Jerusalem with Barnabas, taking Titus also with me.[1]

After the manner of his race Saul withdrew for a time to the wilderness to consider the tremendous idea which had entered his mind. The conception of Jesus as the Messiah who had come already and would presently return to inaugurate the Kingdom of God came easily to one of his Pharisee training. But he went beyond some of the personal followers of Jesus, as well as the Pharisees, in conceiving that the Kingdom of Messiah was intended for the benefit of the Gentiles no less than of the Jews. For Saul was a Roman-citizen-born and proud of the status it gave him, as well as of being a Jew by race. He looked on himself as the instrument ordained to convey this message to the whole Empire, and naturally aspired to begin this work in the country of his birth. Before setting out for Asia Minor he wished to hear more of the teaching of Jesus from those who had heard it. So he visited Jerusalem, saw Peter, and doubtless discussed the conclusions he had reached during his sojourn in Arabia. For the next fourteen years he was preaching in Cyprus, Asia, Thrace, Macedonia and Greece, and often found a more ready hearing in streets than in synagogues. For the rest of his life he was known by a latinised nickname, Paulus, the little man, a reference to the smallness of his body in contrast with the greatness of the soul it contained. Facing the question whether Jesus would have refused Gentiles as followers unless they submitted to the painful and, to them, degrading ordinance of circumcision, he answered it in the negative, and reached the conception that his teaching was intended to supersede the Mosaic law with its tedious and costly ritual.

The destruction of the Temple at Jerusalem, where this ritual had centred, finally established the movement initiated by Paul. The Christian Churches which observed the Mosaic law were thereafter limited to Palestine and died out in the course of a few generations.

For centuries before, the thoughts of Xenophanes, Socrates and Plato had been slowly leavening the Graeco-Roman world. The popular belief in a number of gods and goddesses with a standard of morality lower than that of the best human beings had been undermined. Judaism with its conception of one righteous God was attracting proselytes in growing numbers. But Judaism insisted that the one God must be served by the ritual prescribed in the Law of

Moses. This belief, founded only on Jewish tradition and contrary to reason, was a fatal obstacle to the general adoption of Judaism as a world religion. In Christianity, as interpreted by Paul, the creed of monotheism was freed from this parasitic condition. It appeared no longer as a sect of Judaism, but as a separate faith which Gentiles could adopt more easily than the Jews themselves. The destruction of Jerusalem in A.D. 70 settled the issue. Paul had started Christianity on the road which led to its adoption as the official religion of the Empire within three centuries.

The mind of Paul was none the less completely possessed by another side of the Jewish tradition. He viewed Jesus, whom he had not known in the flesh, through the medium of the Messianic idea in its supernatural form. His course was determined by the thought that Jesus would reappear to inaugurate the Kingdom of God for those who had accepted his teaching, and that this would happen as soon as his followers had conveyed his message to every part of the civilised world. His mission in life was to fulfil this condition and so hasten the second coming. Italy had already received the message. The great Jewish community in Rome sent thousands of pilgrims to Jerusalem, some of whom must have seen Jesus or listened to his followers after his death. It is quite unnecessary to suppose that the Church to which Paul addressed his great epistle was founded by missionaries sent by the churches in Palestine. We know that Paul was fired by the idea of hastening the coming of his Lord by announcing the message to the countries east and west of Italy.

The idea of human society, based on the infinite duty of men to each other, and so organised in harmony with the will of God, was thus viewed through the medium of Jewish legend and transferred to the supernatural plane.

Our earliest Christian records are the letters of Paul written while many of the personal followers of Jesus were living. In these letters we see how confidently they expected to see him return and change the order of the universe by a miracle as stupendous as that of the creation described in Genesis. They continually repeated their stories of what he had said, done and suffered in Galilee and Judea, and some of their hearers who wished to spread the good news to others may have made notes for their own use. But the need of comprehensive and authoritative accounts of his life and teaching was not felt in the first generation, which expected to see him return in the lifetime of some who had previously known him. As, one by one, those who had seen his face and listened to his words passed away, a demand for authoritative records began to arise and was presently met. The first biography of Jesus was produced by Mark, shortly before the time of the great upheaval which led to the fall of Jerusalem. Peter, in whom Jesus had recognised qualities which distinguished him from the rest of his followers, seems to have used Mark as a secretary. It is likely that Peter and Paul both perished at Rome in the massacre ordered by Nero, and that Mark then hastened to put into writing his version of the stories which Peter must very often have told in his hearing. His account was largely embodied and amplified in the two biographies issued some decades later under the names of Matthew and Luke. In any case the statements contained in these three gospels had been constantly repeated and handed from mouth to mouth for a number of years before they were written down. Every middle-aged man must have noticed how a story told by the same person over a long period gradually changes and takes its colour from the mind of the teller, however truthful. The change is of course far more rapid when the story is passed from mouth to mouth. But even when deeply coloured and freely embellished by repetition it often preserves the essential point. The sayings and doings of Jesus were subject to this process for a whole generation before they were placed on record. For several decades they lived on the tongues of simple followers inspired by a personal devotion which has never been equalled; and during that time were steeped in the very ideas he had tried to combat. These ideas, moreover, were greatly strengthened by the belief that his dead body had been raised to life. We thus have detailed accounts of what Jesus said and did, encrusted with legend and often distorted by the crust, side by side with stories which are all crust and with no genuine truth inside. It is only by breaking the crust and examining the contents that we find the truths and see how completely their living tissues differ from the composition of the legendary shell.

NOTE

[1] Gal. i. 11-24, ii. 1.

CHAPTER XXV

To begin with, the Christians were regarded by the Gentile world as the most obnoxious sect of the Jews. In the cities they offended the mob by their puritan morality and their open condemnation of idols and also of the public games. They were treated as atheists, as Socrates had been. In time of public calamity the gods were thought to be visiting their anger on a world which allowed their very existence to be questioned. As Tertullian puts it:

If the Tiber rises too high or the Nile does not rise high enough, or if there be drought or earthquake or famine, or pestilence, then straightway the Christians to the beasts.[1]

The mob were pleased to see these spoil-sports made to furnish the spectacles they denounced, and the Jews, in their hatred of the Christians, were only too ready to excite their passions. In A.D. 64 Nero gratified the rabble by torturing and burning the Christians in Rome. Meanwhile the doctrines of Paul, the destruction of Jerusalem and the open hatred of the Jews were having their effect. By the reign of Domitian the Churches had lost even the appearance of a Jewish sect, and with it the privileges which the Romans had accorded to the Jewish religion.

After the manner of despotisms the Empire was suspicious of private associations. It had tried to suppress pagan cults which attempted to practise secret rites. The existence of the Churches was in principle contrary to the spirit of its laws. The refusal of Gentile Christians to render divine honours to the emperors brought them into open conflict with the civil authorities. Merely to profess Christianity was an act of rebellion against the Empire. The magistrates had thus a legal excuse for gratifying the popular lust for blood, whenever they felt disposed to do so, by exposing Christians as victims at the games.

For nearly three centuries the Churches were the object of persecution, never so persistent as to destroy them, but severe enough, so long as they were active, to purge their ranks of all but people of the highest courage and noblest purpose. The metal of which they were wrought was extracted in a furnace and forged to steel on the terrible anvils of the amphi-theatres.

This conviction that they were a *people—i.e.*, the transference of all the prerogatives and claims of the Jewish people to the new community as a new creation which exhibited and realized whatever was old and original in religion—this at once furnished adherents of the new faith with a *political and historical* self-consciousness. Nothing more comprehensive or complete or impressive than this consciousness can be conceived. Could there be any higher or more comprehensive conception than that of the complex of momenta afforded by the Christians' estimate of themselves as "the true Israel", "the new people", "the original people", and "the people of the future", *i.e.*, of eternity ? This estimate of themselves rendered Christians impregnable against all attacks and movements of polemical criticism, while it further enabled them to advance in every direction for a war of conquest. Was the cry raised, "You are renegade Jews"—the answer came, "We are the community of the Messiah, and therefore the true Israelites". If people said, "You are simply Jews", the reply was, "We are a new creation and a new people". If, again, they were taxed with their recent origin and told that they were but of yesterday, they retorted, "We only seem to be the younger People; from the beginning we have been latent; we have always existed, previous to any other people; we are the original people of God". If they were told, "You do not deserve to live", the answer ran, "We would die to live, for we are citizens of the world to come, and sure that we shall rise again".[2]

Their sufferings at the hands of the Roman Empire naturally disposed the Christians to regard it as the kingdom of Satan. They held themselves aloof from its civil and military life and made no attempt to improve its polity. As Tertullian said, "No interest concerns us so little as that of the state".[3] To Christians, their Church was the Kingdom of Heaven in embryo. The more they endured the more earnestly they looked for the second coming of Christ to inaugurate its miraculous birth. This idea assumed in the minds of some of them a form alien to the spirit of their founder. Tertullian looked forward

with fierce exultation to the glorious gains of the day of judgement, when we shall see (and that full soon) gods and deified emperors, philosophers and poets, actors and jockeys, all burning together in the fires of hell at Christ's triumphant coming. These are *our* games; where is the praetor that can show us their like?[4]

Messianic ideas in their supernatural aspect had a strong hold on Paul. To this extent Judaism has continued to influence Christianity to the present day. It led the followers of Jesus to interpret the Kingdom of Heaven as propounded by him in the light of their national traditions, and to look for miraculous events which have never happened and are not destined to happen. Their master had taught that men must no longer look to the Mosaic law as interpreted by priests, Pharisees or scribes, as the source of truth, but to their own conscience and reason purified by direct intercourse with God. When, after his death, they had come to conceive him as a supernatural being, as divine rather than human, they thought of him as the only source of truth. He had said that God would bestow his spirit on those able to receive it. He had also said that his spirit would still be with them when

they no longer saw him in the flesh. The spirit of
God which descended on Christ and by him could be
given to themselves was conceived in their minds as
an essence and finally as an actual person. Truth was
a matter of revelation vouchsafed to apostles, prophets and elders who had received the Holy Spirit
from Christ himself.

In its early days the Church thus reverted to the
same principle of authority which Jesus had attacked.
The centralised organisation, ruled by a hierarchy,
which it presently developed, was the natural result
of regarding truth as finally revealed by God through
Christ to men. The apostles, who had known Jesus
and received his message, had clearly a right to
prior authority; though, even in their day, there was
Paul claiming to stand on the same footing by virtue
of a special revelation vouchsafed to himself. His
example was presently followed by various sectaries
inspired by the old eastern idea of associating goodness with mind and evil with matter. On the basis of
dualism they constructed a great variety of fantastic
beliefs which they spoke of as 'science' (gnosis). But
this science, as they claimed, was not the fruit of study
or learning, but specially inspired by divine revelation. The Church was undoubtedly right in holding
that the dualism of the Gnostics was contrary to the
teaching of Jesus; but arguing the matter on the
basis of authority rather than reason it was forced to
deny the claim of the Gnostics to direct inspiration,
and therefore to restrict the right of interpreting
the teaching of Jesus to the apostles and to those
ordained for the purpose by the apostles and their
authorised successors. In the second century the
Church was thus developing a hierarchy which
claimed to prescribe to Christians not only what they
should do but also what they must think.

In their earliest form the churches were schismatic
congregations of Jews who recognised in Jesus the

Messiah or Christ, and were separated by that fact from the synagogues where orthodox Jews refused to accept him as such. Amongst Greek-speaking Jews who were also Christians their congregation was known as κυριακὸν δῶμα, the house of the Lord, a term which survives as *Kirche* in German and in English as church. Amongst western Gentiles the term used was often ἐκκλησία, a word which recalled the sovereign assembly of a city-state. The French *église* is derived from this word. As the Catholic movement developed, the name of 'church' was broadened to cover the larger organisation in which the local congregations were embodied.

It is safe to assume with Streeter that in their earlier stages a certain variety of organisation existed in the various churches.[5] In Jerusalem James the brother of the Lord seems to have been accorded a great measure of personal authority. In western churches the use of the word ἐκκλησία suggests that more democratic ideas prevailed. Generally speaking, the churches were ruled by bodies of elders or presbyters. Of these one was usually appointed as ἐπίσκοπος or overseer to manage the corporate property. He thus became the chief administrative officer, and also the channel through whom one church corresponded with another. The office would tend to be filled by the ablest of the presbyters and also to be continued for life where he proved himself as such. In the second century these overseers appear as the virtual rulers of the local church, though still assisted by councils of elders. From this time the office begins to assume the monarchical functions we have come to associate with the title of bishop. The sacraments were now filling the same place in Christian worship as the mysteries in pagan or the sacrifices in Jewish religion. The clergy required to administer them were almost as necessary to intercourse with God as the priests of the older faith. They received their

P

commissions from the bishops, who in turn were held to receive their authority from the apostles through their successors.

The bishops were thus the living repositories of the truth as delivered to the apostles. When they differed on points of doctrine or discipline, gatherings or synods were held to settle their differences. The areas from which bishops were gathered were often those of the Roman provinces. The bishop of the leading city presided and acquired a certain primacy under the title of 'metropolitan'. In the Latinised western provinces the Bishop of Rome came to be recognised as superior to the others, the lineal successor of Peter and the Vicar of Christ, at whose hands the rest of the bishops received their commissions. As Christians thought of themselves as a separate people, they came to regard their church as the Kingdom of God to be finally established at the second coming of Christ. It was to them an organised state, more permanent than the Empire, with a higher claim to their loyalty. In moulding its institutions they were deeply influenced by those of the Empire, and especially by the discipline of the Roman army, of which the Emperor was head. From this early period date the military terms which have found their way into Christian language, 'the sword of the spirit', 'the church militant' and such-like; expressions to us worn so threadbare that we almost forget their origin.

Suffer hardship with me, as a good soldier of Christ Jesus. No soldier on service entangleth himself in the affairs of this life; that he may please him who enrolled him as a soldier.[6]

The Salvation Army has more in common with the primitive Church than General Booth perhaps realised.

By Marcus Aurelius the Church was seen as a movement fatal to Greek culture and the Roman

Empire. In seeking to destroy it he had called the philosophy of Greece to the aid of imperial authority. At his death in A.D. 180, the Church, though widely diffused, still embraced but a fraction of his subjects. By A.D. 250 its numbers and the strength of its organisation had grown to such an extent that it openly described itself as a third race in distinction from pagans and Jews. The Emperor Decius declared that:

He would hear of a rival prince being set up against himself with far more patience and equanimity than of a priest of God being appointed in Rome.[7]

The Emperor had learned to regard the Bishop of Rome as a dangerous rival. Barbarian armies threatening its frontiers were no greater menace to the Emperor than an organisation which claimed an authority higher than his own, and attracted to its service the best of his subjects. As Celsus wrote to Origen:

If all men were to do as you do, nothing would prevent the Emperor from being deserted, and all things . . . falling into the power of . . . savages.[8]

It ceased to be a question of punishing the Christians for breaking the law as Trajan had done. Decius was resolved to extinguish the Church by requiring all Christians on pain of torture and death to recognise the gods of the Empire. To begin with these measures secured more apostates than martyrs and looked like succeeding. But presently the example of the few who preferred to die rather than yield revived the fainting spirit of the Church. Prisons and arenas were glutted with victims and within ten years the persecution which Decius began was abandoned by his successor. Purged of her weaklings, the Church emerged with enhanced prestige and rapidly increased the roll of her converts.

In some of the provinces, and especially in Asia, the pagans scarcely outnumbered the Christians at the close of the century.

Diocletian was called to the purple in A.D. 284. His vigorous methods restored the discipline of the army and the fortunes of the Empire. In A.D. 293 he called to his aid three colleagues, Maximian and Constantius in the west, and Galerius in the east. The anxiety aroused in their minds by the growing power of the Church can be read in the edict issued by Galerius when the last and most formidable effort of the Empire to crush its rival had failed.

> Amongst our other efforts for the public good we formerly desired so to reform the state in accordance with the old laws and public discipline of the Romans, that the Christians also, who had given up the manner of life laid down by their own ancestors, might return to a better mind. For these Christians had reasoned so strangely, and become so possessed with self-will and folly, that they were not following those institutes of the ancients which perhaps their own ancestors had first established, *but were making laws for themselves after their own good-will and pleasure and by divers means collecting assemblies of divers peoples.*[9]

In A.D. 303 the emperors resolved on one final attempt to extinguish the Church. At the instigation of Maximian and Galerius, Diocletian condemned its buildings to destruction and its Scriptures to be burned. Christian officials were ordered to renounce their religion, or else to be stripped of their offices, and also of all civil rights and to be sold as slaves.

Two fires occurred in the palace which Diocletian attributed to Christian officials. Inflamed with fury he authorised a policy of general massacre. But the state could no longer count on the hatred of the mobs which a century before had clamoured for the Christians to be thrown to the lions. By A.D. 311 the attempt to exterminate the Church had palpably failed. It was ended by an edict issued by Galerius on his death-bed some words of which have been quoted above.

NOTES

[1] Tertullian, *Apology*, 40.
[2] Harnack, *The Mission and Expansion of Christianity*, vol. i. pp. 240-41.
[3] Tertullian, *Apology*, 38.
[4] Gwatkin, *Early Church History*, vol. i. p. 178.
[5] Streeter, *The Primitive Church*.
[6] 2 Tim. ii. 3, 4.
[7] Cyprian, Ep. LV. 9.
[8] Origen VIII. 68, quoted by Glover in his *Conflict of Religions in the Roman Empire*, p. 256.
[9] Gwatkin, *Early Church History*, vol. ii. p. 346.

CHAPTER XXVI

THE CHURCH TRIUMPHANT

THE division of the imperial power which Diocletian had made naturally led to a conflict between his colleagues or their heirs, from which the son of Constantius emerged as Emperor. In A.D. 313 Constantine proclaimed the principle of religious liberty and legalised the position of the Church in the edict of Milan. It was now, as he saw, the most vital element in the system of the Empire. Having made it his policy to enlist its support, he sought to strengthen it by composing its internal dissensions. In A.D. 325 he summoned at Nicaea a council of bishops from the whole Empire and gave to its decision the force of law. By the institution of the Ecumenical Council the principle of authority thus acquired its appropriate vehicle.

Under Theodosius (A.D. 379–395) orthodox Christianity, as defined at Nicaea, was finally established as the sole official religion of the Empire. Heathenism was now proscribed, and the relative positions which pagan and Christian worship had filled before Constantine were reversed. The emperors abandoned their claim to divinity, but not their claim to derive their authority from God. Henceforth they ruled as vicegerents of Christ pending his return finally to establish the Kingdom of God upon earth.

Constantine moved his capital to Byzantium, and gave it the name of Constantinople. He died in A.D. 337. The burden of government again proved too heavy for a single ruler, and in A.D. 364 was divided between two emperors, one at Constantinople and the other at Rome.

It was reunited by Theodosius in A.D. 379, and divided once more on his death. In A.D. 395 Honorius became Emperor in the west. Alarmed by the Gothic invasion of Italy, he left Rome in A.D. 404 and retired for safety behind the marshes which surround Ravenna. Henceforward Rome saw little of its emperors. In A.D. 410 it was stormed and sacked by the Goths under Alaric, who had served in the Roman army and had learned its technique.

The like had not happened since the days of Brennus. Italy lay at the mercy of northern barbarians. Nobles and landowners fled from her shores, leaving their property behind them. The poverty of these emigrants revealed to the provinces how low the majesty of Rome had fallen. Pagans saw in the catastrophe the vengeance of the gods whom the Empire had abandoned.

At this period an exchange of letters took place between Volusian, the pro-consul of Africa, a pagan of lofty character who had shown an intelligent interest in Christian teaching, and Augustine, the Bishop of Hippo. Volusian had expressed doubts whether Christianity could be reconciled with the loyalty which he felt for the Empire. Augustine was thus led, in A.D. 413, to survey the whole problem in a treatise entitled *De Civitate Dei*, issued from time to time in a series of books and finally completed in A.D. 426.[1]

The general argument of this monumental work may best be described in his own words:

Rome having been stormed and sacked by the Goths under Alaric their king, the worshippers of false gods, or pagans, as we commonly call them, made an attempt to attribute this calamity to the Christian religion, and began to blaspheme the true God with even more than their wonted bitterness and acerbity. It was this which kindled my zeal for the house of God, and prompted me to undertake the defence of the city of God against the charges and misrepresentations of its assailants. . . . This great undertaking was at last completed in twenty-two books. Of these, the first five refute those who fancy that the polytheistic worship is necessary in order to secure worldly prosperity, and that all these overwhelming calamities have befallen us in consequence of its prohibition. In the following five books I address myself to those who admit that such calamities have at all times attended, and will at all times attend, the human race. . . . In these ten books, then, I refute these two opinions, which are as groundless as they are antagonistic to the Christian religion.

But that no one might have occasion to say, that though I had refuted the tenets of other men, I had omitted to establish my own, I devote to this object the second part of this work, which comprises twelve books. . . . Of these twelve books, the first four contain an account of the origin of these two cities—the city of God, and the city of the world. The second four treat of their history or progress; the third and last four, of their deserved destinies. And so, though all these twenty-two books refer to both cities, yet I have named them after the better city, and called them The City of God.[2]

In the opening pages of Book XI. St. Augustine accepts divine revelation as the necessary basis of his system.

Since the mind itself, though naturally capable of reason and intelligence, is disabled by besotting and inveterate vices not merely from delighting and abiding in, but even from tolerating His unchangeable light, until it has been gradually healed, and renewed, and made capable of such felicity, it had, in the first place, to be impregnated with faith, and so purified. And that in this faith it might advance the more confidently towards the truth, the truth itself, God, God's Son, assuming humanity without destroying His divinity, established and founded this faith, that there might be a way for man to man's God through a God-man. For this is the Mediator between God and man, the man Christ Jesus. For it is as man that He is the Mediator and the Way. Since, if the way lieth between him who goes, and the place whither he goes, there is hope of his reaching it; but if there be no way, or if he know not where it is, what boots it to know whither he should go? Now the only way that is infallibly secured against all mistakes, is when the very same person is at once God and man, God our end, man our way.

3. *Of the authority of the canonical Scriptures composed by the Divine Spirit*

This Mediator, having spoken what He judged sufficient, first by the prophets, then by His own lips, and afterwards by the apostles, has besides produced the Scripture which is called canonical, which has paramount authority, and to which we yield assent in all matters of which we ought not to be ignorant, and yet cannot know of ourselves.[3]

In Book XV. the origin of the two polities is described. They were latent in society from the time of Adam and Eve.

Of these two first parents of the human race, then, Cain was the first-born, and he belonged to the city of men; after him was born Abel, who belonged to the city of God. . . . Accordingly, it is recorded of Cain that he built a city, but Abel, being a sojourner, built none. For the city of the saints is above, although here below it begets citizens, in whom it sojourns till the time of its reign arrives, when it shall gather together all in the day of the resurrection; and then shall the promised kingdom be given to them, in which they shall reign with their Prince, the King of the ages, time without end.[4]

Thus the founder of the earthly city was a fratricide. Overcome with envy, he slew his own brother, a citizen of the eternal city, and a sojourner on earth. So that we cannot be surprised that this first specimen, or, as the Greeks say, archetype of crime, should, long afterwards, find a corresponding crime at the foundation of that city which was destined to reign over so many nations, and be the head of this earthly city of which we speak. For of that city also, as one of their poets has mentioned, "the first walls were stained with a brother's blood", or, as Roman history records, Remus was slain by his brother Romulus.[5]

For practical purposes the earthly city is identified with the Roman Empire.

Babylon, like a first Rome, ran its course along with the city of God, which is a stranger in this world. But the things proper for insertion in this work in comparing the two cities, that is, the earthly and heavenly, ought to be taken mostly from the Greek and Latin kingdoms, where Rome herself is like a second Babylon.[6]

Later on we are told that the malignant demons rule that city, whose eternal punishment is to be shared by it.[7]

Miserable, therefore, is the people which is alienated from God. Yet even this people has a peace of its own which is not to be lightly esteemed, though, indeed, it shall not in the end enjoy it, because it makes no good use of it before the end. But it is our interest that it enjoy this peace meanwhile in this life; for as long as the two cities are commingled, we also enjoy the peace of Babylon. For from Babylon the people of God is so freed that it meanwhile sojourns in its company. And therefore the apostle also admonished the Church to pray for kings and those in authority, assigning as the reason, "that we may live a quiet and tranquil life in all godliness and love".[8]

The whole of Book XXI. is devoted to discussing the ultimate fate of the earthly city.

I propose with such ability as God may grant me, to discuss in this book more thoroughly the nature of the punishment which shall be assigned to the devil and all his retainers, when the two cities, the one of God, the other of the devil, shall have reached their proper ends through Jesus Christ our Lord, the Judge of quick and dead.[9]

In contrast with this awful prospect the reader is asked to

survey the progress of the city of God from the era of the patriarch Abraham, from whose time it begins to be more conspicuous, and the divine promises which are now fulfilled in Christ are more fully revealed.[10]

The Church founded by Christ is in fact

the city of the great King.[11] Yet because the churches are also full of those who shall be separated by the winnowing as in the threshing-floor, the glory of this house is not so apparent now as it shall be when every one who is there shall be there always.[12]

The final constitution of the City of God awaits the return of Christ.

That the last judgement, then, shall be administered by Jesus Christ in the manner predicted in the sacred writings is denied or doubted by no one, unless by those who, through some incredible animosity or blindness, decline to believe these writings, though already their truth is demonstrated to all the world. And at or in connection with that judgement the following events shall come to pass, as we have learned: Elias the Tishbite shall come; the Jews shall believe; Antichrist shall persecute; Christ shall judge; the dead shall rise; the good and the wicked shall be separated; the world shall be burned and renewed. All these things, we believe, shall come to pass; but how, or in what order, human understanding cannot perfectly teach us, but only the experience of the events themselves. My opinion, however, is, that they will happen in the order in which I have related them.[13]

In this work St. Augustine formulated and placed on record the outlook on life developed by the Church in the course of the four centuries which followed the life and death of Jesus. It shows how far the new Judaism, freed by Paul of nationalist and exclusive limitations, assimilated to the Roman Empire and rendered applicable to all human society, effaced the principles which inspired the Greek and Roman commonwealths. The spiritual conquest of Rome by the Greeks was surpassed by the grip which Jewish ideas had slowly acquired in the Roman world through the medium of the Church. Theocracy, in its transcendental form, had ousted the principle of the commonwealth, excluding the tests of conscience, reason and experience, asserting supernatural authority as the final basis of truth. The pen of Augustine was mighty as those that reduced to writing the laws of Manu, of Moses or of Rome. It crystallised the Jewish idea as refined in the crucibles of the Christian Church. In the depths of that crystal the Christian world was to read its destiny.

In the pages of St. Augustine the sermon on the mount is submerged and lost in the Jewish Scriptures. From ideas so rooted in supernatural sanctions some kind of monarchy was bound to spring. And the first and noblest exponent of a spiritual autocracy was at hand. In one of his letters [14] Augustine refers to an acolyte Leo who was very likely the Leo who ten years after his death became Bishop of Rome in A.D. 440. A Roman by birth, of lofty character and powerful mind, he raised the position of his see from *primus inter pares* to an absolute monarchy, claiming obedience in matters spiritual from the whole Church. In suppressing heretics, not only in Rome but in Spain and Gaul, he was supported by the Emperor Valentinian III., who in A.D. 445 ordained that nothing should be done in Gaul contrary to ancient usage without the authority of the Bishop of Rome, and that the decree of the apostolic see should henceforth be law.

But the claims of Leo went far beyond this. In his sermons he propounded the doctrine that the apostles Peter and Paul had given to Rome a dominion in spiritual matters which extended beyond the regions she actually governed to the whole world. He laid the foundations of a new and wider authority, at the very moment when the political sovereignty of Rome was about to collapse. The fifth century was one of those epochs when central Asia, stricken perhaps by a period of drought, was discharging its hordes on China, Persia, India and Europe. In A.D. 452 Attila stormed Aquileia, massacred the garrison, and was marching on Rome when Leo met him on the banks of the Mincio, and, by sheer force of his personality, persuaded the terrible Mongol to retreat. Three years later he saved Rome from massacre at the hands of the Vandal Gaiseric. It is not to be wondered that henceforward a quaking civilisation looked for leadership to the Bishop of Rome rather than to any of the nine puppets who jostled each other on the throne of Ravenna in the next twenty-one years.

Their end was nigh. In A.D. 476 the barbarian auxiliaries of the Empire claimed for themselves one-third of the lands in Italy. When their claim was refused their leader, Odoacer, dethroned the boy emperor, Romulus Augustulus, and, acknowledging the titular sovereignty of the Emperor at Constantinople, agreed to rule Italy as its king.

In A.D. 527 Justinian became Emperor in Constantinople. Before his death in A.D. 565 he had re-conquered Africa, Italy and Sicily, and was governing Italy through an exarch stationed in Ravenna.

Since the time of Leo the Italians had learned to think of the Bishop of Rome as their virtual leader. The tradition that entitled the populace of Rome to live at the public expense was older than the Empire, and, when it fell, the task of feeding the proletariat was assumed by the Church. When threatened with spoliation by barbarian invaders thousands of land-owners made over their property to the Church which could hold the conquerors in awe. The Church was thus furnished with revenues to meet the growing demands of charity. When Gregory was elected Pope in A.D. 590 he found himself called upon to administer estates which are estimated to have covered no less than 1800 square miles. So vast an ownership was inseparable from political power.

Italy was now in the throes of the Lombard invasion. Rome was cut off from Ravenna by their armies. We find Gregory issuing orders to the cities within his reach and giving directions for their defence as their recognised ruler in political no less than in spiritual matters.

Gregory, the greatest man who ever sat in the chair

of St. Peter, largely completed the work begun by Leo in establishing the authority of the Papacy in western Christendom. The Visigoth kings of Spain had abandoned the Arian heresy and recognised the spiritual authority of Rome no less than France. That part of the British Isles which is now called England had been lost to the Church in the earlier decades of the fifth century when the Roman legions had left its shores to the mercy of the Anglo-Saxon invaders. Under Gregory the Church accomplished the often repeated process of a spiritual conquest. In A.D. 597 Ethelbert and most of his nobles and people were converted to Christianity by Augustine, the missionary sent to England by Gregory. With the enthusiasm of recent converts the Saxons became protagonists of the papal authority. It was Wynfrith, a native of Devonshire and trained at Exeter, who under the name of Boniface inspired and led the missionaries who converted a great part of Germany to the Christian faith and organised the German Church in obedience to Rome.

NOTES

[1] *De Civitate Dei* (Dod's translation), vol. i. p. viii.
[2] *Ibid.* p. vii.
[3] *Ibid.* p. 438.
[4] *Ibid.* vol. ii. pp. 50-51.
[5] *Ibid.* p. 54.
[6] *Ibid.* p. 219.
[7] *Ibid.* p. 313.
[8] *Ibid.* p. 341.
[9] *Ibid.* p. 413.
[10] *Ibid.* p. 124.
[11] *Ibid.* p. 172.
[12] *Ibid.* p. 281.
[13] *Ibid.* p. 411.
[14] St. Augustine, Ep. 104.

CHAPTER XXVII

ISLAM

In the north, the Teutonic destroyers of the Empire were fast submitting to the Bishop of Rome. In the south, Christendom was presently to be threatened by invaders armed with a sword tempered to match the spiritual weapons of the Church.

The Kingdom of God upon earth, as conceived by Judaism, lay buried in Jerusalem. Over her ruins a Roman city, peopled by Greeks, had been raised by Hadrian. In the sixth century the smouldering hostility of Asia to Graeco-Roman civilisation was showing signs of renewed activity in the oldest crater of the Semite world. Arabia had always been skirted by Greek and Roman armies alike. In deserts inviolate to phalanx and legion tribal society had remained as it was in the age of Abraham and Job. At the period now reached in our narrative the desert was devouring its own children. Whether by reason of exceptional drought or the natural increase of the people, their numbers had reached and exceeded the margin of subsistence. The proclivity of the clans to prey on each other was accentuated by hunger. To the north, east and west of Arabia fertile and thickly inhabited regions lay inviting the ravages of starving nomads; but the crumbling defences of the Roman Empire were as yet protected from Arab invasion by the internecine feuds of the tribes.

In this arid peninsula life naturally centres round isolated places where wells, or some local condition of rainfall, provide the moisture necessary for vegetable growth. In certain oases the springs are strong enough to supply the needs of considerable towns like Mecca and Medina. Before the age of mechanical transport communication between these centres of tribal life depended for the most part on camels, which of all the beasts of burden can travel furthest without the necessity of drinking and can also transport food and water for the Arab cavalry. By means of the camel the tribes have always been able to pillage as well as to trade with each other. Their natural mobility has also enabled them to keep in touch with civilisations beyond the deserts. From the earliest times caravans have connected Mecca and Medina with the shores of the Mediterranean.

At the period under review a few Christian and a large number of Jewish communities had settled in Arabia. At Medina the Jews had made a number of proselytes but in general the Arabs were still in the clutch of a primitive paganism. As usually happens with a people in this condition, they worshipped idols which were often rude inanimate objects, like the meteoric stone which Ephesians in the time of St. Paul revered as the Goddess Diana. Of all the Arabian sanctuaries the most distinguished was a kind of rectangular hut at Mecca which was called the Ka'ba or Cube which contained the figure of a god. The city of Mecca had long been the centre of an annual pilgrimage. In the walls of the Ka'ba was a black stone which the pilgrims came to adore.

In this city of Mecca Mahomet was born about A.D. 570. As a young man he entered the service of a prosperous widow, by name Khadijah. About the time when Augustine was landing in Kent Mahomet went as her agent with the caravans which were trading with Syria. On returning to Mecca he married Khadijah and for several years after prospered in trade.

The question whether Mahomet could read or write is of little importance, for the strength of his mind and his personality are beyond dispute. No youth of his calibre could visit a place like Damascus and discuss round the camp-fire what he there had seen and heard without obtaining some general knowledge of ideas current in the Empire ruled from Byzantium. In Syrian towns he probably felt as a trader from central Asia feels when he sojourns for a time in Peiping or in one of the Treaty Ports. He must have been conscious that Arabia was regarded in the Graeco-Roman Empire as a cultural back-water. From his contact with the Jewish and Christian world he had clearly grasped the idea of monotheism. He had also seen that it could not be reconciled with the worship of images.

The ideas of the Arabs were narrowly tribal. What seemed best for the tribe was right for its members, including vengeance on a hostile tribe. Along with monotheism Mahomet inbibed the idea it implies of a moral law which is universal, and propounded the duty of forgiving injuries instead of avenging them. He accepted the further conclusions which Hebrew prophets had gradually drawn from their notion that the ultimate reality behind the universe is a spirit of righteousness. Like others in the stage of paganism, the Arabs conceived the dead as surviving only in the shadowy form of wraiths. Mahomet adopted the Jewish and Christian conception of a future existence in its cruder form: the body itself would rise from the grave. His conceptions of Heaven and Hell were derived from those which were current in Christian literature; with this difference, that joys which were physical as well as spiritual were promised to believers.

Ere long these ideas secured such a hold on his mind that he turned from trade to the project of lifting his people from superstition to the plane of religion. He retained, however, to the end the practical shrewdness of a man trained in affairs. To begin with, at any rate, he sought to reform rather than abolish the paganism of his people, exhorting them to worship, not the image in the Ka'ba, but 'the Lord of the House', the god of Mecca, as one with the God of the Jews and Christians, the one universal deity. At first he encouraged his followers to turn in prayer to Jerusalem.

In all this were points of resemblance with the movements initiated by Hindus and Buddhists who have realised that the impact of western ideas cannot be met by mere negation. Such reforms are in these days taking the line of interpreting the national religion on lines conformable to Christian teaching.[1]

That Mahomet's ideas were largely inbibed from Jewish and Christian teaching is scarcely in doubt. That he and his followers thought that God had directly revealed them to Mahomet himself is equally clear. He recognised Moses and Jesus as prophets to whom God had revealed some of his truths; but the final revelation was reserved for Mahomet himself. After his death his teaching was placed on record in the Koran, which came to be regarded as a final and unalterable statement of truth. The new religion was epitomised in the dogma, "There is one God and Mahomet is his prophet". It was this which brought Islam into conflict with both the creeds from which it was derived. In the Christian religion, at any rate, the Greek idea that human knowledge of realities must be found in the mind and conscience of man, as revealed and verified in experience, has always been dormant like seed, ready to germinate again in favourable conditions. The revelation of Mahomet as recorded in the Koran left little room for further development and has therefore sterilised thought wherever his creed has prevailed. The boasted science of the Moslems in Spain is no real exception to this rule, for its source was the science of the Greeks introduced by Christians whom these least intolerant of Moslems employed.

The political results were tremendous, for the principle of authority asserted by Mahomet in its absolute and most uncompromising form enabled the tribes of Arabia to achieve, for a time, the structure of a state. This principle of authority was not limited in its range, as it was with the Jews, by a spirit of nationalism. Islam, as projected by its founder, was capable of becoming a world theocracy, in which all nations and kindreds and tongues could unite in common and equal obedience to the God of the universe. As a project of government for mankind, Christendom, begotten of the Greek and Roman Empires by Judaism, was at last confronted with a formidable rival.

To begin with, Mahomet had no political thoughts in his mind. In Mecca he formed groups of the people about him who held their meetings in privacy and engaged in prayer under the guidance of the prophet himself. They were pledged to renounce infanticide and other immoral practices and also to control the lusts of the flesh. Much stress was laid on 'surrender' to the will of God. Islam is the Arabic word for 'surrender'. The term Moslem means 'one who surrenders himself' to God.

The movement quickly aroused the antagonism which reformers who challenge established ideas and vested interests must always expect. Mahomet encountered the obstacles which had hampered the mission of Jesus, and barely avoided a similar fate.

Some members of his own family . . . bitterly opposed him. . . . It would be a mistake to suppose that the enemies of the new faith were actuated by religious fanaticism. They were, for the most part, simply men of the world who, proud of their social position, objected to recognising the claims of an upstart and dreaded any sweeping change as likely to endanger the material advantages which they derived from the traditional cult. To the majority of the citizens Mahomet appeared a madman. . . . That he had to endure many affronts was quite natural, but actual violence could not have been employed against him without risk of a blood-feud, which the Meccans were always most anxious to avoid.[2]

Like Jesus before him, he turned from the people who lived in the Holy City to the pilgrims who came to it. As noticed above, Medina was largely settled by Jews and was, therefore, a centre where the monotheistic idea was already familiar. In and about this populous centre the Arabian tribes were at war with each other and the peace of the place was constantly threatened by their feuds. Pilgrims who met Mahomet at Mecca conceived the idea that this prophet of monotheism with his masterful personality might command obedience and establish peace between the discordant factions that centred in and about Medina. Mahomet, whose life was in jeopardy from the Meccans, listened to these overtures. In A.D. 622 he and his followers escaped from Mecca and took refuge in Medina.

Thus was accomplished the great event known as the Emigration (*hijra*, distorted by Europeans into *hegira*) which forms the starting-point of the Moslem era.[3]

The claim of Mahomet to unique and final authority as the prophet of God brought him into conflict with the Jewish community of Medina. This antagonism is shown by the fact that in A.D. 624 Mahomet commanded his followers to turn in prayer to Mecca instead of to Jerusalem.

His mind was now concentrated on the task of welding the Arab clans who obeyed him into one organised community. These clans were forbidden to make war on each other and any matter at issue between them was to be brought for settlement to "God and Mahomet". They were all to unite to defend Medina. By the logic of events he was led to issue a stream of edicts which are now embodied in the Koran. They prescribed the ceremonies which

Moslems should observe in religion, their civil and criminal relations to each other and also the principles governing their military organisation, including conscription. They also created a system of public finance. Though in all probability he did not realise it, Mahomet was, in fact, creating a state.

Ere long Mahomet was able to make war on his enemies in Mecca, and an early though trifling engagement with superior numbers secured to him the credit of miraculous powers. This victory is ascribed in the Koran to the intervention of angels. He was now strong enough to expel from Medina the Jews who, as usual, were weakened in the face of an enemy by their own intestine dissensions.

A small expedition despatched to the north in A.D. 629 was signally defeated near the Dead Sea by the Byzantine Empire. This was, in all probability, a raid projected to satisfy the Arab propensity for pillage. By A.D. 630 his main forces were encamped within sight of Mecca. Its people, who realised that further resistance was futile, abandoned their weapons and retired to their houses. Mahomet then entered the city in triumph. He proclaimed an amnesty, but hastened to destroy images wherever he found them and defaced paintings which adorned the walls of the Ka'ba. A concession to paganism was made, however, in the case of the black stone, which Mahomet declared had been placed there by Abraham. The custom of adoring the stone, which from ancient times had attracted pilgrims to Mecca, was sanctioned and incorporated in Moslem worship. This concession to paganism, though resented by some of his followers, availed to conciliate the traditions and interests of the Meccans.

The new power established in Mecca as well as Medina was felt as a threat to their independence by the Bedouin tribes of the desert. Again Mahomet was victorious in a battle which established his authority over regions now covered by the modern kingdom of Hedjaz.

In A.D. 631 he issued a proclamation excluding all unbelievers from the pilgrimage to Mecca and the cult of the Ka'ba. In the following year he conducted the pilgrimage in person and finally settled its ritual. Henceforward this pilgrimage, pagan in origin and in some of its rites, was the visible bond which united Moslems throughout the world.

In A.D. 632 Mahomet was busy preparing an expedition against the Byzantine Empire when he suddenly died.

The death of the prophet was the signal for a further conflict between the Islamic state and the outlying tribes who clung to paganism. But Mahomet had left behind him followers who had grasped his ideas, and also a political organisation sufficiently developed to serve as their instrument. They realised that the dominating fact was a hunger which could never be satisfied so long as the tribes of Arabia preyed on each other. The obvious remedy was for all these tribes to unite in invading the fertile and populous countries beyond the deserts.

The faith of Islam provided the necessary bond, the theocracy which centred in Medina, the means required for effective action. A raid into Mesopotamia was quickly followed by an organised attack on the Syrian dominions of the Emperor Heraclius. The Semite inhabitants in these regions had been alienated by his crushing taxation. In the field of ideas the weeds of paganism had largely smothered the seed which Jesus had sown six centuries before. The doctrine of the Trinity was dangerously near to polytheism in minds too simple to follow the gymnastics of metaphysicians. The worship of images was not merely sanctioned but directly enjoined by the Church. Islam, asserting that God was one and not to be worshipped in visible form, was now confronting the eastern Church as a genuine reform in the sphere of religion.

Like Israel before them, the tribes of Arabia were drawn by the lure of the fertile belt. A similar creed had enabled Moses to unite the Hebrew tribes for the conquest of Canaan. By A.D. 636 the Byzantine armies were finally defeated and Damascus was taken. Jerusalem fell in A.D. 638 and Caesarea, which Heraclius could provision from the sea, was betrayed to the Arabs in A.D. 640.

In the course of the Syrian campaign the Arabs had realised the difficulty of seizing and holding the fertile lands on the coast while the enemy, however feeble on land, commanded the sea. The Byzantine Empire had some of its principal shipyards at the mouths of the Nile. The desert, moreover, was hungry for corn from Egypt, that unfailing supply which grew on its irrigated lands. In A.D. 640 the Arab cavalry invaded Egypt. By A.D. 642 Alexandria was occupied and Egypt was organised as a province of the Arabian Empire. Reversing the strategy which Pausanias had followed in 478 B.C., the Arabs attacked and seized the naval base of the Greek Empire in Cyprus in A.D. 649.

The Arabs were now in a position to attack the heart of the Byzantine Empire on the Bosphorus by land and sea. But the Arab invasion broke in vain on the walls of Constantinople. The tremendous defences which Constantine and his successors had thrown round the eastern gate of Europe were inviolate to Asia for more than eight centuries.

The Arabs were thus impelled by the logic of events to attack Europe from its western flank.

The invasion of Africa opened in 642 B.C. was a necessary sequel to the conquest of Egypt by the Arabs. The basic population of the African littoral was Berber. No stranger to desert life, the Berber had more in common with the Arab than with the

Latin or Greek colonist of the towns on the coast. They were not, however, so near akin to the Arabs as the Semite inhabitants of Syria, nor so easily detached from the Empire and religion of Constantinople and Rome. The process of absorbing the Berbers into Islam took longer. To the last the Arab power was weakened by racial dissension between themselves and the Berbers. The fall of Carthage and the conquest of Africa was only completed in A.D. 708.

Gibraltar still preserves the name of Tarik (Gebel Tarik, *i.e.* Mount Tarik), the leader who crossed the Straits in A.D. 711 with a mixed force of Arabs and Berbers and defeated Roderick, king of the Goths. The large Jewish population, whom the Goths had persecuted without mercy, at once made common cause with the Semite invaders. In six years the Arabs were masters of Spain and ready to attempt the invasion of France.

At the time when the western Empire was extinguished in Rome, Clovis, grandson of Merovech, king of the Franks, was extending his conquests in northern Gaul. In the hope of securing the support of the bishops he accepted baptism on Christmas Day in A.D. 496. His capital was established at Paris on an island in the Seine, and before he died in A.D. 511 his dominions extended to the Loire. The French kings looked back on Clovis as the founder of their monarchy; but the House of the Merovings followed the course which is usual with dynasties. Enfeebled by luxury, the descendants of Clovis allowed their authority to be exercised by powerful nobles. At the time of the Arab invasion, a mayor of the palace called Charles, a name which signified courage, was ruling the realm in the name of the Meroving monarch.

By A.D. 717 the Arabs and Berbers were crossing the Pyrenees. Their onset was opposed with varying fortunes by Eudo, the duke who ruled Aquitaine. In A.D. 732 a host of Arab horsemen were led by 'Abd-ar-Rahman, a fanatical Amir, across the passes. The Amir defeated Eudo and chased him north till he took refuge at Tours, behind the ranks of an army led by Charles. Day after day waves of the Arab horse broke on the shields of the Frankish warriors. 'Abd-ar-Rahman fell in one of these charges and his leaderless hosts fled in confusion, leaving their camp and baggage in the hands of Charles. His soldiers gave him the name of the Hammer, which, centuries before, a Semitic leader had won when he saved his people from the tyranny of the Greeks. The Franks might better have called their leader the Anvil; for the Arab squadrons had hammered on his infantry till they broke into pieces and were scattered to the wind. So the great onslaught on Christendom, which Mahomet had inspired in the heart of Arabia, was at length turned and broken in the centre of France exactly a century from the day of his death.

NOTES

[1] *Vide* Farquhar's *Crown of Hinduism.*

[2] *The Cambridge Mediaeval History*, vol. ii. p. 310. In chapters x., xi. and xii. of this volume the results of modern research into the early history of Islam are brilliantly summarised by Professor Bevan and Dr. Becker. In this chapter their statement of facts has been closely followed, though not always the conclusions they draw from them.

[3] *Ibid.* p. 313.

CHAPTER XXVIII

THE prestige which Charles Martel, the competent leader of the bravest army in Europe, won for his house as well as for himself, was, perhaps, the most far-reaching result of his victory at Tours. A glance at the map is sufficient to show that the Arab failure to conquer Christendom from the west was mainly due to the facts of geography. The real danger lay on the eastern flank. Europe had been saved from subjection to the Arabs when in A.D. 717 Leo the Isaurian had finally broken their attack on Constantinople by land and sea.

As so often happens, the victor was launched by his very success on a sea of troubles. In the course of the struggle Leo had felt the moral disadvantage at which he was placed, as the champion of Christendom, by the Arab claim that Islam was a faith purer and higher than his own. He resolved, therefore, to purge the Church from the taint of idolatry. In Italy his attempts to enforce this reform met with a fierce resistance. Gregory III. accused him of heresy and excommunicated iconoclasts in Rome.

The Arab wars had emptied the treasury of the Empire, so Leo ordered the exarch of Ravenna to levy tribute in Italy. The revenues of the Papacy were touched and the Pope joined with the people in resisting the levy. There was also Liutprand, king of the Lombards, seeking to extend his power in Italy at the Emperor's expense. In A.D. 727 Liutprand besieged Ravenna.

The Lombard king and the Pope, though opposed to the Emperor, were, none the less, at odds

with each other. In Rome itself the Pope was now
the temporal ruler, and in various parts of Italy
claimed the revenues of vast landed estates. These
claims in fact barred the hopes which the Lombard
monarchy entertained of uniting Italy under their
rule, just as those of the Pope in the nineteenth
century were opposed to the projects of the Pied-
mont dynasty. Then, as now, the weapons of the
monarchy were those of a government backed by
its own national armies, while those of the Papacy
were a spiritual influence which extended beyond the
limits of Italy.

For the moment the Lombard king bowed to the
ghostly authority of Gregory II., but, enraged by
the intrigues of his successor, Gregory III., threatened Rome with his armies in A.D. 739. In this predicament the Pope adopted the expedient of using
his spiritual influence in Europe to redress his political weakness in Italy. He appealed to Charles
Martel to cross the Alps and act as the champion of
the Church against the aggressions of a Lombard
monarchy.

For the moment this attempt to make the two
Teutonic kingdoms fight each other failed, for their
courts and nobles were in cordial relations and
Charles Martel refused to stir.

In A.D. 741 Charles Martel died, leaving his sons,
Carloman and Pepin, as joint mayors of the palace.
In A.D. 747 Carloman retired to a monastery which
he founded on Mount Soracte. Changes were soon
to follow which placed Pepin under deep obligations
to the papal chair. In A.D. 749

Burchard, Bishop of Würzburg, and Folrad the chaplain
were sent to Pope Zacharias to ask concerning the kings in
Frank-land who at that time had no royal power, whether
this was good or no. And Pope Zacharias commanded
Pippin that it would be better that *he* should be called king
who had the power, rather than he who was remaining

without any royal power. That order might not be disturbed, by his apostolic authority he ordered that Pippin should be made king.

Pippin, according to the manner of the Franks, was elected king, and anointed by the hand of archbishop Boniface of holy memory, and he was raised to the kingdom by the Franks in the city of Soissons. But Hilderic, who was falsely called king, was tonsured and sent into a monastery.[1]

The election was according to Teuton custom, the anointing a Jewish rite prescribed by the Church as the symbol of divine authority. The coronation of Pepin took place in A.D. 750. When, in A.D. 749, Aistulf had succeeded to the Lombard throne, the conflict with Rome on the question of the papal estates became acute. Pope Stephen II., who succeeded Zacharias in A.D. 752, fled to the court of Pepin. By A.D. 756 Pepin had invaded Italy, restored the Pope to his see, and placed him in possession of the papal estates. He also transferred to him that territory which the eastern emperors had ruled through the exarch at Ravenna.

In A.D. 758 Pepin was succeeded by his son Charles the Great, who in A.D. 773-4, on the invitation of Pope Hadrian I., invaded Italy, dethroned Desiderius, king of the Lombards, annexed his dominions and recognised the Pope's sovereignty over two-thirds of the Italian peninsula.

Before the end of the century Charles had thrust the Saracens out of France, had conquered Spain up to the Ebro, Germany to the Elbe, and was recognised as the most powerful ruler which the civilised world had known since the days of Constantine.

The Isaurian dynasty in Constantinople had fallen meanwhile on evil days. In A.D. 780 Leo IV. died, leaving as joint sovereigns his widow Irene and her boy Constantine VI. When Constantine reached the age of twenty his mother, unwilling to share the power she had wielded alone during his boyhood, threw him into prison, put out his eyes, and reigned as Empress in Constantinople. This behaviour of a woman on the throne of the Caesars quenched any feeling of loyalty to Byzantium which was still flickering in the west.

Until Pepin was crowned, in A.D. 750, the Popes had recognised the Byzantine Emperor as in theory the supreme ruler of Christendom. Zacharias, who died in A.D. 752, was the last Pope who applied to him to confirm his election. What projects were now simmering in clerical brains can be gathered from a document which probably found its way into the papal archives during the pontificate of Stephen II. This document purports to record an imperial decree in terms of which Constantine on his conversion to Christianity recognised that

St. Peter is on earth the appointed Vicar of God, so also the Pontiffs his vicegerents should receive from us and from our empire power and principality greater than belongs to our earthly empire. For we choose the same Prince of the Apostles and his vicars to be our patrons before God, and we decree that even like unto our own earthly imperial power so shall the sacro-sanct Church of Rome be honoured and venerated, and that higher than our terrestrial throne shall the most sacred seat of St. Peter be gloriously exalted.

This forged decretal goes on to recognise the power of the Pope to control the whole Christian priesthood and to regulate all matters appertaining to worship or faith. It details the gifts and properties purported to be conferred by Constantine on the Church, the dignities to be enjoyed by its subordinate officers, and especially confers on the Pope himself

the imperial sceptre, with all standards and banners and similar imperial ornaments, and in short the whole array of our imperial dignity and the glory of our power. . . .

Wherefore, that the pontifical crown may not grow too cheap, but may be adorned with glory and influence even

beyond the dignity of the earthly empire, lo! we hand over
and relinquish our palace, the city of Rome, and all the
provinces, places and cities of Italy and [or] the western
regions, to the most blessed Pontiff and universal Pope,
Silvester; and we ordain by our pragmatic constitution
that they shall be governed by him and his successors, and
we grant that they shall remain under the authority of the
holy Roman Church.

Wherefore we have thought it fitting that our empire
and our royal power be transferred to the Eastern regions,
and that a city bearing our name be built in an excellent
place in the province of Byzantia, and that there our empire
be founded, since where the sovereign of priests and the
head of the Christian religion has been placed by the
Heavenly Emperor, it is not fitting that there the earthly
Emperor should also bear sway.

The document [says Hodgkin] ends with solemn in-
junctions to all future Emperors, to all nobles, 'satraps',
and senators, to keep this grant for ever inviolate. Ana-
themas are uttered on anyone who shall dare to infringe it;
and hell fire is invoked for his destruction.[2]

Writing to Charles in A.D. 778, Pope Hadrian
refers to this fabulous grant of Constantine in the
following words:

And as in the time of St. Silvester the Holy Catholic and
Apostolic Church of Rome was exalted by the generosity
of the most pious Constantine, the great Emperor, of holy
memory, and he deigned to bestow on it power in these
regions of Hesperia, so in these times, which are so prosperous for you and for us, may the Holy Church of God,
that is of the blessed Apostle Peter, grow and flourish and
be more than more exalted, that all the nations when they
hear of it may shout, "O Lord, save the King, and hear us
in the day when we call upon Thee, for, lo, a new and most
Christian Emperor Constantine has arisen in our day,
through whom God has been pleased to bestow all gifts
on His Holy Church."[3]

Thus was the authority of Constantine invoked for
reversing his policy, for restoring to the banks of the
Tiber the capital of the world transferred by him to
the shores of the Bosphorus.

That wellnigh impregnable fortress had long guarded and was still longer to guard a title too large for the narrowing territories governed from its walls. But the Frankish nobles felt with the Roman priests that the imperial title usurped by an infamous woman more properly belonged to the real champion of Christendom, the greatest potentate in Europe, who in every sense was a king of men. Charles himself evidently thought that a time was approaching when forms must be reconciled with facts, as when his father had sent Childeric to a monastery and mounted the throne. But his long experience of priestcraft made him hesitate to accept the imperial title as his father had accepted the royal title at the hands of the Papacy. For years the popes had pestered him with appeals to enlarge their temporal powers and possessions supported by blasphemous promises and threats. We know the effect which these letters left on his mind from his own words:

We wish to ask the chief ecclesiastics and all those who are engaged in teaching from the Holy Scriptures, who are those to whom the Apostle saith, "Be ye imitators of me"? or what he meant when he said, "No one who is a soldier of God entangleth himself with the things of this world"? How is the Apostle to be imitated? How is anyone to be a soldier of God? Pray let them show us truly what is meant by that "renouncing the world" of which they so often speak, and explain how we are to distinguish between those who renounce and those who follow the world. Is the difference only in this, that the former do not bear arms and are not publicly married? I would enquire also if that man can be said to have renounced the world who is unceasingly striving to augment his possessions by drawing persuasive pictures of the blessedness of heaven, and by threatening men with the everlasting punishments of hell? or that man who, in the name of God or of some saint, is for ever stripping simpler people, rich or poor, of their possessions, disinheriting the lawful heirs, and driving men thus unjustly deprived of their paternal estates to robbery and all sorts of crimes? [4]

In A.D. 795 Hadrian died. On April 25 Leo III. was attacked on his way to St. Peter's by two clerics of his own household who attempted to blind him and cut out his tongue. Though badly injured in the eyes and mouth, he escaped and sought refuge at the court of Charles, which he reached in July. Charles' most trusted adviser was an Englishman, Alcuin of York, who had now retired as Abbot of Tours. On hearing of the outrage he wrote to Charles urging that he "as more excellent in power" than Pope or Emperor, "more illustrious in wisdom, more sublime in the dignity of your kingdom", was now called upon to deal with the growing corruption of both papal and imperial courts.

In the autumn of A.D. 799 Charles sent Leo III. back to Rome under an escort strong enough to protect him, intending to follow him presently. As Alcuin, who frankly described the atmosphere of Rome as poisonous, was unwilling to go there with him, Charles paid him a visit at Tours in the spring of A.D. 800. His queen, Liutgarda, died and was buried there during the visit.

We know that Charles and Alcuin were equally alive to the danger of accepting the imperial title, as Pepin had accepted his crown, at the hands of the Pope. They agreed in regarding the disorders at Rome and Constantinople as intolerable. The question before their minds was how Charles could acquire the authority to cleanse both these Augean stables.

On November 24 the Frankish king reached Rome, and on Christmas Day went in state to pay his devotions at the Basilica of St. Peter. He knelt on the spot where the body of the Apostle was supposed to rest, and, as he rose, the Pope placed on his head a golden crown, while the vast congregation burst into a cry: "To Carolus Augustus, crowned of God, mighty and pacific Emperor, be life and victory".

Charles accepted the *fait accompli*; but, according to Einhard, his biographer, he much disliked the title, and afterwards "declared that he would never have entered the church on that day, though it was a high festival, if he could have foreknown the pontiff's design". Apart from his disinclination to accept the position of Emperor at the hands of the Pope, Charles was anxious to avoid a rupture with Constantinople, and even entertained the repulsive idea of a matrimonial union with the infamous Irene. The manœuvre of the Pope had this far-reaching result—that Charles and his successors were never accepted at Constantinople. In his eagerness to restore the Empire to Rome under papal authority Leo finally frustrated the ideal of uniting Christendom under one emperor.

If Charles had acquired the imperial crown in succession to the emperors who had reigned in Constantinople, the popes could scarcely have claimed, as they afterwards did, to exercise the sovereignty of God upon earth. The dexterity of Leo in placing the crown on his head enabled the successors of Leo centuries later to advance that claim.

Charles the Great was a constant student of the *De Civitate Dei*; but he certainly did not view the Empire restored under his authority as in any respect the kingdom of Satan. When Augustine began his treatise, in A.D. 410, the persecution of the Church by the pagan emperors was still fresh in the memory of the Christians. In the centuries which divided Augustine from Charles, Church and Empire had become so closely identified as to be regarded merely as different aspects of the same institution. To Charles the Empire was the Kingdom of God as conceived by Augustine; but the successful and experienced statesman perhaps valued peace and order in this world at a higher rate than the Bishop of Hippo, and felt also that he knew how to achieve it. Nor did he

R

ever allow his position as supreme head of the divine polity to be questioned. His right to rule the Church no less than the state was vigorously asserted.

What a pope had done on that eight-hundredth Christmas morning other popes might do again. In the centuries to come aspirants to the imperial throne were constantly suitors for the crown which Leo had assumed the right to bestow. It is true that for more than two centuries the popes applied to the emperors to confirm their elections. By the eleventh century the Papacy had fallen into such discredit that the emperors sought to reform it by themselves appointing vigorous bishops from Germany. The reform recoiled on the Empire by its very success. At the council of A.D. 1059 it was finally decreed that in future the elections of popes should rest with the cardinals at Rome.

This reform was really the work of the great Hildebrand, who in A.D. 1073 became Pope under the name of Gregory VII. By the thirteenth century Innocent III. was claiming the right of the Pope to appoint the Emperor on the strength of the fact that Leo III. had placed the crown on the head of Charles the Great.

The messianic idea as formulated in the pages of Augustine thus dominated the history of Europe. In the Middle Ages human society was conceived as organised in one polity in preparation for that time when Christ would return to judge the quick and dead, to decide the future of each individual soul, to separate the wheat from the tares and the sheep from the goats, to condemn the wicked to eternal torment and gather the righteous to enjoy for ever the blessings of the heavenly kingdom.

In the eastern Empire where, since Constantine, emperors had reigned in unbroken succession, there was no doubt that the Emperor alone was the supreme representative of God upon earth. He appointed the Patriarch of Constantinople, and used him at his pleasure. And so the Byzantine Empire became indistinguishable from a typical eastern despotism.

With the Holy Roman Empire as reconstituted by Charles and Leo it was otherwise. The conditions under which it was instituted implied the coexistence of two powers, both claiming an authority which was sovereign in nature. The theories by which it was argued that Emperor and Pope were sovereign in different spheres could only mask the essential antagonism, for in practice their spheres were widely overlapping. There is in principle no room in one theocracy for two vicegerents of God. When their spheres conflict, each will claim that the other has received his power through himself, and the conflict between these claims can never be finally reconciled. The divine polity of the Middle Ages was delivered to the world unblemished by any conspicuous birthmark. And yet from the manner in which that delivery was handled it contracted a radical weakness which proved fatal to its normal development as a system of government based on authority. It carried that weakness to the grave. It brought not peace but the sword. From the ninth century to the nineteenth it frustrated the very blessings it was meant to provide, the unity and order of a Christian world.

In the eleventh century Hildebrand had asserted the principle that the pope's appointment should lie with the Church itself and in no way depend on the Emperor's sanction. Thenceforward the popes began to claim an authority as unlimited in the civil as in the spiritual sphere. In A.D. 1139 Innocent II. was addressing the Lateran Council as though he were the absolute master of Christendom:

Ye know that Rome is the capital of the world, that ye hold your dignities by the Roman pontiff as a vassal holds his fiefs of his sovereign, and that ye cannot retain them without his assent.

A Byzantine ambassador was heard to exclaim, "Your Pope Innocent is not a bishop, but an Emperor". Sixty years later Innocent III. had travelled further along this road, and was claiming sovereignty over all the kingdoms of Europe. In the case of England the claim was enforced by closing the churches to public worship, till in A.D. 1213 John surrendered his kingdom to be held from the Pope subject to a quit-rent of 1000 marks.[5] And till 1333 the tribute was paid. In A.D. 1299 Boniface VIII. received the envoys of the Emperor, Albert I., seated on a throne, crowned with the diadem of Constantine, holding a sceptre and girt with a sword. "Am not I", he said to them, "the supreme pontiff? Is not this the throne of Peter? Is it not mine to guard the laws of the Empire? I, I am the Emperor."

NOTES

[1] *Annales Laurissenses*, quoted by Hodgkin, vol. vii. p. 128.

[2] Hodgkin, vol. vii. pp. 145-50.

[3] *Codex Carolinus*, 61, quoted by Hodgkin, vol. viii. pp. 43-4.

[4] *Cap. Duplex Aquisgranense* (811), ap. Migne 330, quoted by Hodgkin, vol. viii. p. 132.

[5] H. W. C. Davis, *England under the Normans and Anjevins*, p. 368.

CHAPTER XXIX

THE PRINCIPLE OF AUTHORITY IN APPLICATION

THE claims of the Papacy could go no further. The authority of the Popes over temporal rulers was used to enforce obedience in spiritual matters. Since the time of Theodosius the powers of the state had been used to punish deviations from belief as prescribed by the Church. The infliction of torture and death as a punishment for heresy had indeed been condemned by the fathers, including Augustine. But the principle of authority overrode the sentiment of the early Christians with ruthless logic. Through the dark ages heretics were executed from time to time in various localities.

The first stirrings of the intellectual revival which eventually led to the Reformation were felt just at the moment when the Papacy was asserting its claim to unlimited sovereignty, and was imitating the Empire of Justinian's time by producing a jurisprudence of its own. At the close of the twelfth century there developed in Provence a formidable movement against sacerdotalism. In order to meet it, Innocent III. declared that treason against God was at least as heinous a crime as treason against temporal rulers, and admitted the logical consequence of this doctrine. Its practical expression was an organisation centralised in Rome for the suppression of heresy throughout Christendom. In every country of western Europe ecclesiastical courts were created for the purpose under the direction of the Grand Inquisitor in Rome. The inquisitors were authorised by papal decree to use torture in obtaining evidence or confession of guilt. They devised a procedure which deprived their victims of all ordinary means of defence, and left them at the mercy of their accusers. The ecclesiastical court, having sentenced the heretic, handed him over to the secular authorities to be burned alive, with a formal recommendation to mercy which was never observed in practice, and was in fact a conventional relic of the earlier Christian feeling against the infliction of capital punishment.

In most countries these ecclesiastical courts were viewed with some jealousy by the secular authorities. In Spain they were largely directed against Moors and Jews, who had falsely adopted the Christian religion, or were thought to have done so, and they worked in the closest alliance with the state. It is estimated that in Spain alone more than 31,000 persons were burned alive, while 290,000 were condemned to lesser punishments at the instance of the Inquisition. No less than 50,000 perished for their religion in the Netherlands under the reign of Charles V. These holocausts of victims became a public spectacle as popular as the gladiatorial games had been in Rome. They were used to celebrate the marriages of princes. This mighty engine for the suppression of thought financed itself by confiscating the property of its victims and even by selling licences to those able to pay for the privilege of holding beliefs contrary to the Catholic faith.

The Papacy, which had acquired the functions of a state without its normal resources, learned to replenish its treasury by similar methods. It began by remitting penalties imposed for infractions of Church law for a money payment. The penance imposed on a sinner by the Church operated to relieve him of so many ages of purgatory.

Historically speaking it is indisputable that the practice of Indulgences in the medieval Church arose out of the authoritative remission, in exceptional cases, of a certain proportion of this canonical penalty. At the same time, according to Catholic teaching, such Indulgence was not a mere permission to omit or postpone payment, but was, in fact, a *discharge* from the debt of temporal punishment which the sinner owed. The authority to grant such discharge was conceived to be included in the power of binding and loosing committed by Christ to His Church, and when in the course of time the vaguer theological conceptions of the first ages of Christianity assumed scientific form and shape at the hands of the Schoolmen, the doctrine came to prevail that this discharge of the sinner's debt was made through an application to the offender of what was called the "Treasure" of the Church. The infinite merits of Christ our Redeemer and the superabundant penance of the Saints, who offered to God a greater atonement than was required for the expiation of their own sins, were conceived of as creating a fund of satisfactions which the Church dispenses at will, and which she applies to those offenders who seem specially to deserve her favour.[1]

By the Middle Ages the Church had learnt to bestow her favours for cash and replenish her treasury by professing to relieve sinners from the penalties of their sins. Pardoners hawked indulgences through Europe like modern travellers in silks or soap.

A few words attributed to Jesus by one of his biographers, and pressed to their logical conclusion by the Church, had yielded an enormous and poisonous growth:

Verily I say unto you, What things soever ye shall bind on earth shall be bound in heaven: and what things soever ye shall loose on earth shall be loosed in heaven.[2]

The Church has dwelt on these words with eager insistence and applied them in a literal and even mechanical sense. The doctrine that Jesus intended to create a machine for controlling the minds and consciences of men is at variance with that part of his teaching which bears the stamp of original thought, and also with the line of action which brought him into conflict with the Jewish hierarchy. He cannot have used these words with this meaning unless he had two minds, and on different occasions preached contrary principles. It is easier to suppose that his hearers had missed the profounder significance of some such phrase as that which he used in his last interview with Peter, and had all unconsciously twisted it into something which expressed their own ideas. His biographers, writing a whole generation after his death, believed him to have vindicated the truth of his teaching by working miracles. It was just as inevitable that they should make him propound the principle of authority against which his genuine doctrine and conduct are both directed.

In the long run principles issue in practice and are tested by results. The tares and the wheat may be hard to distinguish while still in the blade; but once they have ripened to seed the difference between them is plain to all who have eyes to see. It needed a mind powerful as Paul's to realise that Jesus had meant utterly to abolish the Mosaic law, and a courage and force no less than his to convince the world that this was so. But it never dawned on that mind that the teaching of Jesus could rest on any authority other than that upon which the law of Moses was presumed to rest. In Paul's view the truth about life could only be known through a supernatural revelation. His belief that Jesus had wrought miracles, had been raised from the dead and years later had commissioned Paul himself to preach the gospel to the Gentiles, was to him proof that God had chosen to reveal his truth to man through Christ, and also through successors divinely appointed by Christ. In controversy it was vital to Paul to establish his own apostolic commission. The principle of authority in human affairs was a postulate he never thought of examining. He failed to perceive that the system attacked by Jesus with fatal results to himself was the necessary outcome of that principle. Nor could he foresee how the principle inspiring the Mosaic system, renewed in the name of Christ, would reproduce a like system on a vastly extended scale; how the mockery of his trial by ecclesiastics and his execution by the secular arm would be multiplied through centuries, how the Church would derive its revenues from a traffic more flagitious than that which Jesus himself had expelled from the courts of the Temple.

Do men gather grapes of thorns, or figs of thistles? Even so every good tree bringeth forth good fruit; but the corrupt tree bringeth forth evil fruit. A good tree cannot bring forth evil fruit, neither can a corrupt tree bring forth good fruit. Every tree that bringeth not forth good fruit is hewn down, and cast into the fire. Therefore by their fruits ye shall know them.[3]

The ultimate goal of our quest is not to discover what Jesus said or did not say, but that pearl beyond price for which his career was a tireless search, the truth about life, the principles upon which men ought to live. The words just quoted impress our minds with a sense of profound intuition and impel us to believe that they fell from the lips of a master. They point to the test whereby principles based on the truth are in process of time separated and distinguished from those which are false. They afford no hope to our childlike yearning to be shown what is true by the supernatural light of direct revelation. They call on men to trust like Job only to the light that is in them, to the natural resources of their own minds. In the long run the validity of principles is proved in their application, and therefore only in the course of ages. It is this which vests history with its special importance, because it enables abstract principles to be studied in their application to life. With the light of eighteen centuries to guide us we are better able than the early Christians to discern what is really valuable in the gospel records. Over long periods of time the principle of authority and that of the commonwealth have found expression in institutions. In the past and present their effect on society can be closely studied. It is now possible for ordinary minds to discern, as it was not in the dawn of the Christian era, which of them is based on the verities of life.

Revolutions are often disguised by keeping old names, and reactions by changing them. The principle of authority challenged by Jesus in the guise of Judaism was all unconsciously re-established by his followers under the name of Christianity. Seed from the old tree reverently planted on his grave yielded fruit after its kind. In the course of ages the new system of authority exceeded Judaism by the measure that Europe exceeded Judea. Beyond question the Church has conferred on those who came under its influence benefits without number of immeasurable value. Its genuine achievements are fully admitted by competent historians outside the ranks of its own followers who are far from admitting its spiritual claims.[4] To the Church, as to its parents, Judaism and the Roman Empire, the structure of society owes an incalculable debt. Yet the fullest acknowledgment of its merits cannot alter the fact that Christendom, as organised in the Middle Ages, was, in principle and therefore in its ultimate effect, the direct antithesis of the polity which Jesus had conceived as essential to the ever continuous growth of virtue in men.

NOTES

[1] Father Thurston, S.J., *The Holy Year of Jubilee*, pp. 315-16.
[2] Matthew xviii. 18.
[3] Matthew vii. 16-20.
[4] See for instance A. L. Smith's *Church and State in the Middle Ages*.

CHAPTER XXX

THE instinct of men to serve one another has been seen in the mind of Jesus as the element of absolute value in life. In a social system based on its exercise this instinct was capable of infinite growth. But the world in which he uttered these truths was rapidly moving in the opposite direction. The Roman Empire had failed to devise any system whereby the control of society could be based on the duty of men to each other. Even Roman citizens were learning to obey a divine authority backed by force. The mechanism of a commonwealth and some of its spirit still lingered in towns like those of Decapolis. But the Roman Empire had closely integrated the lives of all the communities surrounding the Mediterranean. The direct government of men by themselves was applicable only to the local interests of communities so small that their members could meet to discuss and settle them. It was narrowed to municipal limits. The various cities and races surrounding the Mediterranean were now integral parts of a great society with a common civilisation. Its existence depended on its general security. The Graeco-Roman world had developed no mechanism through which a community too large or too scattered to meet in one spot could govern its own affairs. To maintain a civilisation which had sprung from the principle of the commonwealth it was forced to accept the principle of autocracy, by virtue of which not cities only, but nations widely varying in race, language and thought, could be held together. The sense of permanence, which the Empire gave to its civilisation, was highly deceptive; for the spirit from which it had drawn its vitality languished and died for want of exercise.

In the barbarous tribes which burst through the northern frontiers and submerged the decadent Empire was the crude but vigorous germ of political life. The relation of chiefs to the peoples they led was not that of a Byzantine emperor to his cringing subjects. Charles the Great, at the zenith of his power, had constantly to pause on his tireless journeys to hold a *placitum* or diet. The warriors who followed a northern king expected to know what he meant to do and why he was doing it, as something which closely affected themselves. He must always be thinking how to retain or secure their approval. Here was the instinct which, centuries before, had developed commonwealths in Greece and the sense of a public interest in Rome. In the village communes of the Alps this instinct survived the Roman autocracy and was destined in course of time to produce the Helvetian republic. It burst into sudden and transitory life in the Lombard cities of northern Italy. It found expression in Sweden and Hungary, in the French estates, in those of the Netherlands and also in the diets of central Europe. In various directions and in different degrees the principle of the commonwealth was reduced to practice in institutions. But none of them ripened sufficiently to spread their seed into wider fields. Europe as a whole was in chaos. The Papacy, strong enough to emasculate the Empire, was unequal to the task of creating a genuine government for Christendom. Anarchy prevailed, especially in Italy and central Europe, the home of the Holy Roman Empire.

In conditions like these the people of every locality were accustomed to obey the military leader who was best able to afford them protection. The feudal system developed and in time the strongest leaders welded localities into organised kingdoms. Such rulers claimed to base their title on divine authority, some through the Emperor, some through the Pope and others direct from God, as best suited their immediate interests. The principle of autocracy was never at issue; but only the medium through which it was claimed. Popes, emperors and kings alike viewed with suspicion attempts on the part of ordinary men to manage their own affairs for themselves. The imperial tradition of Rome, though never expressed in a genuine system of government, pervaded the atmosphere and stifled the instinct for freedom in the northern regions of Europe, its natural home.

The revival of the commonwealth, its new development on a national scale, like its first appearance in the cities of Greece, was destined to occur where physical conditions had provided the degree of security needed for the purpose. Rome, saturated and transformed by Jewish tradition, had silently mastered its northern invaders, a reconquest that might have endured, but for a fact of physical geography. As the polar ice-caps melted at the close of the last glacial age, the sea had risen, submerging the estuary of the Rhine, till a group of territories was isolated from the continent of Europe by turbulent waters.

Before this age, when men have learned to fly, the British Isles were a fortress—inviolable whenever their inhabitants could unite to defend them. When Roman legions invaded them the Celtic tribes had acquired no semblance of national union. They were easily conquered and by the end of the fourth century had adopted the civilisation and language of Rome and also the Christian religion.

St. Augustine had scarcely finished his *De Civitate Dei* when in A.D. 430 Rome was withdrawing her legions and abandoning Britain to the rising tide of savage invaders. It may even be that the general disturbance caused by the Hunnish invasion of Europe may have set in motion this westward thrust. To pass from guess-work to fact, we know that Anglo-Saxons from Schleswig-Holstein swarmed to these shores and conquered the island so far as Devon and the mountainous regions of Scotland and Wales. Wherever they conquered and settled the Christian religion was extinguished. The culture and language of Rome was submerged. No contemporary records exist from which the history of this period can be framed because these barbarians were unable to write them. From evidence which the spade is constantly yielding we know that they everywhere burned the houses of the Romanised Britains and put their inhabitants to the sword. They had no desire to use for themselves the solid and comfortable dwellings of civilised men. They simply destroyed the traces of civilisation wherever they found them. As they reached these shores, our Saxon fathers were savages in the ordinary sense of that word.

We all know from our school-books how some English captives, exposed for sale in the Roman slave-market, attracted the notice of Gregory, Abbot of St. Andrews. Touched by their youth and their beauty, the Abbot was led to conceive the idea of converting England from heathenism. He had actually started on his mission when he was recalled and raised to the Chair of St. Peter. In A.D. 596 he commanded Augustine, his successor to the abbacy, to fulfil his still unaccomplished purpose. The mission was successful and in A.D. 601 Augustine was consecrated Archbishop of Canterbury. The Church in the south of England thus owed its foundation to the Papacy more directly than most in that age and the early English churchmen were eager champions of the papal claims. Geography was in time to prove stronger than history.

In Wales Christianity had survived the Saxon invasion. St. Patrick, a Welsh missionary, had carried it to Ireland in the fifth century. In A.D. 563 St. Columba carried it from Ireland to Scotland, whence it spread to Northumbria about A.D. 635. These Celtic churches and their English converts were less ready to acknowledge the authority of Rome than the church founded in the province of Canterbury.

The seeds of civilisation were thus replanted by Christianity. Churchmen were able to write. To them we owe it that once again we begin to know what was happening in England.

The Saxon settlers had lost their taste for the sea and were mainly devoted to farming. The lands they had left vacant in Denmark had been occupied by settlers of a kindred race from further north. In the course of ages the character of these Norsemen had been moulded in the fiords of Scandinavia, valleys of a mountainous country partly submerged at the close of the glacial age. On the edge of these fiords the Norsemen had settled wherever ground could be ploughed and cattle could be grazed on the slopes above. They could hunt in the forests and fish in the sea. As a rule the fishermen's boats were the only means of communication between the villages. In these stormy latitudes the primitive Norsemen became the most skilful and daring of mariners. At the period with which we are now dealing they were learning to build vessels which could traverse the open seas and thus to embark on distant adventures. They crossed the Baltic, founded the Russian Empire at Novgorod, descended the Dnieper and occupied Constantinople. They planted colonies in Iceland, Scotland, England and Ireland, in Normandy, Sicily and Calabria. They visited Greenland and Labrador.

Their amphibious life made them of all men the most resourceful and raised their energy to the highest voltage. But the discipline of the sea also developed an instinct for method and exactness. These opposite qualities naturally led to contrasts in the various colonies they founded. In Iceland these sea lawyers established

a government developed only upon its judicial and (to a much smaller extent) upon its legislative side omitting altogether the executive and international sides.[1]

In Sicily they ruled a medley of races, languages and creeds, much as England ruled India in the nineteenth century. The despotism they founded in England was the crucible in which its refractory races were fused.

In the eighth century the heathen Norsemen began to plunder, conquer and occupy Christianised England from Denmark, much as the Anglo-Saxons had done three centuries earlier. At the close of this century the Saxon Alfred stopped their advance and drove them into the north-east. To the south of this 'Danelaw' Alfred established his power as king. The Danes were converted to Christianity and rapidly fused with the kindred Saxons. They had brought with them the word 'law' and some of the ideas which that word connotes. They had also established fortified towns on the rivers, often repairing old Roman walls. The English began to copy this practice in Wessex and, as they reconquered the Danelaw, parcelled it out into shires—military areas surrounding fortified towns.

For a brief period at the opening years of the tenth century a great part of the Viking world, Denmark, Norway, the Hebrides and England, was organised as an empire by the Danish king Canute. He conquered England and was elected as its king in A.D. 1017. Thereafter he ruled Saxons and Danes alike on a footing of equality. It is idle to speculate what might have happened if this great Norsemen had lived longer and left competent successors. When he died at the age of forty in A.D. 1035 his Empire dissolved and Edward the Confessor, of the House of Alfred, was elected by the English as king.

In the ninth century the Norsemen had preyed on both sides of the English Channel. They had pushed up the Seine as far as Rouen and had ravaged the country surrounding it. In the early years of the tenth century one of them, Rollo by name, had decided to settle there with his followers. By a treaty with Charles the Simple, king of France, he acquired a considerable area surrounding Rouen as duke of Normandy. He himself was baptized and ere long the Normans had adopted the French language, the feudal system as developed in France and the art of fighting on horseback. In his youth Edward the Confessor was trained in a Norman monastery and as king of England depended largely on Norman advisers. The Saxon earl Godwin had expelled these advisers and, when Edward died, Godwin's son Harold was elected to succeed him.

In A.D. 1035, the year of Canute's death, Robert the Devil, duke of Normandy, had also died on a pilgrimage to Jerusalem, bequeathing his dukedom to William, a bastard born to him by the daughter of a tanner. In A.D. 1064 Harold was wrecked on the Norman coast and fell into the power of William, who made him swear to support his claim to the throne of England on the death of Edward the Confessor. When Harold, ignoring his oath, was elected to the throne, William prepared to assert his claim. Through the influence of Hildebrand he secured the approval of the Pope for his enterprise. This was strictly in accordance with the theory of world sovereignty, which Hildebrand claimed for the Papacy. He was thus helping to temper the axe which, centuries later, would be laid to its root.

The death of Edward had fired the king of Nor-

s

way, Harald Hardrada, with the hope of reviving the Empire of Canute. He landed in Yorkshire, where he and his host were destroyed by Harold at Stamford Bridge on September 28, A.D. 1066. Harold marched rapidly to the south to meet William, who had landed at Hastings. On October 14 their armies met; but the Saxon infantry were no match for the Norman cavalry and Harold was defeated and slain.

Within five years William had mastered the country up to the Cheviots and Wales. For the first time an effective political unity was forced on the English and was afterwards maintained, until it had become to them a habit of mind. This unity made the island impregnable and the conquest which created it was therefore the last to which it submitted. Henceforward English society acquired the character of a lake which is troubled only by the winds that reach it. In the atmosphere of Europe any local disturbance could raise a swell which spread through society to its furthest limits.

William brought to the task of government the superlative energy of his race and also their genius for organisation. While the feudal system as developed in France was imposed in its leading features, William made it clear that holders of land owed a duty to himself prior to the duty they owed to their lords. The duties imposed by the feudal system as well as the rights were accurately specified in a vast cadastral survey which bears comparison with the land settlement applied to India centuries later under William's successors. By making it clear that the king was paramount in the feudal system he prepared the way for its supersession.

The word 'feudalism' coined in the eighteenth century was unknown to the people who lived under that system. It developed, when the government provided by the Roman Empire had collapsed, as a means whereby the people in each locality could obtain some kind of security for life and property. A barbarian chief, who had seized the land, parcelled it out amongst his followers, to be held by them in return for military service and certain dues. He was thus provided with a force with which to resist the encroachments of neighbouring chiefs. His tenants allowed the people who lived on their land specified rights, again in return for military service, and also dues to be paid in cash, in kind or in actual labour. The labourers at the base of the system were serfs attached like chattels to the land. One chief, more powerful than the rest, would claim their allegiance and assert his title to be recognised as king. His nobles, tenants in chief, would then try to assert the principle that the royal authority could only be exercised through themselves. When justice had to be done between their henchmen it was they who must do it in courts of their own. The king could only do justice as between the tenants in chief. A strong king, on the other hand, was always seeking to extend his direct authority over the henchmen of his tenants in chief, to assert his right to decide their disputes in courts of his own, to make laws which applied to them all and commanded their obedience as against a lord in rebellion against him. In course of time he would claim that everyone in his dominions was liable to pay taxes to him direct and not to his lord only. It was only in so far as kings succeeded in establishing these rights that states in the real sense of the word were brought into being. Feudalism, based on the principle of contract, was incompatible with the principle of sovereignty, which is founded on dedication; and sovereignty is the essence of the state. As contrasted with systems like caste or feudalism the state is a vertebrate structure. The Norman and Plantagenet kings provided England with the backbone of a genuine government, a paramount authority which all their subjects had, in the last resort, to obey, even as against their local lords.

In parcelling out the land he had conquered to his barons or tenants in chief William the Conqueror was careful to see that he put no one of them in the kind of position which his ancestor Rollo had established for himself as duke of Normandy. To each of his barons he allotted a number of manors, but in different parts of the country. Great earldoms like Wessex, Mercia and Northumbria vanished under his system. He adopted the shires, which were relatively small, as administrative units.

NOTE

[1] Bryce, *Studies in History and Jurisprudence*, vol. i. p. 333.

CHAPTER XXXI

THE COMMONWEALTH RAISED TO THE NATIONAL SCALE

Norman and early Plantagenet kings would scarcely have understood the distinctions we draw between the judicial, executive and legislative branches of government. Conflicting claims to a piece of land, the penalties which were to be inflicted for crimes or the measures for suppressing a rising were all matters which the king must decide. His decision was expressed by a seal on a document prepared by a clerk who could read and write. His seal was, therefore, entrusted to a highly responsible officer, called a chancellor, who was usually a churchman. Yet, before making a decision and ordering his chancellor to impress the seal, the Nordic king felt it wise to secure the approval and support of his leading men. He therefore instructed the chancellor to summon the barons, bishops and some abbots to his court. This summons, issued in writing, was known as a writ.

In the great council, more often held in the camp than the palace, like the durbars held by an Indian prince, the king listened to rival claimants, discussed appropriate punishments for misconduct or the measures to be taken for suppressing a rebellion, and made his decisions after hearing what his councillors had to say. Judicial, executive and legislative action might all be involved in a single decision. In the king's absence his chancellor would preside over the council.

Throughout the kingdom there existed a great variety of Saxon, Danish and Norman customs. The practice adopted by the Norman kings in settling the disputes brought to their courts led to the development of a law common to the realm. Bishops and barons with a taste for judicial work became expert in the law that the court was developing.

In a country so large as England it was clearly impossible that all matters at issue could be brought for settlement to the king in his court. The Norman and Angevin kings realised the danger of leaving the local cases, which they could not deal with themselves, to be settled by feudal barons. They, therefore, instructed the sheriffs, who acted as their officers in the shires, to hold courts like their own, in which the business of the shire could be done. These county courts were the king's courts, no less than the court that he held in person.

The county courts naturally tended to settle cases in accordance with local custom. A notable step was taken when Henry II. commissioned members of his great council, barons skilled in the law there administered for the realm, to tour through the land and hold assizes in the county courts. In the composition of these courts the principle of representation begins to appear.

By the terms of the royal writs ordering the sheriff to summon the county court for the visit of the itinerant justices, each *villa* had on that occasion to be represented by the reeve and four lawful men, each borough by twelve lawful burgesses.[1]

At these county assizes civil and criminal cases were adjudged in accordance with the law common to England, the law developed by the king in council. Henceforward the English were accustomed to obey a law common to all of them and came to regard it as binding, not only on themselves, but also on their rulers. The rule of law was thus established for a whole nation, as centuries before in the cities of Greece.

This increase of power, asserted by Henry II. on

behalf of the crown, was so abused by his son John that he drove into armed opposition not only the barons, but also the lesser gentry and merchants, the classes on whom his father had leaned for support. At Runnymede he was forced by the barons to sign a charter defining their privileges. Magna Carta went further than, perhaps, its authors had meant towards defining the rights of the subject irrespective of rank.

These troubles recurred when John's infant successor, Henry III., reached his majority and assumed his powers. Once more the barons rebelled under the leadership of Simon de Montfort. In A.D. 1264 the king and his son Edward were defeated at the battle of Lewes and imprisoned. As Simon de Montfort had now to govern the country himself he sought to strengthen his position by widening the basis of the great council. Even Henry III. had gone so far as to summon to his council knights from the shires. The towns had resented the taxes which the king had levied on their trade; so Simon now went a step further and summoned to the great council burgesses from the towns as well as knights from the shires. His period of authority was brief. In A.D. 1265 Prince Edward, who had cleverly escaped from his prison, defeated and slew him at the battle of Evesham.

Under Edward I., who came to the throne in A.D. 1272, experienced judges were appointed to sit in Westminster Hall and deal with most of the cases; though the right of appeal to the king in council was preserved. It was Edward I. who started the practice of declaring important aspects of law in the form of statutes framed by the judges and carefully discussed in the great council, the high court of parliament, which was thus becoming less of a court and more of a legislature.

The struggles of John and Henry III. with their

barons largely arose out of questions of money. In the feudal theory of that age the king was supposed to "live of his own" on the rents and dues paid by his vassals, just as they in turn were expected to live on the dues paid by their tenants. The king, conceived as a baron-in-chief, was less than a sovereign and until the principle of sovereignty was established no state in the real sense of the word could be founded. The kings could not in fact meet the costs of a genuine government from customary dues which were fixed in amount. They were constantly bargaining with barons, bishops, abbots and towns to increase or to supplement the customary dues. At times the relations of the king to his subjects were strained to the breaking-point. The results were Runnymede or the battle of Lewes.

Edward I. realised the mistake which his father and grandfather had both made in alienating the gentry and merchants and driving them to support the barons and bishops against the crown. He decided, therefore, to get into touch with them and bring them to his council. But thousands of writs could not be issued to knights and merchants as writs could be issued to the few hundred barons and bishops. His fallen enemy, Simon de Montfort, had shown him the way out of this difficulty and Edward I. followed his example in issuing writs ordering the county courts each to select a couple of knights and provide the money for sending them to attend the meetings of his council. Similar writs were issued to the boroughs. These knights and merchants were to settle with the king the revenue to be paid him from the shires and towns. The king, in the writs he issued from chancery, was careful to specify that the settlements made with him in council by these knights and merchants were to be final and not to be subject to further confirmation by the county courts and the borough councils which had sent them to bargain on their behalf. The settlements they made were to bind their constituents.

> The said knights are to have full and sufficient power for themselves and for the community of the aforesaid county, and the said citizens and burgesses for themselves and the communities of the aforesaid cities and boroughs separately, there and then, for doing what shall then be ordained according to the Common Council in the premises, so that the aforesaid business shall not remain unfinished in any way for defect of this power.[2]

It is needless here to discuss whether the Plantagenet king had copied this provision from church assemblies. This at least is clear that when issuing these writs he had all-unconsciously supplied the link which Aristeides had missed when he planned the synod of Delos. The members of the synod might agree that so much money from each state was necessary to ensure the safety of Greece from Persian aggression; but the money was not payable until it was voted by every city which sent them to Delos. The estimates framed by the league were thus rendered abortive by the failure of constituent members to vote their quotas. The synod became a farce and, to save Greece from Persia, Athens, the dominant member of the league, forcibly collected the quotas due from members in default. The league ceased to be a league and became an empire, ruled by force in the hands of its strongest member, and Athens went down the primrose path to the bonfire prepared for those who deny all sanctions but physical force. If Edward I. had allowed the principle to develop that the knights and burgesses could only arrive at settlements with him, subject to approval by the counties and boroughs which sent them to his court, the whole arrangement would have broken down. The English kings must either have established an absolute monarchy, as in France, or else have drifted into the position which the Holy

Roman Emperors accepted as heads of a polity which was always futile because it was feudal.

On an earlier page we have seen how practical effect was first given to the principle of the commonwealth by nameless statesmen who taught village assemblies in Greece and Italy to end their discussions by taking a vote and allowing the majority to decide the issue. The statesman who made self-government possible for areas wider than city-states was Edward I. when he issued his writs to the counties and boroughs. The idea that spokesmen could voice the views of electorates had slowly developed in county courts. But the principle, at once more difficult and vital, that a majority of the spokesmen could commit not merely their own electors, but also the total electorate and pledge the wealth of the taxpayers as a whole, was finally established by Edward I. It was this that enabled Burke to tell his angry constituents at Bristol that he was elected by them as a pillar of the British constitution and not as a weather-cock on the top of the edifice. In creating a parliament which could bind its constituents, Edward I. had unknowingly created a body which could bind his successors by law. In the history of the commonwealth the principle that majorities can bind minorities is not more important than the principle that electors can be bound by those they elect.

The knights and burgesses called to parliament were expected to do more than agree to aids which the shires and boroughs were to make to the king. They were also to assess and collect the amounts due from the local taxpayers. So onerous were the duties that owners whose holdings were worth less than forty shillings a year had to be relieved from the burden of taking part in elections. Boroughs often petitioned to be freed from the burden of sending members to parliament. These ungrateful tasks, however, were faced by knights and merchants in sufficient numbers to establish the system. The shires and towns which sent them to parliament were broadly described as the 'communes'. So the body of men who represented these communes came to be known as the 'commons'.

It was clearly felt that even this limited number of people might make the council too large for practical purposes. The commons were also shy of raising their voices in the presence of the king and the lords of nobility. Arrangements were therefore made for the commons to appoint from amongst themselves a speaker who would say to the king in council whatever there was to be said for them all. They met behind closed doors in the chapter-house of Westminster to select their speaker and discuss what he should say.

Finance was only one part of their business. The commons were to bring to the king in council matters which aggrieved the people at large; for the king was thus to secure their support as against the feudal power of the nobles. So knights and burgesses came to parliament loaded with petitions from the shires and towns. When they came to compare them in the chapter-house of the Abbey they naturally found that some of the troubles complained of in different counties and towns arose from a general defect in the law. The king in council would then be petitioned by the speaker to make the necessary change in the law. The king was presently to find that the aids which the knights and burgesses were asked to approve were not forthcoming until he himself had promised to grant the petitions made by the commons. He was thus constrained to promise the enactment of statutes to redress their grievances. When the commons had adjourned, he would then promulgate statutes drafted by the judges which purported to give effect to the petitions. But when parliament met once more it was often complained that these laws were not in accord with that which the commons had asked for and the king had said should be done. So the commons began to prepare for themselves drafts of the statutes they wished the king to enact; and in this they were helped by lawyers practising in Westminster Hall on the other side of the road. The king in council was then petitioned by the commons to enact these drafts, which were called 'bills', and to give them the force of law as statutes. In A.D. 1414 a pledge was exacted from Henry V.

that fro hens forth nothyng be enacted to the Petitions of his Commune that be contrarie of his askyng, wharby they should be bounde withoute their assent.[3]

In the course of centuries the principle was established that the king of himself could enact nothing except in the form of a statute which parliament had approved; and, finally, that bills which parliament had approved must be enacted. By then the position was also established that the title of the king himself to his throne was settled by an act of parliament.

The exact terms of the bills which the commons presented to the king in council had first to be settled by themselves in the chapter-house. Like the Greek and Roman assemblies they had learned the art of translating talk into action by dividing the house and allowing the majority to decide. But even so the decision could only be 'aye' or 'no' and, as everyone sees who has sat on the smallest committee, the task of settling the terms of a document in a large assembly is laborious and difficult. A way in which this can be done was developed little by little in the course of centuries and is now embodied in the procedure of the house of commons. The methods followed by legislative bodies throughout the world are largely based on it. As to how this procedure

developed in the Middle Ages we have little information; for the commons, jealous of royal interference,
met behind closed doors and kept no journals till the
sixteenth century. This much we know, that a bill
had in the first instance to be submitted to the house
by an individual member. He would then describe
his proposal and move that the bill be read out from
the manuscript which he handed to the clerk of the
house. Until bills could be printed, few of the members would have before them the text of the measures
they were asked to discuss. They must have been
largely limited to the question whether to accept or
reject the draft as read out by the clerk. The amend-
ment of bills had for the most part to be dealt with
in committees small enough to handle a draft in
writing.

The commonwealth is a system which enables the
structure of society to be moulded by its own members in the light of experience. The invention of
writing was a necessary step in its evolution, because
no body of citizens could express their experience in
laws until their decisions could be placed on record.
Yet the power of popular assemblies to found laws
on the general experience must have reached a certain point and stopped there, so long as the measures
under discussion were presented only in hand-
writing. How greatly this power must have increased when each member could be furnished with
a printed copy of a bill and also of amendments
proposed, and still further when, by movable types,
members could be given revised copies showing the
amendments carried on previous days, will be best
understood by anyone who has sat in a legislative
body.

Acts of parliament were published in print as
early as the reign of Henry VII. not many years
after the time of Caxton. Yet so fearful were the
commons of royal interference, and so jealous of the

secrecy of their proceedings, that up to the eighteenth century, bills continued to be handled in
manuscript only, until they had received the royal
assent.

The first bill which the House directed to be printed and
circulated amongst members before it was discussed was a
bill of 1708, concerning large sums of public money which
had passed through the hands of one Edward Whitaker,
and about which discussion had been going on intermit-
tently since 1702. It was an elaborate financial bill, giving
acquittance to Edward Whitaker for all sums which he had
handled since the death of William III.[4]

The use of printing to give members notice of
proposed amendments and to show the amendments
made in previous sittings was not introduced till the
nineteenth century. The power of the house to deal
with amendments was greatly increased by these
expedients. In time the work became so technical
that parliament called to its aid a staff of experts.
The appointment of professional draftsmen in the
middle of the nineteenth century is another landmark
in parliamentary procedure.

Thus, with the aid of printing, representative
bodies have acquired an unlimited power of moulding law in the light of common experience. Acts of
parliament are no longer confined to brief declara-
tions of general principles for judges to interpret.
A modern statute is sometimes a volume in itself.
Its chapters and sections are a complicated mechanism which reflects the intricate delicacy of the
human relations to which it is applied. A parliament
to-day is a mechanism which differs from that of
Edward I. as a modern railway differs from a
wheel-barrow. The difference is largely due to the
invention of printing with movable types.

So far we have dealt with the commons rather
than parliament. We must now go back to the early
stages when the commons had framed a bill behind

closed doors in the chapter-house of Westminster for their speaker to present to the king in council. When this happened the peers summoned to the council in their own right naturally wished to discuss in private what attitude to adopt towards the measure proposed by the commons. They also developed the habit of meeting without the king under the presidency of the lord chancellor. They often differed from the commons as to the principle of the measure or as to its details. If they could not agree as to the principle it was not presented to the king for his approval. If they differed only on details the lords and commons had then to agree on the terms of amendments. The procedure whereby this is done by the two houses sitting apart was developed. When both were agreed on principle and detail the bill was submitted to the king and enacted as law. The formula was as follows:

Be it therefore enacted by the King's most Excellent Majesty, by and with the advice and consent of the Lords Spiritual and Temporal, and Commons, in this present Parliament assembled, and by the authority of the same as follows. . . .

The commons, however, asserted their exclusive right to settle the details of supply.

The high court of parliament had thus developed from the great council of the Norman kings and was destined in course of centuries to become a legislature with complete control of supply. Its judicial work, except for ultimate appeals, was devolved on separate courts, which also asserted their independence of royal interference. Executive matters remained in the hands of the king, and were dealt with by him and his privy council, a body which peers claimed a technical right to attend.

Legislative, judicial and executive functions were thus to a great extent distributed into three separate organs. Montesquieu, with his logical French mind, announced that this separation of powers was the essence of the British constitution, and indeed the secret of freedom itself, obscuring thereby the fact that the making, interpretation and enforcement of law are merely three aspects of sovereignty which can never be wholly divorced one from the other. Lord Haldane once opened an official interview with a government servant by saying, "I need hardly tell you that the judges have nothing to do with making or altering the law. They have only to interpret the law." "We are all familiar with that legal fiction", the government servant replied. "You, lord chancellor, know better than I do that where there are no precedents to follow the judges decide and in deciding they make the law." The official expression on Lord Haldane's face relaxed in a smile. "Within the four walls of this room I had better admit then that we judges are constantly making the law, and in fact legislate. So now let us talk of this matter on the basis of realities."

Of greater importance is the intimate connection between legislative and executive functions. The man or men responsible for administering the law will, as a rule, know better than any body of elected legislators what changes in the law are necessary to secure the safety of the realm. This applies especially to those laws which decide from year to year the contributions which each citizen must make to meet the expenses of government. In seeking to levy the ship-money from the inland counties Charles I. was right in believing that the cost of naval defence could not be left to counties washed by the sea. The soundness and equity of his claim was obscured by the fact that Charles I. was also set on asserting his claim to rule by divine authority, a claim which cost him his head. By the revolution, in which James II. lost his throne, it was settled once for all that whoever sat on that throne thereafter would sit there by virtue of an act of parliament and not by divine right.

The essential problem was still unsolved. The king and his ministers and parliament, the executive and legislature, might still be at odds as to what changes in the law, especially in the law of supply, were necessary for the safety of the realm. The king, though he could not legislate without parliament, could stop legislation and could, therefore, be removed only by another revolution. The cause of most revolutions is a deadlock in government, not oppression. In England the problem was solved, almost unconsciously, by transferring the executive power from the king to the minister able for the time being to command a majority in the house of commons. Such a minister could ask the house to frame the laws and vote the supplies which he deemed necessary for the safety of the realm. If they refused to support him, his place would be taken by a leader whom parliament was prepared to support; or else the defeated minister could dissolve parliament and ask the country to return one prepared to support him and abide the result. In the British constitution of to-day the real heir to the sovereignty of the Norman and Plantagenet kings is the prime minister, who is brought to office or can be removed from it by the will of parliament or else of the electorate. But, so long as he holds office, parliament must in the last instance do what he says or else remove him. Under British institutions the executive thus controls the legislature, so long as it is the executive.

By this process the lineal descendants of the Norman and Plantagenet kings have become the hereditary presidents of a republic. Just when the change had been made in England the founders of the American constitution, misled by the theories of Montesquieu, established an elective monarchy in

T

the United States. The king who sits on the throne of Washington can only be changed every four years. In the interval the safety of the state may be jeopardised by a deadlock between the executive and legislature.

The first question to be asked about any system of government is not whether it represents the will of the people governed, but whether it is competent to meet their essential needs. History shows that good government cannot continue unless it is moving towards self-government. But it also shows that self-government cannot begin, or continue to exist, unless there is government in the real sense of the word. The instinct for realities that guided the English from Norman times was expressed in the Duke of Wellington's favourite phrase, "The king's government must be carried on". If the king was bound to consult the people through their representatives before taxing them, the people themselves were held to be bound by the settlements made by their representatives with the king. And if parliament could not be pledged to obey an hereditary king, they must then learn to obey the ruler whom they and the people had clothed for the time being with kingly power. The factor which enabled the English to construct a commonwealth on the national scale was this instinct that government must not be popularised beyond a point at which the system loses the quality of government.

NOTES

[1] Pasquet, *An Essay on the Origins of the House of Commons*, p. 15.
[2] Stubbs, *Select Charters*, pp. 476-77.
[3] Redlich, *The Procedure of the House of Commons*, vol. i. p. 15.
[4] Letter to the author from Sir C. Oman, who used the facilities he enjoys as a member of parliament to examine its records.

CHAPTER XXXII

REACTIONS ON CHARACTER

THE great service which parliaments rendered in the middle ages was not, in fact, to make England a constitutional state, but to foster its growth into a national state based on something broader and deeper than monarchical centralisation, to make national unity a thing of the spirit rather than a territorial expression or a mechanical matter of administration, to evoke a common political consciousness at Westminster and then to propagate it in the constituencies. The value of parliaments consisted not so much in what members brought with them as in what they took away. Nationalism in the middle ages came nearer to Napoleon III.'s *la volonté de chacun* than to Rousseau's *la volonté générale*, and it was in and through parliaments that local and social prejudice was merged in a common sense. Every Englishman of to-day feels and realises his nationality to some extent; the degree is a matter of individual imagination, education, and interest. Generally speaking, his attachment to his country overrides every other affection except, perhaps, his devotion to himself and his family and in some cases his addiction to his religious or moral faith. But in the middle ages we are dealing with men whose nationalism came comparatively low in the scale of their affections. Men of the highest mind and character agreed with Archbishop Winchelsey that the loyalty they owed the pope came before the loyalty they owed the king. Barons were, as a rule, more devoted to their class than to either pope or king; the ordinary burgess or squire valued his local affinities more than his national bonds, and to the villager the parish was his world. When he threw himself upon his country—*posuit se super patriam*—his country consisted of his neighbours, and everyone else was a foreigner.

*   *   *   *   *   *

The difference between modern and medieval Englishmen's patriotism is one of degree; in the middle ages locality

275

preceded the nation, and it was through parliaments that the order was reversed.[1]

Trevelyan is expressing the same thought when he says that it was not England that made parliament but parliament which made England. Like Herodotus and Thucydides these historians see the character of their countrymen as shaped in the mould of their own institutions. There is also a darker side to the picture, as in Thucydides.

Perhaps the first European war that can be called national was the Hundred Years' War as waged by England. The armies she sent year after year to lay waste and plunder France were indeed very small, but their efficiency was the outcome of a national organization and a national spirit. England, on account of her insular and remote position, and her strong kings, had since the Norman Conquest outstripped the rest of Europe in obtaining a certain measure of internal peace, and was passing from feudalism to nationhood. As soon as King and Parliament had endowed her with administrative machinery and national self-consciousness, she exercised these new powers at the expense of that clumsy giant, the French feudal Kingdom. She became for a while the plunderer and bully of her continental neighbours, not because she had less conscience than they, but because she had more power.[2]

The victories of Crécy, Poitiers and Agincourt were due, so Trevelyan believes, to the structure of English society. It was this which enabled the English to wrest the control of the seas from Spain, to hold it against the French monarchy, to colonise or control a great part of the continents opened by Columbus and Vasco da Gama and to plant where they conquered the seed of their institutions. It was these institutions that led them to master the forces of nature and so to dominate the industry, commerce and finance of the world in the nineteenth century.

The air of superiority we too often betray in our dealings with foreigners is a remnant of the spirit which led the English to bully the French in the Middle Ages. This arrogance, whether in Athens or England, was not the product of free institutions, but sprang from the sense of superior strength which those institutions had given. It was due, not to the principle of the commonwealth, but rather to the fact that the principle was limited, in one case to a city, in the other to a nation. The principle can never be free from dangerous reactions on character until it is applied to society as a whole. We persist in thinking and acting as though the national commonwealth is the last word in human development. So Aristotle thought in his day that no commonwealth could ever exist on a scale larger than the Athens he knew. To have brought into being a commonwealth on the national scale is the greatest achievement in history and one, therefore, which points to a further and far more difficult task. When a real commonwealth of nations is created on a scale, however restricted, the most difficult stage will have been passed on the road to the ultimate goal, which can be no other than the organisation of all human society in one state based on the principle of the commonwealth.

On the continent of Europe the achievements of England were seen as results of her institutions, which were widely copied; though with very unequal success. In many directions attempts to apply the principle of the commonwealth have failed so completely that, as in the cities of ancient Greece, tyrannies have arisen to restore order and call into being governments which are really effective. More conspicuous still was the failure of China to establish republican government on the ruins of her ancient autocracy. Since the revolution of 1911 one-fifth part of humanity, and by no means the least cultured or intelligent part, has been plunged into anarchy.

In the light of these failures, it is often said that self-governing institutions can only be worked by peoples derived from the Anglo-Saxon stock which produced them. I myself have heard that view expressed by one who in former years had held offices of major importance in Liberal cabinets. One generally finds that the people who take this point of view believe that the qualities which enable Anglo-Saxon communities to govern themselves are derived from obscure biological causes, too complex to analyse and, therefore, not subject to human control. If the opposite view, that taken by Pollard and Trevelyan, is correct there is reason to hope that a like experience may in time develop these same qualities in all kinds of people. How far such qualities can be fostered by a conscious policy in domestic, imperial and foreign affairs is clearly a question of cardinal importance.

In order to form an opinion on this question one must have in one's mind some definite conception of the qualities which a people must develop in order to work a self-governing system. There must, to begin with, be a certain willingness on the part of minorities to accept the decisions of majorities. Such willingness can develop only in so far as majorities are felt to use their power of decision in the general interest rather than in their own. Minorities accustomed to think that the power of majorities is used in the interest of majorities alone lose their sense of membership in the state, develop the minds of aliens and resort to organised force for their own protection. If a state is to govern itself there must be a certain sense in a certain number of its members that the general interest is higher than their own. Where self-government can be made to operate at all this sense of the general interest will grow with exercise. As Trevelyan and Pollard have shown, the growth of this sense in the Middle Ages united

the English and made them the first nation in
Europe.

Enough citizens must also be found to devote
their time to the public interest. The reluctance in
Plantagenet times of knights and burgesses to attend
parliament and of counties and towns to find their
expenses was, perhaps, the most critical juncture
in the history of the English commonwealth. To
begin with they attended only because the king
ordered them to attend. "The function of force in
human affairs is", as Mahan has said, "to give moral
ideas time to take root." By the close of the Middle
Ages election to parliament was felt as a privilege
and so too was the right to elect. The system also
had this effect that it brought an ever-increasing
number of Englishmen into contact with facts and
obliged them to pass judgement on the facts. It was
this, I suggest, which developed in England a somewhat higher sense of realities and also a somewhat
deeper instinct for truth than is commonly found
elsewhere.

In a word my contention is that the quality which
enables a people to govern themselves is not the
instinct of men to insist on their own interests, but
the instinct, weaker in some, but stronger in others,
which enables them to put the public interest before
their own. It is in fact the moral sense which alone
differentiates men from animals ; the faculty without
which, as Aristotle said, men, equipped with the
power of their intellect, would be only the most
dangerous of the beasts. As remarked in an earlier
chapter, a community of people clever and selfish as
Iago could only be governed like a convict settlement. A community of people as simple and selfless
as Humphry Clinker could, from the outset,
govern themselves, and in doing so would acquire
a wisdom and knowledge sufficient for the task.

The reader whose patience has lasted to this point

may well ask why he should be wearied with chapters on constitutional history which is or should be familiar to every child who has passed through a high school. The answer is that I see in these threadbare and commonplace details the first beginnings in the Christian era of the process whereby that creative and potent idea, the Kingdom of God, as viewed and expounded by Jesus of Nazareth, is destined to be realised. I believe that the process here begun will still be continued, till the rule of law produced from the mind and conscience of those who obey it will not be confined to national frontiers. I look forward to a time when the commonwealth will no longer be limited to the national state, when nations, conscious of their own distinctive histories and structures, will have learned to function as organs of one international commonwealth. I do not believe that the still small voice which was first overheard in the cities of Greece and was raised to the sound of a trumpet in England will be silenced till all men have heard it and learned to obey one paramount law, based on the mind and conscience of all.

Such ideas, it is safe to guess, never crossed the minds of those nameless knights and merchants through whose struggles and labours the English commonwealth was brought into being. As foretold by the Master who first projected an order of society based on realities, the Kingdom of Heaven was destined to come without observation.

NOTES

[1] Pollard, *The Evolution of Parliament*, pp. 133-4.
[2] Trevelyan, *History of England*, pp. 222-3.

CHAPTER XXXIII

THE Christian era began in a country where civilisations in conflict were preparing the stage for a great catastrophe. "The Kingdom of God is at hand" was the watchword of Judaism. To Zealots this meant that the God of Israel was about to destroy the Roman Empire and to put in its place a kingdom ruled by a scion of David. They looked on themselves as the instruments of a purpose to be gained by force. In the schools of the prophets the Kingdom of God had come to mean a supernatural transformation, a new heaven and a new earth, from which sorrow and sin would be banished for ever.

The founder of Christianity was trying to divert the attention of his countrymen from violent or visionary projects to realities as he saw them. To him the final reality was the spirit of goodness personified—God, conceived as a Father possessed with desire to perfect the children he had made in his likeness and not as a despot absorbed in the thought of his own glory and power. Goodness cannot exist without doing good and desiring to do it. It is, from its nature, creative. Some faint expression of this spirit, this essential reality, was immanent and incarnate in men. He saw it as the bond which unites society, as the principle of life, and something, therefore, capable of growth. God, who had made men in his likeness, had given them the power to distinguish evil from good. He taught that the ultimate good for men is to serve each other and not themselves. To become like their Father they must exercise his supreme faculty of creation.

But this they could only do in so far as they per-
fected the likeness for themselves. The means to this
end was an order of society which would exercise
and develop the instinct in men to serve one another.
To develop the best in themselves they must strive
to create a system based on realities, a divine polity,
as the work of their own hands. His view of life was
the outcome of faith that the ultimate reality was
mind, not matter; that mind was eternal. So also
was its work of creation in which men could share
in communion with God.

His life was cut short by his enemies; but not
before his ideas had been stated in sayings and
parables that his followers remembered and placed
on record, together with much else that in course of
time they had come to believe that he had said and
done. They lived in an empire from which its rulers
were rapidly removing all traces of the parent
commonwealth. Imperial Rome, no less than Judaism, was based on obedience to a supernatural
authority. It is not to be wondered that disciples, so
soon deprived of their Master, should have failed
to see that the principles embodied in the church
and state under which they lived were the very
negation of those he had sought to expound. From
the fury of the Zealots he had made them immune;
but they viewed his teaching through the medium
of those transcendental ideas which had found expression in the book of Enoch.[1] They saw in Jesus
the Messiah of prophecy. He himself would return
clothed with the power of God to establish his
kingdom. Their task was to warn men of this and
prepare them for it. From the writings of Paul we
know how completely this outlook possessed their
minds. Till a few generations ago it possessed all
Christendom and still possesses a great part of it.

A belief rooted in unreality has produced in the
course of ages a pantheon of idols which dominate

civilisation. No single volume could attempt to analyse the trends of thought which have issued from this mixture and conflict of Greek and Roman with Jewish ideas. The notion of church and state, of two authorities competing for sovereignty, is among them and has led us to seclude religion and politics in separate compartments of our minds. In the teaching of Jesus there is no such distinction. To his mind religion and politics were merely two aspects of life, a sphere viewed from two different angles. He believed that men could grow to perfection in so far as they based their relations on the infinite duty of each to all. This supreme conception could only be realised by gradual developments such as we, in our language, would describe as political. Their fixed belief in supernatural events not destined to happen blinded his followers to these implications. Christianity became from the outset a matter of personal piety, a syncretic religion, heavily charged with older paganisms.

The fact must be squarely faced that for more than eighteen centuries Christendom held the belief, crystallised in the writings of St. Augustine, that the life men live on this earth is destined to end in a sudden cataclysm which may be expected at any moment. A belief held for a period like this creates unconscious habits of mind which determine the conduct of generations which no longer accept it. To this can be traced a political outlook which is short in its range and narrow in scope, which envisages little beyond the immediate interests of national groups. It explains why Christendom has failed to realise its supernational aspirations. No society can learn to think of itself as a whole which does not believe in its own future. Still less can it realise its own capacity for improvement and the structure it ought to attain, and so work on a plan. The growing confusion of the world is due to this failure, and will only be ended by those who face the question where it is going or ought to go. We talk of planning as the great panacea; but intelligent planning can only begin when men have asked and answered the question, what is the ultimate structure they mean to attain for human society? It is only by reference to such a conception that the steps which practical statesmen are taking from day to day can be judged. No political science can guide men far on their journey through life until it can say what is the goal to which the journey should lead.

As noticed in the opening chapter, science has developed an outlook different from that which Christianity adopted from Judaism. We now have reason to expect that society will continue to exist for a period enormously longer than that which has passed since men were first able to distinguish themselves from animals. The reactions on political thought may prove to be greater even than those produced by the speculations of Copernicus or Darwin. All but incurable pessimists would allow that men have attained to a level higher than that reached by their ancestors who lived as carnivorous animals in caves. If this can be done in thousands of years what achievements are possible in the millions which science is leading mankind to expect? This change in our outlook is an undeniable call to harvest the fields which "a greater than Aristotle" scattered with truths and enriched with his life. That the wheat and the tares could not be distinguished till both had grown up and yielded their fruit was itself a profound intuition. For us in our time it is possible to see what his teaching involves as applied to a world still in its infancy, with vistas of experience before it a thousandfold longer than those behind it. Now, at last, it is reasonable to consider the structure which human society as a whole should seek to attain, and to use that conception as a test for deciding what steps can be taken to approach it from day to day and from year to year. If once we allow ourselves to think of a world commonwealth as the goal of human endeavour we shall find that our minds are equipped with a standard which helps us to judge what ought to be done in the politics of a village no less than in those of the greater world. We have then a criterion to the test of which all measures proposed can be brought—how far will the measure in question tend to increase in those to whom it applies their sense of duty one to another? In so far as that test is satisfied, economic and political problems will begin to find unexpected solutions.

A government for the world can never be established merely by the knowledge and skill of technicians. We have knowledge sufficient to create it to-day, if the indispensable factor which binds men together in one society and makes it organic had now been developed enough for the purpose. To strengthen this factor in every part of the social tissue is the necessary process which will move faster as we learn to conceive this as the true purpose of politics, the essential task entrusted to statesmen. We in this age have an experience which those who recorded the gospels had not. We can see in the light of history the kind of society which in course of time slowly but surely increases the sense of duty in men to each other. We can ask how a policy or measure proposed will help to call this sense into play, whether we are ordering the affairs of nations or those of a parish. We can watch what we do to see how far it is having this effect, and revise our policies in the light of experience. All this will be possible as we learn to accept the government of men by themselves as the guiding principle in public affairs.

In the counsel of nations the policy of statesmen

is, indeed, guided by a principle, the avoidance of war. They are ever proclaiming that peace is their aim and are, I believe, more sincere in pursuing it than the cynics, who have not to deal with their practical difficulties, suspect. The reason why peace, accepted as a goal, fails as a principle of direction in policy is inherent in its negative character. A policy which treats the avoidance of war as its final criterion is merely an attempt to apply in the highest sphere of human relations the principle of the decalogue, which the greatest thinker of all time regarded as obsolete. In the place of ten prohibitions he propounded a positive and constructive injunction, that men should seek the good of others as though it were their own. If he was right in believing that "no other commandment is greater than this", it will not suffice for nations to abstain from coercing each other by force. They must learn to think how by steps, slow but patient and persistent, they can bring into being an order of society based on the duty of each to all, irrespective of national limits. International conferences will repeat their record of failures so long as the minds of governments are set on the task of avoiding collisions with each other. The manœuvres they execute are fraught with danger, and can end at best by leading nowhere, until they have recognised an ultimate goal, however remote, in front of them all and are thinking how they can reach it together. It will then be seen that the rule prescribed in the sermon on the mount as superseding the Ten Commandments applies to the whole sphere of conduct—to public no less than private affairs. "Seek ye first the Kingdom of God, and all things else shall be added unto you" was the greatest of all contributions made to constructive thought. Transcendental ideas have obscured from our minds its literal meaning, an order of society based on realities as the goal of human endeavour on this earth.

No political science will furnish guidance in practical politics unless it proceeds from a definite conception of ultimate values. The system propounded by Jesus proceeds from the faith that right and wrong are valid distinctions of infinite importance. It therefore regards mind as the ultimate reality in the universe and as indestructible. Death is conceived as no more than a physical incident in the endless life of the spirit. It opens to man a prospect of achievement for which much time in space is required, time for which we have reason to hope. Yet, while science can tell us that, in all probability, we have ages before us in which to accomplish our work, it also assures us that a time must come when life on this earth and the earth itself will have ceased to exist. Belief in the infinite value of goodness is vain, unless we are justified in the faith that God is the God of the living and not of the dead, which, could it be proved, would cease to be faith. In this twentieth century the inexorable question must be faced, whether this view of reality can be proved by miracles and based on authority.

That spiritual values are the ultimate reality and indestructible cannot be proved. No more can the opposite be proved; though a certain order of scientists would seem to think otherwise. In the search for truth the limits of human knowledge must be recognised. Belief, in the true sense of the word, is not the assertion of knowledge, or dogma, but courage to act on the best hypothesis we are able to conceive. Unbelievers are those too timid or idle to guess at the truth and act on the guess. "The deepest, nay, the unique theme of the history of the world", says Goethe, "to which all other themes are subordinate, is the conflict of faith and unbelief. All epochs in which faith prevails—whatever its form may be—are noble, soul-elevating and fruitful for the present and for after times. All epochs in which unbelief, be it under what form it may, wins an un-happy victory, even though for the moment they are invested with a deceptive halo of glory, vanish and are forgotten by posterity; because no one willingly wastes his pains on what is barren and unfruitful."[2]

NOTES

[1] *Vide supra*, p. 108.
[2] Quoted by Caird, *Lay Sermons and Addresses*, p. 85.

INDEX

THE END

Printed in Great Britain by R. & R. CLARK, LIMITED, *Edinburgh.*